Biology

Guided Reading and Study Workbook

Prentice
Hall

Upper Saddle River, New Jersey
Glenview, Illinois
Needham, Massachusetts

ISBN 0-13-044174-0

2 4 5 6 7 8 9 10   05 04 03 02 01

Contents

Chapter 1 The Science of Biology   5
1–1   What Is Science?.....................................5
1–2   How Scientists Work 6
1–3   Studying Life 9
1–4   Tools and Procedures 10

Chapter 2 The Chemistry of Life   13
2–1   The Nature of Matter..........................13
2–2   Properties of Water 14
2–3   Carbon Compounds 17
2–4   Chemical Reactions and Enzymes.......19

Chapter 3 The Biosphere   22
3–1   What Is Ecology?................................22
3–2   Energy Flow.......................................23
3–3   Cycles of Matter 26

Chapter 4 Ecosystems and Communities   29
4–1   The Role of Climate 29
4–2   What Shapes an Ecosystem? 31
4–3   Land Biomes 33
4–4   Aquatic Ecosystems 36

Chapter 5 Populations   40
5–1   How Populations Grow 40
5–2   Limits to Growth...............................42
5–3   Human Population Growth 44

Chapter 6 Humans in the Biosphere   47
6–1   A Changing Landscape.....................47
6–2   Renewable and Nonrenewable
      Resources..48
6–3   Biodiversity.......................................51
6–4   Charting a Course for the Future 53

Chapter 7 Cell Structure and Function   55
7–1   Life Is Cellular 55
7–2   Cell Structures 56
7–3   Movement Through the Membrane.....59
7–4   The Diversity of Cellular Life 62

Chapter 8 Photosynthesis   64
8–1   Energy and Life..................................64
8–2   Photosynthesis: An Overview..............65
8–3   The Reactions of Photosynthesis 66

Chapter 9 Cellular Respiration   70
9–1   Chemical Pathways 70
9–2   The Krebs Cycle and Electron
      Transport 72

Chapter 10 Cell Growth and Division   77
10–1   Cell Growth.......................................77
10–2   Cell Division 78
10–3   Regulating the Cell Cycle 81

Chapter 11 Introduction to Genetics   83
11–1   The Work of Gregor Mendel 83

11–2   Probability and Punnett Squares 85
11–3   Exploring Mendelian Genetics.............87
11–4   Meiosis..90
11–5   Linkage and Gene Maps 92

Chapter 12 DNA and RNA   94
12–1   DNA..94
12–2   Chromosomes and DNA Replication ..97
12–3   RNA and Protein Synthesis 99
12–4   Mutations 101
12–5   Gene Regulation..............................103

Chapter 13 Genetic Engineering   107
13–1   Changing the Living World................107
13–2   Manipulating DNA 109
13–3   Cell Transformation 111
13–4   Applications of Genetic Engineering....113

Chapter 14 The Human Genome   116
14–1   Human Heredity 116
14–2   Human Chromosomes 118
14–3   Human Molecular Genetics.................121

Chapter 15 Darwin's Theory of Evolution   125
15–1   The Puzzle of Life's Diversity.............125
15–2   Ideas that Shaped Darwin's Thinking...127
15–3   Darwin Presents His Case 129

Chapter 16 Evolution of Populations   133
16–1   Genes and Variation 133
16–2   Evolution as Genetic Change.............135
16–3   The Process of Speciation 137

Chapter 17 The History of Life   140
17–1   The Fossil Record 140
17–2   Earth's Early History 142
17–3   Evolution of Multicellular Life 144
17–4   Patterns of Evolution........................147

Chapter 18 Classification   150
18–1   Finding Order in Diversity.................150
18–2   Modern Evolutionary Classification 152
18–3   Kingdoms and Domains 153

Chapter 19 Bacteria and Viruses   157
19–1   Prokaryotes 157
19–2   Bacteria in Nature 160
19–3   Viruses 162

Chapter 20 Protists   165
20–1   The Kingdom Protista 165
20–2   Animallike Protists: Protozoans 166
20–3   Plantlike Protists: Unicellular Algae.....169
20–4   Plantlike Protists: Red, Brown,
      and Green Algae.................................171
20–5   Funguslike Protists 174

Contents (continued)

Chapter 21 Fungi   **177**
21–1 The Kingdom Fungi 177
21–2 Classification of Fungi..........................179
21–3 Ecology of Fungi 183

Chapter 22 Plant Diversity   **185**
22–1 Introduction to Plants...........................185
22–2 Bryophytes 187
22–3 Seedless Vascular Plants 189
22–4 Seed Plants 191
22–5 Angiosperms—Flowering Plants........194

Chapter 23 Roots, Stems, and Leaves   **197**
23–1 Specialized Tissues in Plants...............197
23–2 Roots 199
23–3 Stems 201
23–4 Leaves 204
23–5 Transport in Plants...............................206

Chapter 24 Reproduction of Seed Plants   **209**
24–1 Reproduction With Cones
       and Flowers..209
24–2 Seed Development and Germination...213
24–3 Plant Propagation and Agriculture 215

**Chapter 25 Plant Responses and
Adaptations**   **218**
25–1 Hormones and Plant Growth..............218
25–2 Plant Responses....................................220
25–3 Plant Adaptations 222

Chapter 26 Sponges and Cnidarians   **225**
26–1 Introduction to the Animal Kingdom...225
26–2 Sponges..228
26–3 Cnidarians...229

Chapter 27 Worms and Mollusks   **233**
27–1 Flatworms 233
27–2 Roundworms 235
27–3 Annelids 237
27–4 Mollusks 240

Chapter 28 Arthropods and Echinoderms   **243**
28–1 Introduction to the Arthropods 243
28–2 Groups of Arthropods...........................245
28–3 Insects 248
28–4 Echinoderms 251

Chapter 29 Comparing Invertebrates   **254**
29–1 Invertebrate Evolution 254
29–2 Form and Function in Invertebrates......256

**Chapter 30 Nonvertebrate Chordates,
Fishes, and Amphibians**   **260**
30–1 The Chordates 260
30–2 Fishes 262
30–3 Amphibians...265

Chapter 31 Reptiles and Birds   **269**
31–1 Reptiles 269
31–2 Birds 271

Chapter 32 Mammals   **275**
32–1 Introduction to the Mammals 275
32–2 Diversity of Mammals..........................277
32–3 Primates and Human Origins.............279

Chapter 33 Comparing Chordates   **283**
33–1 Chordate Evolution 283
33–2 Controlling Body Temperature 285
33–3 Form and Function in Chordates 286

Chapter 34 Animal Behavior   **290**
34–1 Elements of Behavior............................290
34–2 Patterns of Behavior 292

Chapter 35 Nervous System   **295**
35–1 Human Body Systems...........................295
35–2 The Nervous System 297
35–3 Divisions of the Nervous System 299
35–4 The Senses 301
35–5 Drugs and the Nervous System..........304

**Chapter 36 Skeletal, Muscular,
and Integumentary Systems**   **307**
36–1 The Skeletal System 307
36–2 The Muscular System 309
36–3 The Integumentary System 312

**Chapter 37 Circulatory and
Respiratory Systems**   **315**
37–1 The Circulatory System........................315
37–2 Blood and the Lymphatic System.......318
37–3 The Respiratory System 320

**Chapter 38 Digestive and
Excretory Systems**   **324**
38–1 Food and Nutrition...............................324
38–2 The Process of Digestion......................326
38–3 The Excretory System 329

**Chapter 39 Endocrine and
Reproductive Systems**   **332**
39–1 The Endocrine System...........................332
39–2 Human Endocrine Glands....................335
39–3 The Reproductive System....................338
39–4 Fertilization and Development...........340

**Chapter 40 The Immune System
and Disease**   **343**
40–1 Infectious Disease 343
40–2 The Immune System.............................345
40–3 Immune System Disorders 348
40–4 Cancer 350

3. What is the metric system? _____

_____

_____

4. Complete each equation by writing the correct number or metric unit.

a. 1000 meters = 1 _____

b. 1 liter = _____ milliliters

c. 1 gram = _____ milligrams

d. 1000 kilograms = 1 _____

Analyzing Biological Data (page 25)

5. When scientists collect data, what are they often trying to find out? _____

_____

_____

6. What does a graph of data make easier to recognize and understand than a table of data? _____

Microscopes (pages 25–26)

7. What are microscopes? _____

_____

8. What are compound light microscopes? _____

_____

_____

9. How do chemical stains make light microscopes more useful? _____

_____

10. What are the two main types of electron microscopes?

a. _____

b. _____

11. Compare how a TEM and an SEM produce images. _____

_____

_____

_____

12. How must samples be prepared for observation by an electron microscope? _____

Laboratory Techniques (page 27)

13. A group of cells grown in a nutrient solution from a single original cell is called a(an) _____.

14. What technique do biologists use to separate one part of a cell from the rest of the cell? _____

Chapter 1, The Science of Biology *(continued)*

Working Safely in Biology (page 28)

15. What is the single most important rule for your safety while working in a laboratory? _____

_____

WordWise

The block of letters below contains six vocabulary terms from Chapter 1. Use the clues to identify the words you need to find. Then, find the words across, down, or on the diagonal. Circle each word in the hidden-word puzzle.

Clues	**Vocabulary Terms**
A device that produces magnified images of structures that are too small to see with the unaided eye	_____
A well-tested explanation that unifies a broad range of observations	_____
Change over time	_____
The process by which organisms keep their internal conditions relatively stable	_____
An organized way of using evidence to learn about the natural world	_____
Evidence gathered from observations	_____
The chemical reactions through which an organism builds up or breaks down materials	_____
A collection of living matter enclosed by a barrier that separates it from the surroundings	_____

```
h  o  m  e  o  s  t  a  s  i  s
h  n  s  q  a  a  l  e  s  n  m
m  t  c  e  l  l  s  v  m  s  s
h  y  i  d  o  s  z  o  u  p  b
t  m  e  t  a  b  o  l  i  s  m
r  w  n  l  s  t  x  v  m  s  s
m  i  c  l  s  v  a  e  d  a  h
t  h  e  o  r  y  l  m  e  a  n
m  m  i  c  r  o  s  c  o  p  e
```

2. What results from the oxygen atom being at one end of a water molecule and the hydrogen atoms being at the other end? _____ _____ _____ _____

3. Why is a water molecule polar? _____ _____ _____

4. Circle the letter of each sentence that is true about hydrogen bonds.

   a. A hydrogen bond is stronger than an ionic bond.

   b. The attraction between the hydrogen atom on one water molecule and the oxygen atom on another water molecule is an example.

   c. A hydrogen bond is stronger than a covalent bond.

   d. They are the strongest bonds that form between molecules.

5. Complete the table about forms of attraction.

FORMS OF ATTRACTION

Form of Attraction	Definition
Cohesion	
Adhesion	

6. Why is water extremely cohesive? _____ _____

7. The rise of water in a narrow tube against the force of gravity is called _____.

8. How does capillary action affect plants? _____ _____ _____

Solutions and Suspensions (pages 41–42)

9. What is a mixture? _____ _____ _____

10. A mixture of two or more substances in which the molecules of the substances are evenly mixed is called a(an) _____.

11. The greatest solvent in the world is _____.

Chapter 2, The Chemistry of Life *(continued)*

12. What is a suspension? _____

_____

13. Complete the table about substances in solutions.

SUBSTANCES IN SOLUTIONS

Substance	Definition		Saltwater Solution
Solute			
			Water

Acids, Bases, and pH (pages 42–43)

14. Two water molecules can react to form _____.

15. Why is water neutral despite the production of hydrogen ions
and hydroxide ions? _____

_____

_____

16. What does the pH scale indicate? _____

_____

17. On the pH scale below, indicate which direction is increasingly
acidic and which is increasingly basic.

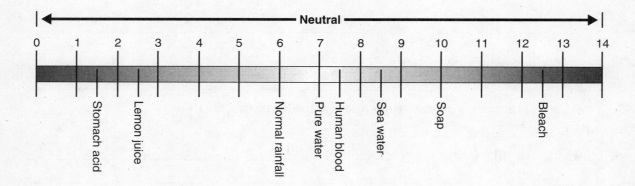

18. How many more H^+ ions does a solution with a pH of 4 have
than a solution with a pH of 5? _____

19. Circle the letter of each sentence that is true about acids.

a. Acidic solutions have pH values below 7.

b. An acid is any compound that forms H^+ ions in solution.

c. Strong acids have pH values ranging from 11 to 14.

d. Acidic solutions contain higher concentrations of H^+ ions than
pure water.

20. Circle the letter of each sentence that is true about bases.

    a. Alkaline solutions have pH values below 7.

    b. A base is a compound that produces OH^- ions in solution.

    c. Strong bases have pH values ranging from 11 to 14.

    d. Basic solutions contain lower concentrations of H^+ ions than pure water.

21. What are buffers? _____

_____

_____

Section 2–3 Carbon Compounds (pages 44–48)

This section explains how the element carbon is able to form millions of carbon, or organic, compounds. It also describes four groups of organic compounds found in living things.

The Chemistry of Carbon (page 44)

1. How many valence electrons does each carbon atom have? _____

_____

2. What gives carbon the ability to form chains that are almost

    unlimited in length? _____

_____

Macromolecules (page 45)

3. Many of the molecules in living cells are so large that they are

    known as _____.

4. What is the process called by which macromolecules are formed? _____

5. When monomers join together, what do they form? _____

6. What are four groups of organic compounds found in living things?

    a. _____

    b. _____

    c. _____

    d. _____

Carbohydrates (pages 45–46)

7. What atoms make up carbohydrates? _____

_____

8. Circle the letter of each sentence that is true about carbohydrates.

    a. Starches and sugars are examples of carbohydrates.

    b. Living things use them as their main source of energy.

    c. The monomers in sugar polymers are starch molecules.

    d. Plants and some animals use them for strength and rigidity.

Chapter 2, The Chemistry of Life (continued)

9. Single sugar molecules are also called _____.

10. Circle the letter of each monosaccharide.

    a. galactose   **b.** glycogen   **c.** glucose   **d.** fructose

11. What are polysaccharides? _____

    _____

12. How do plants and animals store excess sugar? _____

    _____

    _____

Lipids (pages 46–47)

13. What kinds of atoms are lipids mostly made up of? _____

    _____

    _____

14. What are three common categories of lipids?

    a. _____ **b.** _____ **c.** _____

15. Many lipids are formed when a glycerol molecule combines with compounds called _____.

16. Circle the letter of each way that fats are used in living things.

    a. As parts of biological membranes

    b. To store energy

    c. To give plants rigidity

    d. As chemical messengers

17. Complete the table about lipids.

KINDS OF LIPIDS

Kind of Lipid	Description
	Each carbon atom in a lipid's fatty acid chains is joined to another carbon atom by a single bond.
Unsaturated	
	A lipid's fatty acids contain more than one double bond.

Nucleic Acids (page 47)

18. Nucleic acids contain what kinds of atoms? _____

    _____

19. The monomers that make up nucleic acids are known as

_____.

20. A nucleotide consists of what three parts? _____

_____

_____

21. What is the function of nucleic acids in living things? _____

_____

_____

22. What are two kinds of nucleic acids?

a. _____

b. _____

Proteins (pages 47–48)

23. Proteins contain what kinds of atoms? _____

_____

_____

24. Proteins are polymers of molecules called _____.

25. What are four roles that proteins play in living things?

a. _____

b. _____

c. _____

d. _____

Reading Skill Practice

You can often increase your understanding of what you've read by making comparisons. A compare-and-contrast table helps you to do this. On a separate sheet of paper, make a table to compare the four groups of organic compounds you read about in Section 2–3. You might use the heads *Elements, Functions,* and *Examples* for your table. For more information about compare-and-contrast tables, see Organizing Information in Appendix A.

Section 2–4 Chemical Reactions and Enzymes (pages 49–53)

This section describes what happens to chemical bonds during chemical reactions. It also explains how energy changes affect whether a chemical reaction will occur and describes the importance of enzymes to living things.

Chemical Reactions (page 49)

1. What is a chemical reaction? _____

_____

Chapter 2, The Chemistry of Life *(continued)*

2. Complete the table about chemicals in a chemical reaction.

CHEMICALS IN A CHEMICAL REACTION

Chemicals	Definition
Reactants	
Products	

3. Chemical reactions always involve changes in chemical

_____.

Energy in Reactions (page 50)

4. What is released or absorbed whenever chemical bonds form or
are broken? _____

5. What do chemical reactions that absorb energy need to occur? _____
_____

6. Chemists call the energy needed to get a reaction started the

_____.

7. Complete the graph of an energy-
releasing reaction by adding labels
to show the energy of the reactants,
the energy of the products, and the
activation energy.

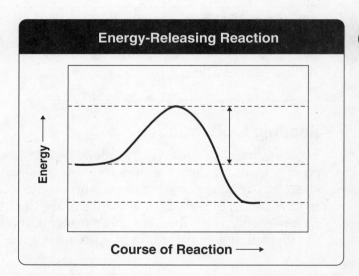

Enzymes (pages 51–52)

8. What is a catalyst? _____
_____

9. Proteins that act as biological catalysts are called

_____.

10. How do cells use enzymes? _____
_____

11. From what is part of an enzyme's name usually derived? _____
_____

Enzyme Action (pages 52–53)

12. The reactants of enzyme-catalyzed reactions are known as

_____.

13. Why are the active site and the substrates in an enzyme-catalyzed

reaction often compared to a lock and key? _____
_____
_____

14. The binding together of an enzyme and a substrate forms a(an)

_____.

15. How do most cells regulate the activity of enzymes? _____
_____
_____

WordWise

Answer the questions by writing the correct vocabulary term in the blanks.
Use the circled letter(s) in each term to find the hidden vocabulary word.
Then, write a definition for the hidden word.

Clues   **Vocabulary Terms**

What is a negatively charged subatomic particle?   __ __ ○ __ __ __ __

What is the basic unit of matter?   __ __ ○ __

What is a large compound formed from
combinations of many monomers?   __ __ __ __ ○ __ __

What is an organic compound called that is used
to store energy and forms important parts of
biological membranes?   __ __ ○ __ __

What is an element or compound called that is
produced by a chemical reaction?   __ __ ○ __ __ __ __

What is the type of mixture whose components are
evenly distributed throughout?   __ __ __ ○ __ __ __ __

What is an atom called that has a positive or negative
charge as a result of gaining or losing electrons?   __ __ ○ __

What is a monomer of nucleic acids called?   __ __ __ __ __ __ __ ○ __

Hidden Word: __ __ __ __ __ __ __ __

Definition: _____
_____

Chapter 3

The Biosphere

Section 3–1 What Is Ecology? (pages 63–65)

This section identifies the different levels of organization that ecologists study. It also describes methods used to study ecology.

Interactions and Interdependence (page 63)

1. What is ecology? _____

_____

2. What does the biosphere contain? _____

_____

_____

Levels of Organization (page 64)

3. Why do ecologists ask questions about events and organisms that

range in complexity from an individual to the biosphere? _____

_____

4. Complete the table about levels of organization.

LEVELS OF ORGANIZATION

Level	Definition
Species	
	A group of individuals that belong to the same species and live in the same area
Community	
Ecosystem	
	A group of ecosystems that have the same climate and dominant communities

5. What is the highest level of organization that ecologists study? _____

_____

Ecological Methods (page 65)

6. What are the three basic approaches scientists use to conduct
modern ecological research?

a. _____ b. _____ c. _____

7. Why might an ecologist set up an artificial environment in a laboratory? _____

_____

8. Why are many ecological phenomena difficult to study? _____

_____

9. Why do ecologists make models? _____

_____

10. Is the following sentence true or false? An ecological model may consist of a mathematical formula. _____

Section 3–2 Energy Flow (pages 67–73)

This section explains where the energy for life processes comes from. It also describes how energy flows through living systems and how efficient the transfer of energy is among organisms in an ecosystem.

Introduction (page 67)

1. What is at the core of every organism's interaction with the environment? _____

Producers (pages 67–68)

2. What source of energy do organisms use that don't use the sun's energy? _____

3. What are autotrophs? _____

_____

4. Why are autotrophs also called producers? _____

_____

5. What do autotrophs do during photosynthesis? _____

_____

_____

6. For each of the following, write which kind of autotroph is the main producer.

   a. Land: _____

   b. Upper layers of ocean: _____

   c. Tidal flats and salt marshes: _____

7. What is chemosynthesis? _____

_____

8. Where do bacteria that carry out chemosynthesis live? _____

_____

_____

_____

Chapter 3, The Biosphere *(continued)*

Consumers (pages 68–69)

9. Heterotrophs are also called _____.

10. Complete the table about types of heterotrophs.

TYPES OF HETEROTROPHS

Type	Definition	Examples
Herbivore		Cows, rabbits
	Heterotroph that eats animals	
Omnivore		Humans, bears, crows
Detritivore		
Decomposer		

11. Plant and animal remains and other dead matter are collectively called _____.

Feeding Relationships (pages 69–71)

12. How does energy flow through an ecosystem? _____
   _____
   _____
   _____

13. Complete the table about feeding relationships.

FEEDING RELATIONSHIPS

Relationship	Description
Food Chain	
Food Web	

14. What does a food web link together? _____
   _____

15. What is a trophic level? _____

16. In a food web, what organisms make up the first trophic level? _____

17. What does a consumer in a food chain depend on for energy? _____

_____

Ecological Pyramids (pages 72–73)

18. What is an ecological pyramid? _____

_____

_____

19. Why is it that only part of the energy stored in one trophic level is

passed on to the next level? _____

_____

20. Complete the energy pyramid by writing the source of the energy
for the food web and how much energy is available to first-,
second-, and third-level consumers.

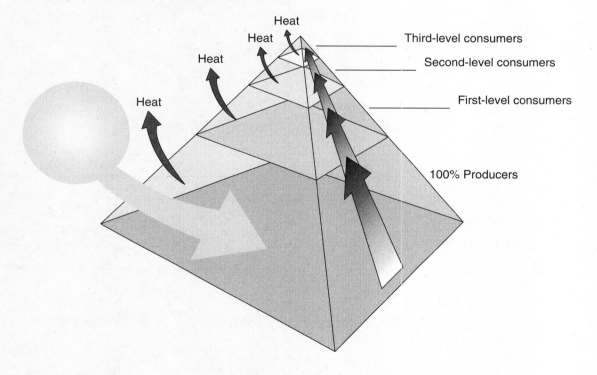

21. What is biomass? _____

_____

22. What does a biomass pyramid represent? _____

_____

23. What does a pyramid of numbers show? _____

_____

24. Why can each trophic level support only about one tenth the

amount of living tissue as the level below it? _____

_____

_____

Chapter 3, The Biosphere *(continued)*

Reading Skill Practice

When you read about complex topics, writing an outline can help you organize and understand the material. Outline Section 3–2 by using the headings and subheadings as topics and subtopics and then writing the most important details under each topic. Do your work on a separate sheet of paper.

Section 3–3 Cycles of Matter (pages 74–80)

This section describes how matter cycles among the living and nonliving parts of an ecosystem. It also explains how nutrients are important in living systems.

Introduction (page 74)

1. What are the four elements that make up over 95 percent of the body in most organisms? _____

Recycling in the Biosphere (page 74)

2. How is the movement of matter through the biosphere different from the flow of energy? _____

_____

3. Matter moves through an ecosystem in _____

_____.

4. What do biogeochemical cycles connect? _____

_____

The Water Cycle (page 75)

5. Water can enter the atmosphere by evaporating from the leaves of plants in the process of _____.

6. Circle the letter of each process involved in the water cycle.

   a. precipitation　**b.** evaporation　**c.** runoff　**d.** fertilization

Nutrient Cycles (pages 76–79)

7. What are nutrients? _____

_____

8. What are the three nutrient cycles that play especially prominent roles in the biosphere?

   a. _____　**c.** _____

   b. _____

9. Why is carbon especially important to living systems? _____

_____

10. Complete the table about the kinds of processes involved in the carbon cycle.

KINDS OF PROCESSES IN THE CARBON CYCLE

Kind of Processes	Examples
Biological processes	
	Release of CO_2 to the atmosphere by volcanoes
Mixed geochemical processes	
Human activity	

11. What are three large reservoirs where carbon is found in the biosphere?

   a. As carbon dioxide gas in the _____

   b. As dissolved carbon dioxide in the _____

   c. As coal, petroleum, and calcium carbonate rock found _____

12. In what process do plants use carbon dioxide? _____

13. Why do all organisms require nitrogen? _____
_____

14. What is the main reservoir of nitrogen in the biosphere? _____
_____

15. What is nitrogen fixation? _____
_____

16. What is denitrification? _____
_____

17. What role does denitrification play in the nitrogen cycle? _____
_____

18. Circle the letter of each sentence that is true about the phosphorus cycle.

   a. Phosphate is released as rocks and sediments wear down.

   b. Plants absorb phosphate from the soil or from water.

   c. Phosphorus is abundant in the atmosphere.

   d. Organic phosphate cannot move through food webs.

19. Why is phosphorus essential to living things? _____
_____
_____

Chapter 3, The Biosphere *(continued)*

Nutrient Limitation *(page 80)*

20. What is the primary productivity of an ecosystem? _____
_____

21. If a nutrient is in short supply in an ecosystem, how will it affect
an organism? _____

22. When is a substance called a limiting nutrient? _____
_____
_____

23. In the ocean and other saltwater environments, what is often the
limiting factor? _____

24. What is the typical limiting factor in streams, lakes, and
freshwater environments? _____

25. When an aquatic ecosystem receives a large input of a limiting
nutrient, what is often the result, and what is this result called? _____
_____
_____

26. Why do blooms occur? _____
_____
_____

WordWise

Complete the sentences by using one of the scrambled words below.

dcreuorps   meiob   aieoeoibgchmcl yeccl
mtssyceoe   ythnssieoemhcs   ttnnreiu

The process by which organisms use chemical energy to produce carbohydrates is

_____.

A collection of all the organisms that live in a particular place, together with their physical

environment, is a(an) _____.

A chemical substance that an organism requires to live is a(an)

_____.

Autotrophs, which make their own food, are also called _____.

A group of ecosystems that have the same climate and dominant communities is

a(an) _____.

A process in which elements, chemical compounds, or other forms of matter are passed
from one organism to another and from one part of the biosphere to another is a(an)

_____.

Chapter 4

Ecosystems and Communities

Section 4–1 The Role of Climate (pages 87–89)

This section explains how the greenhouse effect maintains the biosphere's temperature range. It also describes Earth's three main climate zones.

What Is Climate? (page 87)

1. How is weather different from climate? _____

_____

_____

_____

2. What factors cause climate? _____

_____

_____

_____

_____

The Greenhouse Effect (page 87)

3. Circle the letter of the world's insulating blanket.

    a. oxygen   **b.** the atmosphere   **c.** the oceans   **d.** solar energy

4. Complete the illustration of the greenhouse effect by showing in arrows and words what happens to the sunlight that hits Earth's surface.

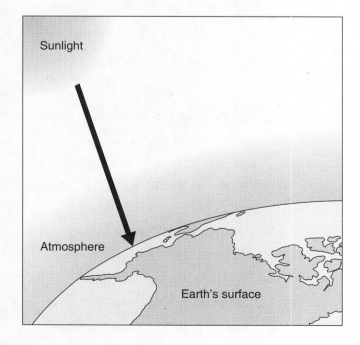

Chapter 4, Ecosystems and Communities *(continued)*

5. What effect do carbon dioxide, methane, and a few other atmospheric gases have on Earth's temperature? _____

_____

6. What is the greenhouse effect? _____

_____

The Effect of Latitude on Climate *(page 88)*

7. Why does solar radiation strike different parts of Earth's surface at an angle that varies throughout the year? _____

_____

8. Circle the letter of where the sun is almost directly overhead at noon all year.

   a. the North Pole   **b.** China   **c.** the equator   **d.** the South Pole

9. Why does Earth have different climate zones? _____

_____

_____

10. Complete the table about Earth's three main climate zones.

MAIN CLIMATE ZONES

Climate Zone	Location	Climate Characteristics
	Areas around North and South poles	
	Between the polar zones and the tropics	
	Near the equator	

Heat Transport in the Biosphere *(page 89)*

11. What force drives winds and ocean currents? _____

_____

12. The process in which water rises toward the surface in warmer regions is called _____.

13. Circle the letter of each sentence that is true about ocean currents.

   a. Patterns of heating and cooling result in ocean currents.

   b. Ocean currents transport heat within the biosphere.

   c. Surface water moved by winds result in ocean currents.

   d. Ocean currents have no effect on the climate of landmasses.

Section 4–2 What Shapes an Ecosystem? (pages 90–97)

This section explains how biotic and abiotic factors influence an ecosystem. It also describes what interactions occur within communities and explains how ecosystems recover from a disturbance.

Biotic and Abiotic Factors (page 90)

1. Complete the table about factors that influence ecosystems.

FACTORS THAT INFLUENCE ECOSYSTEMS

Type of Factor	Definition	Examples
Biotic factors		
Abiotic factors		

2. What do the biotic and abiotic factors together determine? _____
_____
_____

The Niche (pages 91–92)

3. What is a niche? _____
_____

4. In what ways is food part of an organism's niche? _____
_____
_____

5. Circle the letter of each sentence that is true about niches.
   a. Different species can share the same niche in the same habitat.
   b. No two species can share the same niche in the same habitat.
   c. Two species in the same habitat have to share a niche to survive.
   d. Different species can occupy niches that are very similar.

Community Interactions (pages 92–93)

6. When does competition occur? _____
_____

7. What is a resource? _____
_____

Chapter 4, Ecosystems and Communities *(continued)*

8. What is often the result of direct competition in nature? _____
_____
_____

9. What is the competitive exclusion principle? _____
_____

10. What is predation? _____
_____

11. When predation occurs, what is the organism called that does the
killing and eating, and what is the food organism called? _____
_____
_____

12. What is symbiosis? _____
_____

13. Complete the table about main classes of symbiotic relationships.

MAIN CLASSES OF SYMBIOTIC RELATIONSHIPS

	Description of Relationship
Mutualism	
Commensalism	
Parasitism	

14. The organism from which a parasite obtains nutritional needs is
called a(an) _____.

15. Circle the letter of each sentence that is true of parasites.
    a. They generally weaken but do not kill their host.
    b. They obtain all or part of their nutritional needs from the host.
    c. They neither help nor harm the host.
    d. They are usually smaller than the host.

Ecological Succession *(pages 94–97)*

16. What is ecological succession? _____
_____

17. What is primary succession? _____
_____

18. The first species to populate an area when primary succession
begins are called _____.

19. When a disturbance changes a community without removing the soil, what follows? _____

_____

20. An area that was once referred to as a climax community may appear to be permanent, but what might cause it to undergo change? _____

_____

Section 4–3 Land Biomes (pages 98–105)

This section describes the unique characteristics of the world's major land biomes. It also describes other land areas.

Introduction (page 98)

1. What is a biome? _____

_____

_____

Climate and Microclimate (page 98)

2. What does a climate diagram summarize? _____

_____

_____

3. Complete the climate diagram by adding labels to the bottom and both sides of the graph to show what the responding variables are.

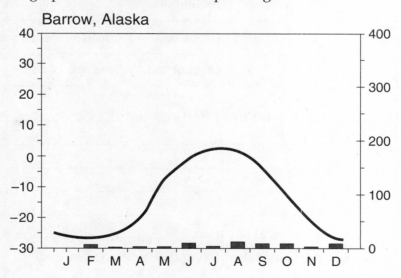

4. On a climate diagram, what does the line plot and what do the vertical bars show? _____

_____

_____

Chapter 4, Ecosystems and Communities *(continued)*

5. What is a microclimate? _____

_____

_____

The Major Biomes *(pages 99–103)*

6. Circle the letter of each sentence that is true about how each of the world's major biomes is defined.

a. Each is defined by a unique set of abiotic factors.

b. Each has a characteristic ecological community.

c. Each is defined by the country it is in.

d. Each is particularly defined by climate.

Use the map in Figure 4–12 to match the biome with its geographic distribution.

Biome	Geographic Distribution
_____ **7.** Tropical rain forest	**a.** Forest biome that occurs almost exclusively in the Northern Hemisphere
_____ **8.** Tundra	**b.** Biome that occurs on or near the equator
_____ **9.** Boreal forest	**c.** Biome that occurs near or above 60°N latitude

10. Complete the table about layers of a tropical rain forest.

LAYERS OF A TROPICAL RAIN FOREST

Layer	Definition
	Dense covering formed by the leafy tops of tall trees
	Layer of shorter trees and vines

11. In what kind of places do tropical dry forests grow? _____

_____

_____

12. What is a deciduous tree? _____

_____

13. What is another name for tropical savannas? _____

14. Is the following sentence true or false? Savannas are found in large parts of eastern Africa. _____

15. Circle the letter of each sentence that is true about deserts.

a. They are hot day and night.

b. The soils are rich in minerals but poor in organic material.

c. Cacti and other succulents are dominant plants.

d. Reptiles are the only wildlife.

16. What amount of annual precipitation defines a desert biome? _____
_____
_____

17. What factors maintain the characteristic plant community of
temperate grasslands? _____
_____

18. Why is fire a constant threat in temperate woodland and shrubland? _____
_____
_____

19. Communities that are dominated by shrubs are also known as
_____.

20. What kinds of trees do temperate forests contain? _____
_____

21. What is a coniferous tree? _____
_____

22. What is humus? _____
_____

23. What is the geographic distribution of the northwestern
coniferous forest? _____
_____

24. Boreal forests are also called _____.

25. What are the seasons like in a boreal forest? _____
_____
_____

26. Circle the letter of each sentence that is true about boreal forests.
 a. Dominant plants include spruce and fir.
 b. They have very high precipitation.
 c. They have soils that are rich in humus.
 d. Dominant wildlife include moose and other large herbivores.

27. What is permafrost? _____
_____

28. What happens to the ground in tundra during the summer? _____
_____
_____

29. Why are tundra plants small and stunted? _____
_____
_____

Chapter 4, Ecosystems and Communities *(continued)*

Other Land Areas (page 105)

30. Number the sequence of conditions you would find as you moved from the base to the summit of a mountain. Number the conditions at the base *1*.

_____ **a.** Stunted vegetation like that in tundra

_____ **b.** Grassland

_____ **c.** Forest of spruce and other conifers

_____ **d.** Open woodland of pines

31. When are the polar regions cold? _____

_____

32. What plants and algae can be found in the polar ice regions? _____

_____

33. In the north polar region, what are the dominant animals? _____

_____

34. The abiotic and biotic conditions of mountain ranges vary with

_____.

Reading Skill Practice

You can often increase your understanding of what you've read by making comparisons. A compare-and-contrast table helps you to do this. On a separate sheet of paper, make a table to compare the major land biomes you read about in Section 4–3. The characteristics that you might use to form the basis of your comparison could include a general description, abiotic factors, dominant plants, dominant wildlife, and geographic distribution. For more information about compare-and-contrast tables, see Organizing Information in Appendix A of your textbook.

Section 4–4 Aquatic Ecosystems (pages 106–112)

This section explains the main factors that govern aquatic ecosystems. It also describes the characteristics of freshwater ecosystems, freshwater wetlands, estuaries, and the different marine zones.

Introduction (page 106)

1. Aquatic ecosystems are primarily determined by what characteristics of the overlying water?

a. _____ **c.** _____

b. _____ **d.** _____

2. What does the depth of the water determine? _____

_____

3. What does water chemistry primarily refer to? _____
_____
_____

Freshwater Ecosystems (pages 106–107)

4. What are the two main types of freshwater ecosystems?

a. _____ b. _____

5. Where do flowing-water ecosystems originate? _____
_____
_____

6. How does the circulating water in a standing-water ecosystem affect the ecosystem? _____
_____

7. What is plankton? _____
_____
_____

8. Complete the table about kinds of plankton.

KINDS OF PLANKTON

Kind	Organisms	How Nutrition Obtained
	Single-celled algae	
	Planktonic animals	

9. What is a wetland? _____
_____
_____

10. What is brackish water? _____

11. What are three main types of freshwater wetlands?

a. _____ b. _____ c. _____

12. What distinguishes a marsh from a swamp? _____
_____
_____

Estuaries (page 108)

13. What are estuaries? _____
_____

14. Tiny pieces of decaying plants and animals make up the
_____ that provides food for organisms at the base
of an estuary's food web.

Chapter 4, Ecosystems and Communities *(continued)*

15. Circle the letter of each sentence that is true about estuaries.

   a. Most primary production is consumed by herbivores.

   b. They contain a mixture of fresh water and salt water.

   c. Sunlight can't reach the bottom to power photosynthesis.

   d. They are affected by the rise and fall of ocean tides.

16. What are salt marshes? _____

_____

_____

17. What are mangrove swamps, and where are they found? _____

_____

_____

Marine Ecosystems *(pages 109–112)*

18. What is the photic zone of the ocean? _____

_____

19. The permanently dark zone below the photic zone is called the

_____.

20. What are the three main vertical divisions of the ocean based on the depth and distance from the shore?

   a. _____ **b.** _____ **c.** _____

21. Circle the letter of each sentence that is true about the intertidal zone.

   a. Organisms there are exposed to extreme changes in their surroundings.

   b. The rocky intertidal zones exist in temperate regions.

   c. Organisms are battered by currents but not by waves.

   d. Competition among organisms often leads to zonation.

22. What is zonation? _____

_____

23. What are the boundaries of the coastal ocean? _____

_____

_____

24. Why is the coastal ocean often rich in plankton and many other

organisms? _____

_____

_____

25. A huge forest of giant brown algae in the coastal ocean is a(an)

_____.

26. Circle the letter of each sentence that is true about coral reefs.

  a. The coasts of Florida and Hawaii have coral reefs.

  b. The primary structure of coral reefs are the skeletons of coral animals.

  c. Almost all growth in a coral reef occurs within 40 meters of the surface.

  d. Only a few organisms are able to live near coral reefs.

27. What are the boundaries of the open ocean? _____

_____

_____

28. The benthic zone covers the ocean _____.

29. What are the boundaries of the benthic zone? _____

_____

_____

30. Organisms that live attached to or near the bottom of the ocean are called _____.

WordWise

Answer the questions by writing the correct vocabulary terms from Chapter 4 in the blanks. Use the circled letter from each term to find the hidden word. Then, write a definition for the hidden word.

What are physical factors that shape ecosystems?

__ Ⓞ __ __ __ __ __   __ __ __ __ __ __ __ __

What is the full range of physical and biological conditions in which an organism lives and the way in which the organism uses those conditions?

__ Ⓞ __ __ __

What are the planktonic animals called?

__ Ⓞ __ __ __ __ __ __ __ __ __ __ __

What is a layer of permanently frozen subsoil in the tundra?

__ __ __ Ⓞ __ __ __ __ __ __ __

What is the average, year-after-year conditions of temperature and precipitation in a particular region?

__ __ __ __ __ __ Ⓞ

Hidden Word: __ __ __ __ __

Definition: _____

_____

Populations

Section 5–1 How Populations Grow (pages 119–123)

This section identifies the characteristics used to describe a population. It also describes factors that affect population size and explains what exponential growth and logistic growth are.

Characteristics of Populations (page 119)

1. What are the four main characteristics of a population?

   a. _____ c. _____

   b. _____ d. _____

2. What is a population's geographic distribution? _____
   _____

3. Another term for geographic distribution is _____.

4. What is population density? _____
   _____

5. What is the equation with which you can calculate population density? _____

Population Growth (page 120)

6. Circle the letter of each sentence that is true about populations.

   a. They can grow rapidly.

   b. They can decrease in size.

   c. They may stay the same size from year to year.

   d. They stay the same size until they disappear.

7. What three factors can affect population size?

   a. _____

   b. _____

   c. _____

8. If more individuals are born than die in any period of time, how will the population change? _____

9. Complete the table about changes in population.

CHANGES IN POPULATION

Type of Change	Definition	Resulting Change in Size
Immigration		
Emigration		

Exponential Growth (page 121)

10. How will a population change if there is abundant space and food and if the population is protected from predators and disease? _____ _____ _____

11. When does exponential growth occur? _____ _____

12. What are three ways that a growth rate may be stated, or expressed? _____ _____ _____

13. Under ideal conditions with unlimited resources, how will a population grow? _____

14. Complete the graph by drawing the characteristic shape of exponential population growth.

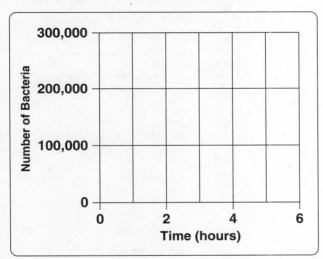

Exponential Growth of Bacterial Population

15. Is the following sentence true or false? Elephants never grow exponentially because their rate of reproduction is so slow.

    _____

Logistic Growth (page 122)

16. Circle each sentence that is true about exponential growth.

    a. It continues until the organism covers the planet.

    b. It continues at the same rate as resources become less available.

    c. It does not continue in natural populations for very long.

    d. It continues in natural populations until the birthrate increases.

17. When resources become less available, how does population growth change? _____

Chapter 5, Populations *(continued)*

18. When does logistic growth occur? _____

_____

_____

19. Circle the letter of each instance when a population's growth will slow down.

    a. The birthrate and death rate are the same.

    b. The birthrate is greater than the death rate.

    c. The rate of immigration is equal to the rate of emigration.

    d. The rate of emigration is less the that rate of immigration.

20. What is the carrying capacity of the environment for a particular

species? _____

_____

21. Complete the graph by drawing the characteristic shape of logistic population growth.

Logistic Growth of Yeast Population

Carrying capacity

Number of Yeast Cells

Time (hours)

Section 5–2 Limits to Growth (pages 124–127)

This section describes what factors limit population growth.

Limiting Factors (page 124)

1. What is a limiting factor? _____

_____

2. How do different limiting factors affect populations? _____

_____

_____

_____

Density-Dependent Factors (pages 125–126)

3. What is a density-dependent limiting factor? _____

   _____

4. When do density-dependent factors become limiting? _____

   _____

5. When do density-dependent factors operate most strongly? _____

   _____

6. What are four density-dependent limiting factors?

   a. _____   c. _____

   b. _____   d. _____

7. When populations become crowded, what do organisms compete

   with one another for? _____

   _____

8. The mechanism of population control in which a population is
   regulated by predation is called a(an)

   _____.

9. What are the prey and what are the predators in the predator-
   prey relationship on Isle Royale? _____

   _____

10. Why does the wolf population on Isle Royale decline following a

    decline in the moose population? _____

    _____

11. How are parasites like predators? _____

    _____

Density-Independent Factors (page 127)

12. A limiting factor that affects all populations in similar ways,
    regardless of population size, is called a(an)

    _____.

13. What are examples of density-independent limiting factors? _____

    _____

    _____

14. Circle the letter of each sentence that is true about changes caused
    by density-independent factors.

    a. Most populations can adapt to a certain amount of change.

    b. Periodic droughts can affect entire populations of grasses.

    c. Populations never build up again after a crash in population size.

    d. Major upsets in an ecosystem can lead to long-term declines in
       certain populations.

Chapter 5, Populations *(continued)*

15. What is the characteristic response in the population size of many
    species to a density-independent limiting factor? _____

    _____

Reading Skill Practice

A graph can help you understand comparisons of data at a glance. By looking
carefully at a graph in a textbook, you can help yourself understand better what
you have read. Look carefully at the graph in Figure 5–7 on page 126. What
important concept does this graph communicate?

Section 5–3 Human Population Growth (pages 129–132)

*This section describes how the size of the human population has changed
over time. It also explains why population growth rates differ in countries
throughout the world.*

Historical Overview (page 129)

1. How does the size of the human population change with time? _____

   _____

2. Why did the population grow slowly for most of human existence? _____

   _____

   _____

3. Circle the letter of each reason why the human population began
   to grow more rapidly about 500 years ago.

   a. Improved sanitation and health care reduced the death rate.

   b. Industry made life easier and safer.

   c. The world's food supply became more reliable.

   d. Birthrates in most places remained low.

Patterns of Population Growth (pages 130–131)

4. Why can't the human population keep growing exponentially

   forever? _____

5. What is demography? _____

   _____

6. What factors help predict why the populations of some countries

   grow faster than others? _____

   _____

   _____

7. The hypothesis that explains why population growth has slowed dramatically in the United States, Japan, and much of Europe is called the _____.

8. Throughout much of human history, what have been the levels of birthrates and death rates in human societies? _____

_____

9. What factors lower the death rate? _____

_____

10. Complete the flowchart about the demographic transition.

```
┌──────────────────────────────────────────────────────────────────┐
│ Changes brought about by modernization lower the _____ rate.   │
└──────────────────────────────────────────────────────────────────┘
                              │
                              ▼
┌──────────────────────────────────────────────────────────────────┐
│ Births greatly exceed deaths, resulting in rapid population _____. │
└──────────────────────────────────────────────────────────────────┘
                              │
                              ▼
┌──────────────────────────────────────────────────────────────────┐
│ As modernization continues, the birthrate _____ and population     │
│ growth _____.                                                      │
└──────────────────────────────────────────────────────────────────┘
                              │
                              ▼
┌──────────────────────────────────────────────────────────────────┐
│ The birthrate falls to meet the death rate, and population growth __. │
└──────────────────────────────────────────────────────────────────┘
```

11. Circle the letter of each sentence that is true about human population growth.

a. The demographic transition is complete in China and India.

b. The worldwide human population is still growing exponentially.

c. Most people live in countries that have not yet completed the demographic transition.

d. The demographic transition has happened in the United States.

12. Is the following sentence true or false? Population growth depends, in part, on how many people of different ages make up a given population. _____

13. What do age-structure diagrams graph? _____

_____

14. What do the age structures of the United States and of Rwanda predict about the population growth of each country? _____

_____

_____

_____

Chapter 5, Populations *(continued)*

Future Population Growth **(page 132)**

15. By 2050, the world's population may reach how many people? _____

_____

16. What may cause the growth rate of the world population to level

off, or even slow down? _____

_____

17. What do many ecologists suggest will happen if the growth in

human population does not slow down? _____

_____

WordWise

Use the clues to help you write the vocabulary terms from Chapter 5 in the blanks. Then, put the numbered letters in order to find the answer to the riddle.

What kind of limiting factor depends on population size?

— — — — — — — — — - — — — — — — — — — — —
　　　　　　　　　　1

What occurs when the individuals in a population reproduce at a constant rate?

— — — — — — — — — — — — — — — — — —
　　　　　2

What is the movement of individuals into an area called?

— — — — — — — — — — — —
　　3　　　　　　4

What occurs when a population's growth slows or stops following a period of exponential growth?

— — — — — — — — — — — — —
　　　　5　　　　　　6

What is a mechanism of population control in which a population is regulated by predation?

— — — — — — — — - — — — — — — — — — — — — — — — — —
　　　7　　　　　　　　　　　　　　　　　　8

What is the tendency of a population to shift from high birth and death rates to low birth and death rates called?

— —
　　　　　9

What is the largest number of individuals a given environment can support called?

— — — — — — — — — — — — — — — — —
　　　10

Riddle: What is the scientific study of human populations called?

Answer: — — — — — — — — — —
　　　1　2　3　4　5　6　7　8　9　10

Humans in the Biosphere

Section 6–1 A Changing Landscape (pages 139–143)

This section describes types of human activities that can affect the biosphere.

Earth as an Island (page 139)

1. Increasing demands on what resources come with a growing human population? _____

_____

Human Activities (page 140)

2. Is the following sentence true or false? Human activity uses as much energy as all of Earth's other multicellular species combined.

_____

3. What four human activities have transformed the biosphere?

a. _____   c. _____

b. _____   d. _____

Hunting and Gathering (page 140)

4. How did prehistoric hunters and gatherers change the environment? _____

_____

_____

5. Hunting that makes relatively few demands on the environment is called _____.

Agriculture (pages 141–142)

6. What is agriculture? _____

7. Why was the spread of agriculture an important event in human history? _____

_____

8. What ecological changes came with the cultivation of both plants and animals? _____

_____

_____

9. What changes in agriculture occurred in the 1800s as a result of advancements in science and technology? _____

_____

_____

Chapter 6, Humans in the Biosphere *(continued)*

10. What was the green revolution? _____

_____

_____

11. What is the farming method called monoculture? _____

_____

_____

12. Circle the letter of each benefit of the green revolution to human society.

   a. It helped prevent food shortages.

   b. China and India depleted water supplies.

   c. It increased food production.

   d. Global food production was cut in half.

Industrial Growth and Urban Development (page 143)

13. What occurred during the Industrial Revolution of the 1800s? _____

_____

14. From what resources do we obtain most of the energy to produce and power the machines we use? _____

_____

15. The continued spread of suburban communities across the American landscape is referred to as _____.

16. How does suburban sprawl place stress on plant and animal populations? _____

Section 6–2 Renewable and Nonrenewable Resources (pages 144–149)

This section explains how environmental resources are classified. It also describes what effect human activities have on natural resources.

Introduction (page 144)

1. How was the commons in an old English village destroyed? _____

_____

_____

_____

The Tragedy of the Commons (page 144)

2. What is meant by the phrase the "tragedy of the commons"? _____

_____

_____

_____

3. Complete the table about types of environmental resources.

TYPES OF ENVIRONMENTAL RESOURCES

Type of Resource	Definition	Examples
Renewable resources		
Nonrenewable resources		

Sustainable Use (page 145)

4. What is sustainable use? _____

_____

5. How do human activities affect renewable resources? _____

_____

_____

6. Upon which principles are sustainable practices based? _____

_____

_____

Land Resources (page 145)

7. What is fertile soil? _____

_____

8. The uppermost layer of soil is called _____.

9. What is soil erosion? _____

_____

10. How does plowing the land increase the rate of soil erosion? _____

_____

11. The conversion of a previously soil-rich, productive area into a

desert is called _____.

12. What can cause desertification? _____

_____

Forest Resources (page 146)

13. Why have forests been called the "lungs of the Earth"? _____

_____

14. Why are forests in Alaska and the Pacific Northwest called old-

growth forests? _____

15. What is deforestation, and how does it affect soil? _____

_____

Chapter 6, Humans in the Biosphere *(continued)*

Ocean Resources (page 147)

16. For what resources are the Earth's oceans particularly valuable? _____

_____

_____

17. The practice of harvesting fish faster than they can reproduce is called _____.

18. What are some important species that have been overfished? _____

_____

_____

19. What is one approach to sustainable use of fisheries? _____

_____

_____

20. What is aquaculture? _____

Air Resources (page 148)

21. What is smog? _____

_____

22. What is a pollutant? _____

_____

23. How does the burning of fossil fuels affect air quality? _____

_____

_____

24. Microscopic particles of ash and dust in the air that can cause health problems are called _____.

25. What does acid rain contain that kills plants and harms soil? _____

_____

26. Complete the illustration by writing the names of the processes that lead to the formation of acid rain.

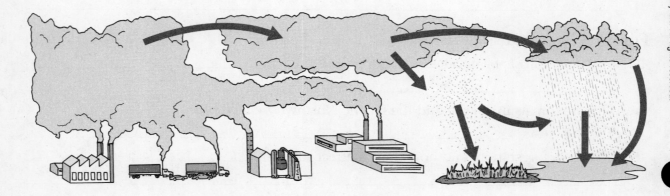

Water Resources (page 149)

27. Why are protecting water supplies from pollution and managing demand for water major priorities? _____

_____

28. What is domestic sewage, and how does it threaten water supplies? _____

_____

_____

_____

29. How can protecting forests ensure sustainable use of water resources? _____

_____

30. Why can conservation in agriculture save large amounts of water? _____

_____

_____

Section 6–3 Biodiversity (pages 150–156)

This section describes what the current threats to biodiversity are. It also explains the goal of conservation biology.

The Value of Biodiversity (page 150)

1. What is biodiversity? _____

_____

2. Complete the table about diversity.

DIVERSITY IN THE BIOSPHERE

Type of Diversity	Definition
Ecosystem diversity	
Species diversity	
Genetic diversity	

3. Why is biodiversity one of Earth's greatest natural resources? _____

_____

_____

_____

Chapter 6, Humans in the Biosphere *(continued)*

Threats to Biodiversity (page 151)

4. What are four ways that human activity can reduce biodiversity?

a. _____

b. _____

c. _____

d. _____

5. When does extinction occur? _____

_____

6. A species whose population size is declining in a way that places it in danger of extinction is called a(an) _____.

7. Why does a declining population make a species more vulnerable to extinction? _____

_____

Habitat Alteration and Fragmentation (page 151)

8. The process of splitting a habitat into small pieces is called

_____.

Demand for Wildlife Products (page 151)

9. Why are species hunted? _____

_____

_____

Pollution (page 152)

10. What is DDT? _____

11. What two properties of DDT make it hazardous over the long term? _____

_____

_____

12. What is biological magnification? _____

_____

_____

Introduced Species (page 153)

13. Plants and animals that have migrated to places where they are not native are called _____.

14. Why do invasive species reproduce rapidly and increase their populations? _____

_____

Conserving Biodiversity (pages 154–156)

15. What is conservation? _____

_____

16. What is the purpose of conservation biology? _____

_____

17. What does protecting an ecosystem ensure? _____

_____

_____

Reading Skill Practice

Writing a summary can help you remember the information you have read. When you write a summary, write only the important points. Write a summary of the information in Section 6–3. Your summary should be shorter than the text on which it is based. Do your work on a separate sheet of paper.

Section 6–4 Charting a Course for the Future (pages 157–160)

This section describes two types of global change that is of concern to biologists.

Ozone Depletion (pages 157–158)

1. What is ozone? _____

_____

2. Where is ozone concentrated in the atmosphere? _____

_____

3. Over what continent has a "hole" in the ozone layer been growing larger and lasting longer over the last 20 years?

_____

4. What is causing the problem of ozone depletion? _____

_____

_____

_____

Global Warming (page 159)

5. What is global warming? _____

_____

6. What is the most widely accepted hypothesis about the cause of global warming? _____

_____

_____

Chapter 6, Humans in the Biosphere *(continued)*

7. Circle the letter of each sentence that is true about the problem of global warming.

   a. The burning of fossil fuels pulls carbon dioxide from the atmosphere.

   b. Some scientists think it is part of natural variations in climate.

   c. The 1990s were the hottest decade ever recorded.

   d. Cutting down and burning forests adds carbon dioxide to the atmosphere.

8. If global warming continues at the current rate, how might sea level be affected? _____

   _____

   _____

The Value of a Healthy Biosphere *(page 160)*

9. What goods and services does a healthy biosphere provide to us? _____

   _____

   _____

   _____

10. What is the most important shift that a society can make to solve today's ecological problems? _____

    _____

11. What is the first step in charting a course that will improve living conditions without harming the environment? _____

    _____

WordWise

Complete the sentences using one of the scrambled terms below.

oouuertlcnm   diiioeytsrvb   lblgao mwgnira   fortaestnoide
eeernwbla eecruosr

1. The loss of forests is _____.

2. The increase in the average temperature of the biosphere is

   _____.

3. A resource that can regenerate and therefore is replaceable is a(an)

   _____.

4. The agricultural method in which large fields are planted with a single crop year after year is _____.

5. The sum total of the genetically based variety of all organisms of the biosphere is

   _____.

Section 10–3 Regulating the Cell Cycle (pages 250–252)

This section describes how the cell cycle is regulated. It also explains how cancer cells are different from other cells.

Controls on Cell Division (page 250)

1. What happens to the cells at the edges of an injury when a cut in the skin or a break in a bone occurs? _____

_____

2. What happens to the rapidly dividing cells when the healing process nears completion? _____

_____

Cell Cycle Regulators (page 251)

3. What do cyclins regulate? _____

_____

4. What are internal regulators? _____

5. Circle the letter of each sentence that is true about external regulators.

   a. They direct cells to speed up or slow down the cell cycle.

   b. They prevent the cell from entering anaphase until all its chromosomes are attached to the mitotic spindle.

   c. They include growth factors.

   d. They prevent excessive cell growth and keep the tissues of the body from disrupting each other.

Uncontrolled Cell Growth (page 252)

6. What is cancer? _____

_____

7. Complete the flowchart about cancer.

```
┌─────────────────────────────────────────────────────────┐
│ Cancer cells don't respond to signals that regulate _____. │
└─────────────────────────────────────────────────────────┘
                            │
                            ▼
┌─────────────────────────────────────────────────────────┐
│ Cancer cells form masses of cells called _____.           │
└─────────────────────────────────────────────────────────┘
                            │
                            ▼
┌─────────────────────────────────────────────────────────┐
│ Cancer cells break loose and spread throughout the _____. │
└─────────────────────────────────────────────────────────┘
```

8. Is the following sentence true or false? Cancer is a disease of the cell cycle. _____

Chapter 10, Cell Growth and Division *(continued)*

WordWise

Complete the sentences by using one of the scrambled words below.

Word Bank

spetmeaha	sdtihcmora	eshaploet	phsaeorp	kniesscitoy	aasehpan
nilpsed	lecl yeclc	elcl voisdini	metonercer	astinhepre	sotimsi
nacecr	cinlyc	tenilorec			

1. The division of a cell's cytoplasm is called _____.

2. The final phase of mitosis is _____.

3. The phase of mitosis in which microtubules connect the centromere of each chromosome to the poles of the spindle is

   _____.

4. At the beginning of cell division, each chromosome consists of

   two sister _____.

5. The longest phase of mitosis is _____.

6. The phase of mitosis that ends when the chromosomes stop

   moving is _____

7. The process by which a cell divides into two new daughter cells is

   called _____.

8. A tiny structure located in the cytoplasm near the nuclear

   envelope is a(an) _____.

9. A disorder in which some of the body's cells lose the ability to

   control growth is called _____.

10. The area where a pair of chromotids is attached is the

    _____.

11. The division of the cell nucleus is called _____.

12. A protein that regulates the timing of the cell cycle in eukaryotic

    cells is _____.

13. The series of events that cells go through as they grow and divide

    is known as the _____.

14. A fanlike microtubule structure that helps separate the

    chromosomes is a(an) _____.

15. The time period between cell divisions is called

    _____.

Section 11–3 Exploring Mendelian Genetics (pages 270–274)

This section describes Mendel's principle of independent assortment. It also tells about traits that are controlled by multiple alleles or multiple genes.

Independent Assortment (pages 270–271)

1. In a two-factor cross, Mendel followed _____ different genes as they passed from one generation to the next.

2. Write the genotypes of the true-breeding plants that Mendel used in his two-factor cross.

Phenotype	Genotype
a. round yellow peas	_____
b. wrinkled green peas	_____

3. Circle the letter that best describes the F$_1$ offspring of Mendel's two-factor cross.

   a. Homozygous dominant with round yellow peas

   b. Homozygous recessive with wrinkled green peas

   c. Heterozygous dominant with round yellow peas

   d. Heterozygous recessive with wrinkled green peas

4. Is the following sentence true or false? The genotypes of the F$_1$ offspring indicated to Mendel that genes assort independently.

   _____

5. How did Mendel produce the F$_2$ offspring? _____
   _____

6. Circle the letter of the phenotypes that Mendel would expect to see if genes segregated independently.

   a. round and yellow

   b. wrinkled and green

   c. round and green

   d. wrinkled and yellow

7. What did Mendel observe in the F$_2$ offspring that showed him that the alleles for seed shape segregate independently of those for seed color? _____
   _____
   _____
   _____

8. What were the phenotypes of the F$_2$ generation that Mendel observed? _____
   _____

9. What was the ratio of Mendel's F$_2$ generation for the two-factor cross? _____

Chapter 11, Introduction to Genetics (continued)

10. Complete the Punnett square below to show the predicted results of Mendel's two-factor cross.

MENDEL'S TWO-FACTOR CROSS
RrYy × RrYy

	RY	Ry	rY	ry
RY				
Ry				
rY				
ry				

11. State Mendel's principle of independent assortment. _____
_____
_____

A Summary of Mendel's Principles (page 272)

12. Circle the letter of each sentence that is true about Mendel's principles.

   a. The inheritance of biological characteristics is determined by genes that are passed from parents to their offspring in organisms that reproduce sexually.

   b. Two or more forms of the gene for a single trait can never exist.

   c. The copies of genes are segregated from each other when gametes are formed.

   d. The alleles for different genes usually segregate independently of one another.

13. When two or more forms of the gene for a single trait exist, some forms of the gene may be _____ and others may be _____.

Beyond Dominant and Recessive Alleles (pages 272–273)

14. Is the following sentence true or false? All genes show simple patterns of dominant and recessive alleles. _____

15. Complete the compare-and-contrast table of the different patterns of inheritance.

PATTERNS OF INHERITANCE

Type	Description	Examples
	One allele is not completely dominant over another. The heterozygous phenotype is somewhere in between the two homozygous phenotypes.	
	Both alleles contribute to the phenotype of the organism.	
	Genes have more than two alleles.	
	Two or more genes control a trait.	

Applying Mendel's Principles (page 274)

16. List three criteria Thomas Hunt Morgan was looking for in a model organism for genetic studies.

a. _____

_____

b. _____

_____

c. _____

_____

17. Is the following sentence true or false? Mendel's principles apply not just to pea plants but to other organisms as well.

_____

18. In humans, the dominant allele for skin pigmentation produces skin coloration. Homozygous recessive individuals have

_____; they lack melanin.

Chapter 11, Introduction to Genetics *(continued)*

Section 11–4 Meiosis (pages 275–278)

This section explains how gametes form in the process of meiosis. It also explains how meiosis is different from mitosis.

Introduction (page 275)

1. List the two things that Mendel's principles of genetics required in order to be true.

   a. _____

   _____

   b. _____

   _____

Chromosome Number (page 275)

2. What does it mean when two sets of chromosomes are

   homologous? _____

   _____

   _____

3. Circle the letter of each way to describe a diploid cell.

   a. 2N

   b. Contains two sets of homologous chromosomes

   c. Contains a single set of homologous chromosomes

   d. A gamete

4. Circle the letter of the number of chromosomes in a haploid *Drosophila* cell.

   a. 8   b. 4   c. 2   d. 0

Phases of Meiosis (pages 276–277)

5. Draw the chromosomes in the diagrams below to show the correct phase of meiosis.

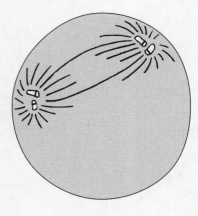
Prophase I

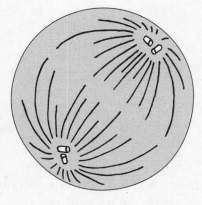
Metaphase I

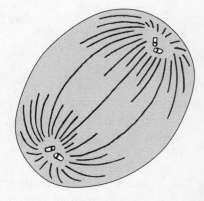
Anaphase II

6. Why is meiosis described as a process of reduction division? _____

_____

_____

7. What are the two distinct stages of meiosis?

a. _____   **b.** _____

8. Is the following sentence true or false? The diploid cell that enters meiosis becomes 4 haploid cells at the end of meiosis.

_____

9. How does a tetrad form in prophase I of meiosis? _____

_____

_____

10. Circle the number of chromatids in a tetrad.

    a. 8   **b.** 6   **c.** 4   **d.** 2

11. What results from the process of crossing-over during prophase I? _____

_____

_____

_____

12. Circle the letter of each sentence that is true about meiosis.

    a. During meiosis I, homologous chromosomes separate.

    b. The two daughter cells produced by meiosis I still have the two complete sets of chromosomes as a diploid cell does.

    c. During anaphase II, the paired chromatids separate.

    d. After meiosis II, the four daughter cells contain the diploid number of chromosomes.

Gamete Formation (page 278)

Match the products of meiosis with the descriptions.

Description	Product of Meiosis
_____ **13.** Haploid gametes produced in males	**a.** eggs
_____ **14.** Haploid gametes produced in females	**b.** sperm
_____ **15.** Cells produced in females that do not participate in reproduction	**c.** polar bodies

Comparing Mitosis and Meiosis (page 278)

16. Circle the letter of each sentence that is true about mitosis and meiosis.

    a. Mitosis produces four genetically different haploid cells.

    b. Meiosis produces two genetically identical diploid cells.

    c. Mitosis begins with a diploid cell.

    d. Meiosis begins with a diploid cell.

Chapter 11, Introduction to Genetics *(continued)*

Section 11–5 Linkage and Gene Maps (pages 279–280)

This section describes how genes that are linked to the same chromosome assort during meiosis.

Gene Linkage (page 279)

1. Is the following sentence true or false? Thomas Hunt Morgan discovered that some genes violated the principle of independent assortment. _____

2. Morgan grouped the *Drosophila* genes that were inherited together into four _____ groups.

3. List the two conclusions that Morgan made about genes and chromosomes.

   a. _____

   _____

   b. _____

   _____

4. Why didn't Mendel observe gene linkage? _____

_____

_____

_____

Gene Maps (pages 279–280)

5. Explain why two genes found on the same chromosome are not always linked forever. _____

_____

_____

_____

6. The new combinations of alleles produced by crossover events help to generate genetic _____.

7. Is the following sentence true or false? Genes that are closer together are more likely to be separated by a crossover event in meiosis. _____

8. What is a gene map? _____

_____

9. How is a gene map constructed? _____

_____

_____

_____

Section 12–5 Gene Regulation (pages 309–312)

This section explains how some genes in prokaryotes and eukaryotes are controlled.

Introduction (page 309)

1. Label the parts of a typical gene in the diagram below.

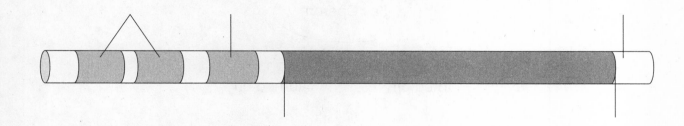

2. Where does RNA polymerase bind? _____

_____

3. Is the following sentence true or false? The actions of DNA-binding proteins help to determine whether a gene is turned on or

turned off. _____

Gene Regulation: An Example (pages 309–310)

4. What is an operon? _____

_____

_____

5. What is the function of the genes in the *lac* operon? _____

_____

_____

_____

6. Circle the letter of each sentence that is true about lactose.

    a. Lactose is a simple sugar.

    b. To use lactose for food, *E. coli* must take lactose across its cell membrane.

    c. The bond between glucose and galactose must be broken in order for *E. coli* to use lactose for food.

    d. Proteins encoded by the genes of the *lac* operon are needed only when *E. coli* is grown on a medium containing glucose.

7. Circle the letter of the number of genes in the *lac* operon found in *E. coli.*

    a. 1   **b.** 2   **c.** 3   **d.** 4

Chapter 12, DNA and RNA *(continued)*

8. What turns the *lac* operon off and on? _____
_____
_____

9. Complete the concept map to show how the *lac* operon is regulated.

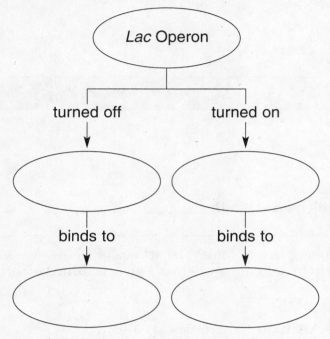

10. How does the repressor protein prevent transcription? _____
_____
_____

11. How does lactose cause the *lac* operon to turn on? _____
_____
_____

12. Circle the letter of each sentence that is true about gene regulation
in prokaryotic genes.

   a. The *lac* operon is the only example of genes regulated by
   repressor proteins.

   b. Many other genes are regulated by repressor proteins.

   c. Some genes are regulated by proteins that enhance the rate of
   transcription.

   d. Cells cannot turn their genes on and off as needed.

Eukaryotic Gene Regulation (page 311)

13. Is the following sentence true or false? Operons are frequently
found in eukaryotes. _____

14. How are eukaryotic genes usually controlled? _____

_____

_____

15. What is the function of the TATA box? _____

_____

_____

16. Eukaryotic promoters are usually found just _____

the TATA box, and they consist of a series of short

_____ sequences.

17. List three ways in which proteins that bind to enhancer sequences of a gene can work to regulate gene expression.

a. _____

b. _____

c. _____

18. Why is gene regulation in eukaryotes more complex than in

prokaryotes? _____

_____

_____

Regulation and Development (page 312)

19. What role do the hox genes play in the development of an

organism? _____

_____

_____

20. Circle the letter of each sentence that is true about hox genes.

a. A mutation in a hox gene has no effect on the organs that develop in specific parts of the body.

b. In fruit flies, a mutation affecting the hox genes can replace a fly's antennae with a pair of legs.

c. The function of the hox genes in humans seems to be almost the same as it is in fruit flies.

d. A copy of the gene that controls eye growth in mice does not function in fruit flies.

21. Why do common patterns of genetic control for development

exist among animals? _____

_____

_____

Chapter 12, DNA and RNA *(continued)*

WordWise

Answer the questions by writing the correct vocabulary term in the blanks.
Use the circled letter from each term to find the hidden word. Then, write a
definition for the hidden word.

1. What is the substance that is made up of DNA and protein tightly
   packed together?

   _ Ⓞ _ _ _ _ _ _ _

2. What are the three bases on the tRNA molecule that are
   complimentary to mRNA?

   _ _ Ⓞ _ _ _ _ _ _

3. What is the process in which one strain of bacteria has been
   changed into another?

   _ _ _ Ⓞ _ _ _ _ _ _ _ _ _ _

4. What is a change in the DNA sequence that affects genetic
   information?

   _ _ Ⓞ _ _ _ _ _

5. What is a group of genes that is operated together?

   _ _ _ Ⓞ _

6. What are the intervening sequences of RNA molecules that are cut
   out before the messenger RNA leaves the nucleus?

   _ _ _ _ Ⓞ _

7. What is the region of DNA to which RNA polymerase binds?

   _ _ _ _ _ Ⓞ _

Hidden Word: _ _ _ _ _ _ _

Definition: _____

_____

Chapter 13

Genetic Engineering

Section 13–1 Changing the Living World (pages 319–321)

This section explains how people use selective breeding and mutations to develop organisms with desirable characteristics.

Selective Breeding (pages 319–320)

1. What is meant by selective breeding? _____

_____

_____

2. Circle the letter of each organism that has been produced by selective breeding.

   a. horses   **b.** dogs   **c.** cats   **d.** potatoes

3. Who was Luther Burbank? _____

_____

_____

4. Complete the compare-and-contrast table of types of selective breeding.

SELECTIVE BREEDING

Type	Description	Examples
	Crossing dissimilar individuals to bring together the best of both organisms	
	The continued breeding of individuals with similar characteristics	

5. Is the following sentence true or false? Hybrids are often hardier than either of the parents. _____.

6. What two plant traits did Luther Burbank try to combine in his crosses?

   a. _____

   b. _____

7. Is the following sentence true or false? To maintain the desired characteristics of a line of organisms, breeders often use hybridization. _____

8. Most members of a breed are genetically _____.

9. What are the risks of inbreeding? _____

_____

_____

Chapter 13, Genetic Engineering *(continued)*

Increasing Variation (pages 320–321)

10. Why are biologists interested in preserving the diversity of plants and animals in the wild? _____

_____

_____

11. Is the following sentence true or false? The genetic variation that exists in nature is enough to satisfy the needs of breeders.

_____

12. Breeders can increase the genetic variation by inducing

_____, which are the ultimate source of genetic variability.

13. Circle the letter of an inheritable change in DNA.

a. variation   **b.** trait   **c.** mutation   **d.** genotype

14. Is the following sentence true or false? Mutations cannot occur

spontaneously. _____

15. Name two methods used by breeders to increase the rate of mutation.

a. _____   **b.** _____

16. Is it easy for breeders to produce mutants with desirable

mutations? Explain. _____

_____

_____

17. Why are radiation and chemicals useful techniques for producing

mutant bacteria? _____

_____

_____

18. Is the following sentence true or false? Scientists have produced

bacteria that can digest oil. _____

19. What technique do scientists use to produce mutant plants? _____

_____

_____

20. Circle the letter of each sentence that is true about polyploidy.

a. Polyploid plants have many sets of chromosomes.

b. Polyploidy is usually fatal in animals.

c. Polyploidy produces new species of plants that are weaker and smaller than their diploid relatives.

d. Bananas and some citrus fruits are polyploid.

Section 13–2 Manipulating DNA (pages 322–326)

This section describes the various techniques used by molecular biologists to study and change DNA molecules.

The Tools of Molecular Biology (pages 322–323)

1. What is genetic engineering? _____

_____

2. Is the following sentence true or false? Making changes to the DNA code is similar to changing the code of a computer program.

_____

3. Scientists use their knowledge of the _____ of DNA and its _____ properties to study and change DNA molecules.

4. List four different techniques that molecular biologists use to study and change DNA molecules.

    a. _____

    b. _____

    c. _____

    d. _____

5. Explain how biologists get DNA out of a cell. _____

_____

_____

6. Biologists use _____ to cut DNA molecules at a specific sequence of nucleotides to make smaller fragments.

7. Circle the letter of the process by which DNA fragments are separated and analyzed.

    a. gel electrophoresis   c. transformation

    b. extraction   d. restriction

8. In the diagram below, label the positive and negative ends of the gel and identify the location of longer and shorter fragments.

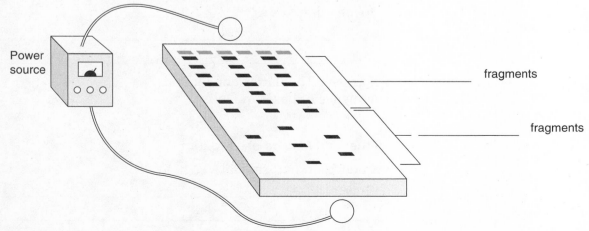

Chapter 13, Genetic Engineering *(continued)*

9. Circle the letter of each sentence that is true about gel electrophoresis.

   a. An electric voltage applied to the gel separates the DNA fragments.

   b. DNA molecules are positively charged.

   c. Gel electrophoresis is used to compare the genomes of different organisms.

   d. Gel electrophoresis can be used to locate and identify one particular gene in an individual's genome.

Using the DNA Sequence (pages 323–326)

10. Complete the concept map to show how researchers use the DNA sequence of an organism.

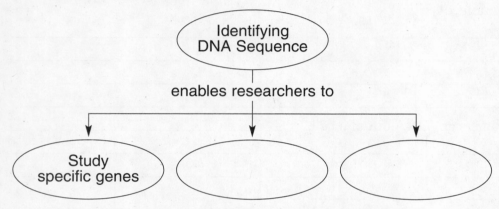

11. List four "ingredients" added to a test tube to produce tagged DNA fragments that can be used to read a sequence of DNA.

   a. _____

   b. _____

   c. _____

   d. _____

12. What does the reaction in the test tube generate when complimentary DNA is made for reading DNA? _____

   _____

   _____

13. Is the following sentence true or false? The pattern of colored bands on a gel tells the exact sequence of bases in DNA.

   _____

14. Enzymes that splice DNA together can also be used to join

   _____ DNA sequences to natural DNA sequences.

15. How is recombinant DNA produced? _____

   _____

16. What is polymerase chain reaction? _____

_____

_____

17. What is the role of the primers in PCR? _____

_____

_____

18. Circle the letter of the first step in the polymerase chain reaction.

    a. The copies become templates to make more copies.

    b. The DNA is cooled to allow the primers to bind to the single-stranded DNA.

    c. The DNA is heated to separate its two strands.

    d. DNA polymerase makes copies of the region between the primers.

Section 13–3 Cell Transformation (pages 327–329)

This section tells what happens during cell transformation. It also describes techniques used to determine if transformation has been successful.

Introduction (page 327)

1. What occurs during transformation? _____

_____

2. Is the following sentence true or false? Griffith's extract of heat-killed bacteria contained DNA fragments. _____

Transforming Bacteria (pages 327–328)

3. Complete the flowchart to show the steps in transforming bacteria.

> Foreign DNA is joined to a(an) _____, which is a small, circular DNA molecule found naturally in some bacteria.

$\downarrow$

> Recombinant plasmids are mixed with bacterial cells. Some bacterial cells take in the recombinant DNA by the process of _____.

$\downarrow$

> The culture is treated with a(an) _____, a compound that kills bacteria.

$\downarrow$

> Only cells that have been transformed survive, because only they carry a(an) _____ for antibiotic resistance.

Chapter 13, Genetic Engineering *(continued)*

4. Give two reasons why a plasmid is useful for DNA transfer.

   a. _____

   _____

   b. _____

   _____

Transforming Plant Cells (pages 328–329)

5. Circle the letter of each sentence that is true about transforming plant cells.

   a. Many plant cells can be transformed by using a bacterium that will, in nature, insert a tumor-producing plasmid into plant cells.

   b. Sometimes plant cells in culture will take up DNA on their own when their cell walls are removed.

   c. It is impossible to inject DNA directly into plant cells.

   d. Plant cells that are transformed cannot develop into adult plants.

6. When researchers transform plant cells using a bacterium that causes plant tumors, how do researchers prevent plant tumors from forming in the transformed cells? _____

   _____

7. Describe what occurs in a successful transformation of cells. _____

   _____

   _____

Transforming Animal Cells (page 329)

8. Describe how animal cells can be transformed by directly injecting DNA. _____

   _____

   _____

9. Is the following sentence true or false? The DNA molecules used for transformation of animal cells do not require marker genes.

   _____

10. How is a DNA molecule constructed so that it will "knock out" a particular gene? _____

    _____

    _____

11. Is the following sentence true or false? Gene replacement has made it possible to identify the specific functions of genes in many organisms. _____

Reading Skill Practice

When you read about related concepts, a compare-and-contrast table can help you focus on their similarities and differences. Construct a table to compare and contrast transformation in bacteria, plants, and animals. Look in Appendix A for more information about compare-and-contrast tables. Do your work on a separate sheet of paper.

Section 13–4 Applications of Genetic Engineering (pages 331–333)

This section explains how transgenic organisms are made. It also describes what a clone is and how animal clones are produced.

Introduction (page 331)

1. How do scientists know that plants and animals share the same

   basic mechanisms of gene expression? _____

   _____

Transgenic Organisms (pages 331–333)

2. What is a transgenic organism? _____

   _____

3. Describe how to make a transgenic organism. _____

   _____

   _____

   _____

4. Genetic engineering has spurred the growth of

   _____, a new industry that is changing
   the way we interact with the living world.

5. Circle the letter of each sentence that is true about transgenic microorganisms.

   a. Transgenic bacteria will never produce useful substances for health and industry.

   b. Transgenic bacteria produce human proteins cheaply and in great abundance.

   c. People with insulin-dependent diabetes are now treated with pure human insulin.

   d. In the future, transgenic organisms may produce the raw materials for plastics.

6. Is the following sentence true or false? Researchers are working on developing transgenic chickens that will be resistant to bacterial infections that sometimes cause food poisoning.

   _____

Chapter 13, Genetic Engineering *(continued)*

7. List four ways in which transgenic animals have been used.

   a. _____

   b. _____

   c. _____

   d. _____

8. Many transgenic plants contain genes that produce a natural

   _____, so the crops do not have to be sprayed
   with pesticides.

9. Circle the letter of each item that might soon be produced by
   transgenic plants.

   a. human antibodies   **c.** rot-resistant foods

   b. plastics   **d.** vitamin A-enriched rice

Cloning (page 333)

10. What is a clone? _____

   _____

11. Is the following sentence true or false? For years, many scientists
   thought that that it was impossible to clone bacteria.

   _____

12. Complete the sentences in the diagram below to show the steps in
   cloning a sheep.

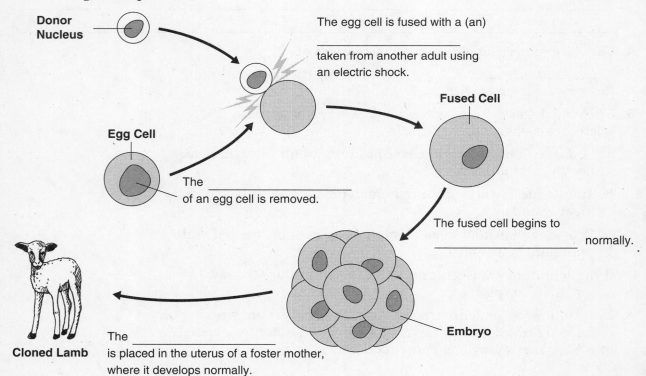

Donor Nucleus

The egg cell is fused with a (an) _____ taken from another adult using an electric shock.

Fused Cell

Egg Cell

The _____ of an egg cell is removed.

The fused cell begins to _____ normally.

Embryo

Cloned Lamb

The _____ is placed in the uterus of a foster mother, where it develops normally.

13. Is the following sentence true or false? All cloned animals are also transgenic. _____

14. What kinds of mammals have been cloned in recent years? _____
_____

WordWise

Use the clues below to identify vocabulary terms from Chapter 13. Write the terms below, putting one letter in each blank. When you finish, the term enclosed in the diagonal will reveal an important tool in transformation.

Clues

1. The condition of having many sets of chromosomes
2. A member of a population of genetically identical cells produced from a single cell
3. An organism that contains genes from other organisms
4. A molecule that cuts DNA molecules at a specific sequence of nucleotides
5. Produced when DNA from different sources is combined
6. The continued breeding of individuals with similar characteristics
7. The process of crossing dissimilar individuals to bring together the best of both organisms

1. _ _ _ _ _ _ _

2. _ _ _ _ _

3. _ _ _ _ _ _ _ _

4. _ _ _ _ _ _ _ _ _ _ _

5. _ _ _ _ _ _ _ _ _ _

6. _ _ _ _ _ _ _

7. _ _ _ _ _ _ _ _ _ _ _

Hidden Word: _ _ _ _ _ _ _

Definition: _____
_____

Chapter 14

The Human Genome

Section 14–1 Human Heredity (pages 341–348)

This section explains what scientists know about human chromosomes, as well as the inheritance of certain human traits and disorders. It also describes how scientists study the inheritance of human traits.

Human Chromosomes (pages 341–342)

1. How do biologists make a karyotype? _____

_____

_____

2. Circle the letter of each sentence that is true about human chromosomes.

   a. The X and Y chromosomes are known as sex chromosomes because they determine an individual's sex.

   b. Males have two X chromosomes.

   c. Autosomes are all the chromosomes, except the sex chromosomes.

   d. Biologists would write 46XY to indicate a human female.

3. Complete the Punnett square below to show how the sex chromosomes segregate during meiosis.

Male (XY) × Female (XX)

	X	X
X		
Y		

4. Why is there the chance that half of the zygotes will be 46XX and half will be 46XY? _____

_____

_____

5. Is the following sentence true or false? Human chromosomes contain both protein and a single, double-stranded DNA molecule.

_____

Human Traits (pages 342–343)

6. What does a pedigree chart show? _____

Match the labels to the parts of the pedigree chart shown below. Some of the parts of the pedigree chart may be used more than once.

Pedigree Chart

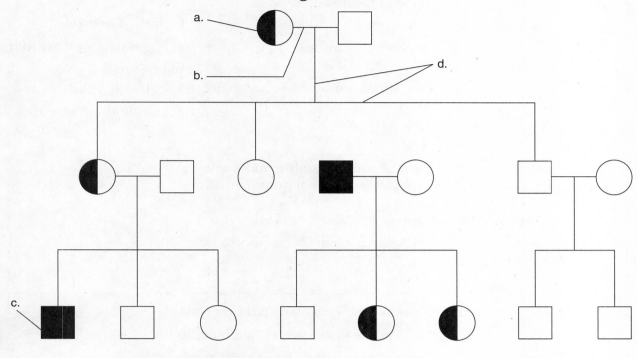

_____ **7.** A person that has the trait

_____ **8.** A male

_____ **9.** A carrier of the trait

_____ **10.** Represents a marriage

_____ **11.** A female

_____ **12.** Connects parents to their children

13. Give two reasons why it is impossible to associate some of the most obvious human traits with single genes.

a. _____

b. _____

Human Genes (pages 344–346)

14. Why is it difficult to study the genetics of humans? _____

_____

15. Circle the letter of each sentence that is true about human blood group genes.

a. The Rh blood group is determined by a single gene.

b. The negative allele (Rh–) is the dominant allele.

c. All of the alleles for the ABO blood group gene are codominant.

d. Individuals with type O blood are homozygous for the *i* allele (*ii*) and produce no antigen on the surface of red blood cells.

Chapter 14, The Human Genome *(continued)*

16. Is the following sentence true or false? Many human genes have become known through the study of genetic disorders.

_____

Match the genetic disorder with its description.

Description

_____ **17.** Nervous system breakdown caused by an autosomal recessive allele

_____ **18.** A form of dwarfism caused by an autosomal dominant allele

_____ **19.** A buildup of phenylalanine caused by an autosomal recessive allele

_____ **20.** A progressive loss of muscle control and mental function caused by an autosomal dominant allele

Genetic Disorder

a. Phenylketonuria (PKU)

b. Tay-Sachs disease

c. Achondroplasia

d. Huntington's disease

From Gene to Molecule *(pages 346–348)*

21. What is the normal function of the protein that is affected in cystic fibrosis? _____

_____

22. A change in just one DNA base for the gene that codes for the protein _____ causes sickle-shaped red blood cells.

23. What is the advantage of being heterozygous for the sickle cell allele? _____

_____

24. What makes an allele dominant, recessive, or codominant? _____

_____

Section 14–2 Human Chromosomes *(pages 349–353)*

This section describes the structure of human chromosomes. It also describes genetic disorders that are sex-linked, as well as disorders caused by nondisjunction.

Human Genes and Chromosomes *(page 349)*

1. Circle the letter of each sentence that is true about human genes and chromosomes.

a. Chromosomes 21 and 22 are the largest human chromosomes.

b. Chromosome 22 contains long stretches of repetitive DNA that do not code for proteins.

c. Biologists know everything about how the arrangements of genes on chromosomes affect gene expression.

d. Human genes located on the same chromosome tend to be inherited together.

Sex-Linked Genes (pages 350–351)

2. What are sex-linked genes? _____

_____

3. Is the following sentence true or false? The Y chromosome does not contain any genes at all. _____

4. Complete the compare-and-contrast table for sex-linked genes.

SEX-LINKED DISORDERS IN HUMANS

Disorder	Description	Cause
Colorblindness		
		A recessive allele in either of two genes resulting in a missing protein required for normal blood clotting.
		A defective version of the gene that codes for a muscle protein

5. Is the following sentence true or false? All X-linked alleles are expressed in males, even if they are recessive.

_____

6. Complete the Punnett square to show how colorblindness is inherited.

$$X^c X^c \times X^c Y$$

	X^c	Y
X^c		
X^c		

X-Chromosome Inactivation (page 352)

7. How does the cell "adjust" to the extra X chromosome in female cells? _____

_____

Chapter 14, The Human Genome *(continued)*

  8. What is a Barr body? _____

_____

_____

  9. Is the following sentence true or false? Barr bodies are found only

in males. _____

10. If you saw a white cat with orange and black spots, could it be a

male or a female? Explain. _____

_____

_____

_____

Chromosomal Disorders (pages 352–353)

11. What occurs during nondisjunction? _____

_____

_____

12. Is the following sentence true or false? If nondisjunction occurs,
gametes may have abnormal numbers of chromosomes.

_____

13. The condition in which an individual has three copies of a

chromosome is known as _____, which means
"three bodies."

14. Is the following sentence true or false? Down syndrome occurs
when an individual has two copies of chromosome 21.

_____

15. Circle the letter of the characteristic of Down syndrome.

   a. dwarfism   **c.** colorblindness

   b. mental retardation   **d.** muscle loss

16. Why does an extra copy of one chromosome cause so much

trouble? _____

_____

17. Circle the letter of each sentence that is true about sex
chromosome disorders.

   a. A female with the genotype XO has inherited only one X
chromosome and is sterile.

   b. Females with the genotype XXY have Klinefelter's syndrome.

   c. Babies have been born without an X chromosome.

   d. The Y chromosome contains a sex-determining region that is
necessary for male sexual development.

Reading Skill Practice

Writing an outline is a useful way to organize the important facts in a section. Write an outline of Section 14–2. Use the section headings as the headings in your outline. Include only the important facts and main ideas in your outline. Be sure to include the vocabulary terms. Do your work on a separate sheet of paper.

Section 14–3 Human Molecular Genetics (pages 355–360)

This section explains how genetic engineering techniques are being used to study the genes and chromosomes in the human genome. It also describes how this information is used for gene therapy.

Human DNA Analysis (pages 355–357)

1. Biologists search the volumes of the human genome using

   _____.

2. Why might prospective parents decide to have genetic testing? _____

   _____

   _____

   _____

3. Circle the letter of each sentence that is true about genetic testing.

   a. It is impossible to test parents to find out if they are carriers for cystic fibrosis or Tay-Sachs disease.

   b. Labeled DNA probes can be used to detect specific sequences found in disease-causing alleles.

   c. Some genetic tests use changes in restriction enzyme cutting sites to identify disease-causing alleles.

   d. DNA testing makes it possible to develop more effective therapy and treatment for individuals affected by genetic disease.

4. What is DNA fingerprinting? _____

   _____

   _____

   _____

5. Circle the letter of each source for a DNA sample from an individual.

   a. blood

   b. sperm

   c. clothing

   d. hair with tissue at the base

6. Is the following sentence true or false? DNA evidence is not reliable

   enough to be used to convict criminals. _____

Chapter 14, The Human Genome (continued)

7. Complete the flowchart to show the steps in DNA fingerprinting.

> Small sample of DNA is cut with a(an) _____ enzyme.

↓

> The fragments are separated by size using _____.

↓

> Fragments with highly variable regions are detected with a(an)
> _____, revealing a series of DNA bands of various sizes.

↓

> The pattern of bands produced is the _____, which can be distinguished statistically from the pattern of any other individual in the world.

The Human Genome Project (pages 357–358)

8. What is the Human Genome Project? _____
_____

9. Circle the letter of each sentence that is true about the Human Genome Project.
   a. The human genome is the first genome entirely sequenced.
   b. The human genome is about the same size as the genome of *E. coli.*
   c. Researchers completed the genomes of yeast and fruit flies during the same time they sequenced the human genome.
   d. The sequence of the human genome was completed in June 2000.

10. What were the three major steps in the process of sequencing the human genome?
    a. _____
    _____
    b. _____
    _____
    c. _____
    _____

11. What is the central question about the human genome that biologists will study next? _____

12. What is an "open reading frame" and what is it used for? _____
_____
_____

13. The mRNA coding regions of most genes are interrupted by
_____, which have special DNA sequences
marking their boundaries.

14. List three other parts of the gene that researchers look for.

  a. _____

  b. _____

  c. _____

15. Why are biotechnology companies interested in genetic
information? _____
_____

16. Is the following sentence true or false? Human genome data is
top secret and can be accessed only by certain people.
_____

Gene Therapy (pages 359–360)

17. What is gene therapy? _____
_____
_____

18. Circle the letter of each sentence that is true about gene therapy.

  a. When the normal copy of the gene is inserted, the body can
  make the correct protein, which eliminates the disorder.

  b. So far, no one has been successfully cured of a genetic disorder
  using gene therapy.

  c. Viruses are often used to carry the normal genes into cells.

  d. Viruses used in gene therapy often cause disease in the patients.

19. Have all gene therapy experiments been successful? Explain. _____
_____
_____
_____

Ethical Issues in Human Genetics (page 360)

20. What other changes could be made to the human genome by
manipulating human cells? _____
_____
_____

21. What is the ultimate goal of biology? _____
_____

Chapter 14, The Human Genome *(continued)*

22. What is the responsibility of society in biology? _____

_____

_____

_____

23. Is the following true or false? Scientists should be expected to
make all ethical decisions regarding advances in human genetics.

_____

WordWise

Use the clues to fill in the blanks with vocabulary terms from Chapter 14.
Then, put the numbered letters in the correct spaces to find the hidden message.

Clues	**Vocabulary Terms**
Occurs when homologous chromosomes fail to separate during meiosis	— — — — — — — — — — — — 1 2 3 4 5
Describes a trait that is controlled by many genes	— — — — — — — — 6 7 8
In humans, Y is a sex ____.	— — — — — — — — — 9 10 11 12
Technique that uses DNA to identify individuals	— — — — — — — — — — — — — — 13 14 15 16 17 18
Chart that shows the relationships within a family	— — — — — — — — 19 20 21
A picture of chromosomes arranged in pairs	— — — — — — — — 22 23 24 25
A gene located on the X or Y chromosome is a _____ gene.	— — — - — — — — — 26 27 28 29
Chromosomes that are not sex chromosomes	— — — — — — — — 30 31 32 33

Hidden Message:

___ ___ ___ ___ ___ ___ ___   ___ ___   ___ ___ ___
 4 10 30 28 20 32 33   16 5   13 14 15

___ ___ ___ ___ ___   ___ ___ ___ ___ ___ ___ ___
 8 22   3 26 21   7 25   1 12 24 18   9

___ ___ ___ ___ ___ ___ ___ ___ ___ .
19 27 31   6 17   2 29 23 11

Darwin's Theory of Evolution

Section 15–1 The Puzzle of Life's Diversity (pages 369–372)

This section outlines Charles Darwin's contribution to science. It also describes the pattern of diversity he observed among organisms of the Galápagos Islands.

Introduction (page 369)

1. The process by which modern organisms have descended from ancient organisms is called _____.

2. A well-supported explanation of phenomena that have occurred in the natural world is a(an) _____.

3. Is the following sentence true or false? Charles Darwin contributed more to our understanding of evolution than anyone else.
   _____

Voyage of the *Beagle* (pages 369–370)

4. Circle the letter of each sentence that is true about Charles Darwin.
   a. He was born in 1809.
   b. He was an English naturalist.
   c. He was 42 when he began the voyage on the *Beagle*.
   d. The voyage lasted 5 years and took him around the world.

5. Label the Galápagos Islands on the map below.

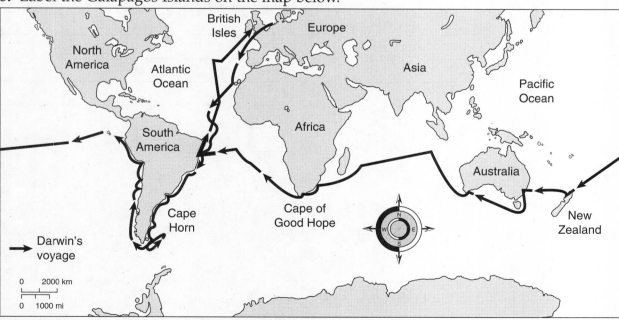

6. Is the following sentence true or false? Darwin was looking for a scientific explanation for the diversity of life on Earth.
   _____

Chapter 15, Darwin's Theory of Evolution *(continued)*

Darwin's Observations (pages 370–372)

7. Circle the letter of each observation that Darwin made.

   a. An enormous number of species inhabit Earth.

   b. Many organisms seem to be poorly suited to their environment.

   c. The same sorts of animals are always found in the same ecosystems in different parts of the world.

   d. Some species that lived in the past no longer live on Earth.

8. The preserved remains of ancient organisms are called

   _____ .

9. As Darwin studied fossils, what new questions arose? _____

   _____

   _____

10. Is the following sentence true or false? Of all the *Beagle's* ports of call, the one that influenced Darwin the most was the Galápagos

    Islands. _____

11. Circle the letter of each choice that is true about the Galápagos Islands.

    a. The islands are far apart.

    b. The smallest, lowest islands are hot and wet.

    c. The higher islands have more rainfall.

    d. All the islands have the same amount of vegetation.

12. How did Darwin explain differences in shell shape of tortoises

    from Hood Island and Isabela Island? _____

    _____

    _____

    _____

13. Darwin observed that small brown birds on the Galápagos

    Islands differed in the shape of their _____ .

The Journey Home (page 372)

14. What did Darwin think about on his journey home to England? _____

    _____

    _____

    _____

15. After he returned to England, what hypothesis did Darwin

    develop to explain his findings? _____

    _____

    _____

Reading Skill Practice

You can focus on the most important points in a section by turning the headings into questions and then trying to find the answers as you read. For each heading in Section 15–1, first write the heading as a how, what, or why question. Then, find and write the answer to your question. Do your work on a separate sheet of paper.

Section 15–2 Ideas That Shaped Darwin's Thinking (pages 373–377)

This section describes the theories of other scientists who influenced Darwin, including Hutton, Lyell, Lamarck, and Malthus.

An Ancient, Changing Earth (pages 374–375)

1. Two scientists who helped Darwin and others recognize how old Earth is were _____ and

   _____ .

2. Circle the letter of each idea that was proposed by James Hutton.

   a. Earth is a few thousand years old.

   b. Layers of rock are moved by forces beneath Earth's surface.

   c. Most geological processes operate extremely slowly.

   d. The processes that changed Earth in the past are different from the processes that operate in the present.

3. Circle the letter of each sentence that is true about Lyell's work.

   a. His book, *Principles of Geology*, was published after Darwin returned from his voyage.

   b. His work explained how awesome geological features could be built up or torn down over long periods of time.

   c. His publications helped Darwin appreciate the significance of the geological phenomena that he had observed.

   d. He stressed that scientists must explain past events in terms of processes that they can actually observe.

4. In what two ways did an understanding of geology influence

   Darwin? _____

   _____

   _____

   _____

Lamarck's Theory of Evolution (page 376)

5. Is the following sentence true or false? Lamarck was among the first scientists to recognize that living things have changed over

   time. _____

Chapter 15, Darwin's Theory of Evolution (continued)

6. Is the following sentence true or false? Lamarck proposed that all organisms have an innate tendency toward complexity and perfection. _____

7. How did Lamarck propose that species change over time? _____
_____
_____
_____

8. How did Lamarck pave the way for the work of later biologists? _____
_____
_____

9. Which step in the diagram below shows the inheritance of acquired traits as proposed by Lamarck? _____

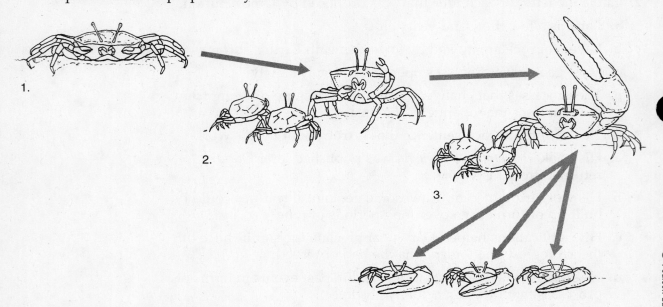

Population Growth (page 377)

10. Circle the letter of each sentence that is true about Thomas Malthus.

    a. He was an important influence on Darwin.

    b. He was an English naturalist.

    c. He believed that war, famine, and disease limit the growth of populations.

    d. His views were influenced by conditions in twentieth-century England.

11. Is the following sentence true or false? The overwhelming majority of a species' offspring survive. _____

Section 15–3 Darwin Presents His Case (pages 378–386)

This section explains the concepts of artificial selection, natural selection, and fitness. It also describes evidence for evolution.

Publication of *On the Origin of Species* (pages 378–379)

1. Is the following sentence true or false? When Darwin returned to England, he rushed to publish his thoughts about evolution.

   _____

2. The naturalist whose essay gave Darwin an incentive to publish his own work was _____.

3. Circle the letter of each sentence that is true about Darwin's book, *On the Origin of Species.*

   a. It was published in 1869.

   b. It was ignored when it was first published.

   c. It contained evidence for evolution.

   d. It described natural selection.

Natural Variation and Artificial Selection (page 379)

4. Differences among individuals of a species are referred to as

   _____.

5. Is the following sentence true or false? Natural variation is found only in wild organisms in nature. _____

6. Circle the letter of each sentence that is true about artificial selection.

   a. It is also called selective breeding.

   b. It occurs when humans select natural variations they find useful.

   c. It produces organisms that look very different from their ancestors.

   d. It is no longer used today.

Evolution by Natural Selection (pages 380–382)

7. What was Darwin's greatest contribution? _____

   _____

8. What does the phrase *struggle for existence* mean? _____

   _____

   _____

Match each term with its definition.

Term	Definition
_____ 9. fitness	a. Any inherited characteristic that increases an organism's chance of survival
_____ 10. adaptation	b. Survival of the fittest
_____ 11. natural selection	c. The ability of an individual to survive and reproduce in its specific environment

Chapter 15, Darwin's Theory of Evolution *(continued)*

12. Is the following sentence true or false? Adaptations can be physical characteristics but not more complex features such as behavior. _____

13. Explain what Darwin meant by the phrase *survival of the fittest.* _____

_____

_____

14. Circle the letter of each sentence that is true about natural selection.

    a. It selects traits that increase fitness.

    b. It takes place without human control.

    c. It can be observed directly in nature.

    d. It leads to an increase in a species' fitness.

15. The principle that living species descend, with changes, from other species over time is referred to as

_____.

16. Is the following sentence true or false? Descent with modification implies that all living organisms are related to one another.

_____

17. The principle that all species were derived from common ancestors is known as _____.

Evidence of Evolution (pages 382–385)

18. Is the following sentence true or false? Darwin argued that living things have been evolving on Earth for thousands of years.

_____

19. Complete the concept map.

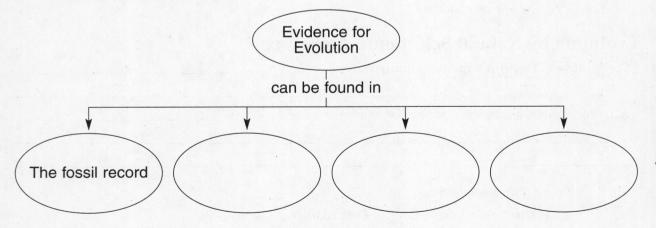

20. How do fossils that formed in different rock layers provide evidence of evolution? _____

_____

_____

21. Circle the letter of the way Darwin explained the distribution of finch species on the Galápagos Islands.

    a. They had descended with modification from a common mainland ancestor.

    b. They had descended with modification from several different mainland ancestors.

    c. They had remained unchanged since arriving on the Galápagos from the mainland.

    d. They had become more similar to one another after arriving on the Galápagos.

22. How did Darwin explain the existence of similar but unrelated species? _____

    _____

    _____

23. Structures that have different mature forms but develop from the same embryonic tissues are called _____.

24. Is the following sentence true or false? Homologous structures provide strong evidence that all four-limbed animals with backbones have descended, with modifications, from common ancestors. _____

25. Organs that are so reduced in size that they are just vestiges, or traces, of homologous organs in other species are called

    _____.

Summary of Darwin's Theory (page 386)

26. Is the following sentence true or false? Darwin's theory was profoundly different from anything known in nineteenth century England. _____

27. What is the status of Darwin's theory today? _____

    _____

28. Circle the letter of each idea that is part of Darwin's theory of evolution.

    a. There is variation in nature.

    b. Fewer organisms are produced than can survive.

    c. There is a struggle for existence.

    d. Species change over time.

29. According to Darwin's theory, what happens to individuals whose characteristics are not well suited to their environment? _____

    _____

30. Darwin believed that all organisms on Earth are united into a single tree of life by _____.

Chapter 15, Darwin's Theory of Evolution *(continued)*

WordWise

Test your knowledge of vocabulary terms from Chapter 15 by completing this crossword puzzle.

Clues across:

1. The type of selection that humans control
3. The ability to survive and reproduce in a specific environment
5. Change over time
9. The kind of structures that have different mature forms but develop from the same embryonic tissues
10. Any inherited characteristic that increases an organism's chance of survival

Clues down:

2. The preserved remains of ancient organisms
4. A well-supported explanation of phenomena that have occurred in the natural world
6. The type of selection that increases an organism's fitness in its environment
7. The kind of organs that are so reduced in size they are just traces of homologous organs in other species
8. The type of descent that explains why all species are linked in a single tree of life

Evolution of Populations

Section 16–1 Genes and Variation (pages 393–396)

This section describes the main sources of inheritable variation in a population. It also explains how phenotypes are expressed.

Darwin's Ideas Revisited (page 393)

1. Is the following sentence true or false? Mendel's work on inheritance was published after Darwin's lifetime.

   _____

2. Which two important factors was Darwin unable to explain without an understanding of heredity? _____

   _____

   _____

3. List the three fields that collaborate today to explain evolution.

   a. _____   b. _____   c. _____

Gene Pools (page 394)

4. A collection of individuals of the same species in a given area is a(an) _____.

5. The combined genetic information of all members of a particular population is a(an) _____.

6. Is the following sentence true or false? A gene pool typically contains just one allele for each inheritable trait.

   _____

7. The number of times that an allele occurs in a gene pool compared with the number of times other alleles occur is called the

   _____ of the allele.

Sources of Genetic Variation (pages 394–395)

8. Complete the concept map.

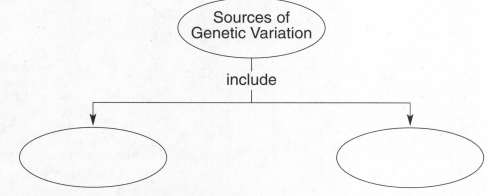

Chapter 16, Evolution of Populations *(continued)*

9. What is a mutation? _____

_____

10. Why do mutations occur? _____

_____

_____

11. Circle the letter of each choice that is true about mutations.

    a. They can be limited to a single base of DNA.

    b. They always affect lengthy segments of a chromosome.

    c. They always affect an organism's phenotype.

    d. They always affect an organism's fitness.

12. Is the following sentence true or false? Most inheritable differences are due to gene shuffling that occurs during the production of gametes. _____

13. Circle the letter of each choice that is true about sexual reproduction.

    a. It is a major source of variation in many populations.

    b. It can produce many different phenotypes.

    c. It can produce many different genetic combinations.

    d. It can change the relative frequency of alleles in a population.

Single-Gene and Polygenic Traits *(pages 395–396)*

14. Is the following sentence true or false? The number of phenotypes produced for a given trait depends on how many genes control the trait. _____

15. Is the following sentence true or false? Most traits are controlled by a single gene. _____

16. Label the two graphs to show which one represents a single-gene trait and which one represents a polygenic trait.

_____   _____

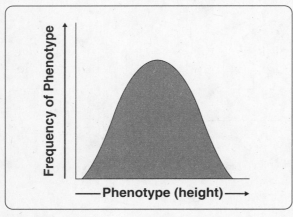

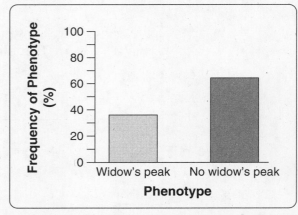

Reading Skill Practice

When you read about related concepts, making a graphic organizer such as a Venn diagram can help you focus on their similarities and differences. Make a Venn diagram comparing and contrasting single-gene and polygenic traits. For more information on Venn diagrams, see Appendix A of your textbook. Do your work on a separate sheet of paper.

Section 16–2 Evolution as Genetic Change (pages 397–402)

This section explains how natural selection affects different types of traits. It also describes how populations can change genetically by chance as well as the conditions that prevent populations from changing genetically.

Natural Selection on Single-Gene Traits (pages 397–398)

1. Is the following sentence true or false? Natural selection on single-gene traits cannot lead to changes in allele frequencies.

   _____

2. If a trait made an organism less likely to survive and reproduce,

   what would happen to the allele for that trait? _____

   _____

   _____

3. If a trait had no effect on an organism's fitness, what would

   happen to the allele for that trait? _____

   _____

   _____

Natural Selection on Polygenic Traits (pages 398–399)

4. List the three ways that natural selection can affect the distributions of phenotypes.

   a. _____   **c.** _____

   b. _____

Match the type of selection with the situation in which it occurs.

	Type of Selection	**Situation**
_____	**5.** Directional	**a.** Individuals at the upper and lower ends of the curve have higher fitness than individuals near the middle.
_____	**6.** Stabilizing	**b.** Individuals at one end of the curve have higher fitness than individuals in the middle or at the other end.
_____	**7.** Disruptive	**c.** Individuals near the center of the curve have higher fitness than individuals at either end.

8. An increase in the average size of beaks in Galápagos finches is an

   example of _____ selection.

Chapter 16, Evolution of Populations *(continued)*

9. Is the following sentence true or false? The weight of human infants at birth is under the influence of disruptive selection.

   _____

10. Draw the missing graph to show how disruptive selection affects beak size.

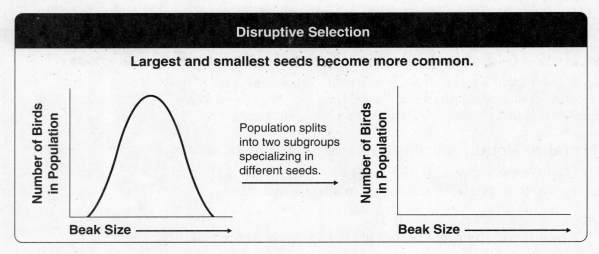

Disruptive Selection

Largest and smallest seeds become more common.

Number of Birds in Population

Population splits into two subgroups specializing in different seeds.

Number of Birds in Population

Beak Size ⟶   Beak Size ⟶

Genetic Drift (page 400)

11. Is the following sentence true or false? Natural selection is the only source of evolutionary change. _____

12. Random change in allele frequencies in small populations is called _____.

13. A situation in which allele frequencies change as a result of the migration of a small subgroup of a population is known as the

    _____.

14. What is an example of the founder effect? _____

    _____

    _____

Evolution Versus Genetic Equilibrium (pages 401–402)

15. What does the Hardy-Weinberg principle state? _____

    _____

    _____

16. The situation in which allele frequencies remain constant is called

    _____.

17. List the five conditions required to maintain genetic equilibrium.

    a. _____   d. _____

    b. _____   e. _____

    c. _____

18. Why is large population size important in maintaining genetic
equilibrium? _____
_____

Section 16–3 The Process of Speciation (pages 404–410)

*This section explains how species evolve and describes the process of
speciation in the Galápagos Islands.*

Introduction (page 404)

1. What is speciation? _____
_____

Isolating Mechanisms (pages 404–405)

2. Is the following sentence true or false? Individuals in different
species can have the same gene pool. _____

3. What does it mean for two species to be reproductively isolated
from each other? _____
_____

4. What must happen in order for new species to evolve? _____
_____
_____

5. List three ways that reproductive isolation occurs.

a. _____   c. _____

b. _____

6. When does behavioral isolation occur? _____
_____
_____

7. Is the following sentence true or false? Eastern and Western
meadowlarks are an example of behavioral isolation.
_____

8. When does geographic isolation occur? _____
_____
_____

9. Abert and Kaibab squirrels in the Southwest are an example of
_____ isolation.

10. Is the following sentence true or false? Geographic barriers
guarantee the formation of new species. _____

11. What is an example of temporal isolation? _____
_____
_____

Chapter 16, Evolution of Populations *(continued)*

Testing Natural Selection in Nature (pages 406–407)

12. Is the following sentence true or false? The basic mechanisms of evolutionary change cannot be observed in nature.

_____

13. Circle the letter of each hypothesis about the evolution of Galápagos finches that was tested by the Grants.

   a. The finches' beak size and shape has enough inheritable variation to provide raw material for natural selection.

   b. The different finch species are the descendants of a common mainland ancestor.

   c. Differences in the finches' beak size and shape produce differences in fitness that cause natural selection to occur.

   d. The evolution of the finches is proceeding slowly and gradually.

14. Circle the letter of each observation that was made by the Grants.

   a. Differences in beak size were more important for survival during the wet season.

   b. When food for finches was scarce, individuals with the largest beaks were less likely to survive.

   c. Big-beaked birds tended to mate with small-beaked birds.

   d. Average beak size increased dramatically.

Speciation in Darwin's Finches (pages 408–410)

15. Complete the flowchart to show how speciation probably occurred in the Galápagos finches.

```
┌─────────────────────────────┐
│      Founders arrive         │
└─────────────────────────────┘
              │
              ▼
┌─────────────────────────────┐
│                             │
└─────────────────────────────┘
              │
              ▼
┌─────────────────────────────┐
│                             │
└─────────────────────────────┘
              │
              ▼
┌─────────────────────────────┐
│                             │
└─────────────────────────────┘
              │
              ▼
┌─────────────────────────────┐
│                             │
└─────────────────────────────┘
              │
              ▼
┌─────────────────────────────┐
│     Continued evolution     │
└─────────────────────────────┘
```

16. How could differences in beak size lead to reproductive isolation? _____

_____

_____

_____

17. Is the following sentence true or false? During the dry season, individual birds that are most different from each other have the highest fitness. _____

WordWise

Test your knowledge of vocabulary terms from Chapter 16 by solving the clues. Then, copy the numbered letters in order to reveal the hidden message.

Clues	Vocabulary Terms
Type of isolation that prevents eastern and western meadowlarks from interbreeding	_ _ _ _ _ _ _ _ _ 1 2 3 4
Type of selection that acts against individuals of an intermediate type	_ _ _ _ _ _ _ _ 5 6 7
Term that means the formation of new species	_ _ _ _ _ _ _ _ _ _ 8 9
Type of selection that causes an increase in individuals at one end of the curve	_ _ _ _ _ _ _ _ 10
Type of selection that keeps the center of the curve at its current position	_ _ _ _ _ _ _ _ _ _ 11 12
Kind of pool that contains all the genetic information in a population	_ _ _ _ _ 13 14 15
Type of isolation that prevents species from interbreeding	_ _ _ _ _ _ _ _ _ _ _ 16 17
Type of isolation that led to the evolution of the Kaibab squirrel	_ _ _ _ _ _ _ _ 18
Type of equilibrium that occurs when allele frequencies do not change	_ _ _ _ _ _ 19
Name of the principle stating that allele frequencies will remain constant unless factors cause them to change	_ _ _ _ _ - _ _ _ _ _ _ 20 21 22 23
Type of trait produced by more than one gene	_ _ _ _ _ _ _ 24

Hidden Message:

‾ ‾ ‾ ‾ ‾ ‾ ‾ ‾ ‾   ‾ ‾   ‾ ‾ ‾ ‾ ‾ ‾ ‾
1 2 3 4 5 6 7 8 9   10 11   12 13 14 15 16 17 18

‾ ‾ ‾ ‾ ‾ ‾ .
19 20 21 22 23 24

The History of Life

Section 17–1 The Fossil Record (pages 417–422)

This section explains how fossils form and how they can be interpreted. It also describes the geologic time scale that is used to represent evolutionary time.

Fossils and Ancient Life (page 417)

1. Scientists who study fossils are called _____.

2. What is the fossil record? _____
_____

3. What evidence does the fossil record provide? _____
_____
_____

4. Species that died out are said to be _____.

5. Is the following sentence true or false? About half of all species that have ever lived on Earth have become extinct. _____

How Fossils Form (page 418)

6. Circle the letter of each sentence that is true about fossils.

   a. Most organisms that die are preserved as fossils.

   b. Fossils can include footprints, eggs, or other traces of organisms.

   c. Most fossils form in metamorphic rock.

   d. The quality of fossil preservation varies.

7. How do fossils form in sedimentary rock? _____
_____
_____
_____

Interpreting Fossil Evidence (pages 418–420)

8. List the two techniques paleontologists use to determine the age of fossils.

   a. _____

   b. _____

9. Circle the letter of each sentence that is true about relative dating.

   a. It determines the age of a fossil by comparing its placement with that of fossils in other layers of rock.

   b. It uses index fossils.

   c. It allows paleontologists to estimate a fossil's age in years.

   d. It provides no information about absolute age.

10. Is the following sentence true or false? Older rock layers are usually closer to Earth's surface than more recent rock layers. _____

11. Is the following sentence true or false? Scientists use radioactive decay to assign absolute ages to rocks. _____

12. The length of time required for half of the radioactive atoms in a sample to decay is called a(an) _____.

13. The use of half-lives to determine the age of a sample is called _____.

14. How do scientists calculate the age of a sample using radioactive dating? _____

_____

_____

15. Is the following sentence true or false? All radioactive elements have the same half-life. _____

Geologic Time Scale (pages 421–422)

16. Fill in the missing eras and periods in the geologic time scale below.

GEOLOGIC TIME SCALE

Era							Paleozoic					
Period	Quaternary		Cretaceous		Triassic	Permian		Devonian		Ordovician		Vendian
Time (millions of years ago)	1.8 – present	65 – 1.8	145 – 65	208 – 145	245 – 208	290 – 245	363 – 290	410 – 363	440 – 410	505 – 440	544 – 505	650 – 544

17. Circle the letter of the choice that lists the eras of the geologic time scale in order from most recent to oldest.

    a. Mesozoic, Paleozoic, Cenozoic **c.** Cenozoic, Mesozoic, Paleozoic

    b. Cenozoic, Paleozoic, Mesozoic **d.** Paleozoic, Mesozoic, Cenozoic

Chapter 17, The History of Life *(continued)*

18. Circle the letter of each sentence that is true about the geologic time scale.

   a. The scale is used to represent evolutionary time.

   b. Major changes in fossil organisms separate segments of geologic time.

   c. Divisions of the scale cover standard lengths of 100 million years.

   d. Geologic time begins with the Cambrian Period.

Section 17–2 Earth's Early History (pages 423–428)

This section explains how Earth formed. It also outlines hypotheses that have been proposed for how life first arose on Earth and describes some of the main evolutionary steps in the early evolution of life.

Formation of Earth (pages 423–424)

1. List the six components of Earth's early atmosphere.

   a. _____   c. _____   e. _____

   b. _____   d. _____   f. _____

2. Is the following sentence true or false? Liquid water first occurred on Earth more than 4 billion years ago. _____

The First Organic Molecules (page 424)

3. Label the diagram to show which part of Miller and Urey's apparatus simulated lightning storms on early Earth.

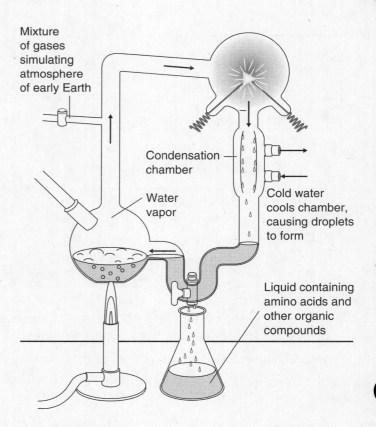

Mixture of gases simulating atmosphere of early Earth

Condensation chamber

Water vapor

Cold water cools chamber, causing droplets to form

Liquid containing amino acids and other organic compounds

4. Circle the letter of each sentence that is true about Miller and Urey's experiments.

   a. Their purpose was to determine how the first organic molecules evolved.

   b. They led to the formation of several amino acids.

   c. They accurately simulated conditions in Earth's early atmosphere.

   d. The results were never duplicated in experiments by other scientists.

How Did Life Begin? (page 425)

5. What are proteinoid microspheres? _____

_____

_____

6. Is the following sentence true or false? Scientists know how DNA and RNA evolved. _____

7. Why do scientists think that RNA may have evolved before DNA? _____

_____

_____

8. Is the following sentence true or false? Under certain conditions, small sequences of RNA could have formed and replicated on their own. _____

Free Oxygen (page 426)

9. Microscopic fossils are called _____.

10. Circle the letter of each sentence that is true about the earliest life forms on Earth.

   a. They resembled modern bacteria.

   b. They were eukaryotes.

   c. They relied on oxygen.

   d. They were not preserved as fossils.

11. How did early photosynthetic bacteria change Earth? _____

_____

_____

12. Is the following sentence true or false? The rise of oxygen in the atmosphere drove some life forms to extinction.

_____

Origin of Eukaryotic Cells (pages 427–428)

13. Is the following sentence true or false? The ancestor of all eukaryotic cells evolved about 2 billion years ago.

_____

Chapter 17, The History of Life (continued)

14. What was the first step in the evolution of eukaryotic cells? _____

_____

_____

15. What does the endosymbiotic theory propose? _____

_____

_____

16. Circle the letter of each choice that provides support for the
endosymbiotic theory.

   a. The membranes of mitochondria and chloroplasts resemble the
plasma membranes of free-living prokaryotes.

   b. Mitochondria and chloroplasts do not have DNA.

   c. Mitochondria and chloroplasts have ribosomes that are similar
in size and structure to those of bacteria.

   d. Mitochondria and chloroplasts reproduce by binary fission as
bacteria do.

Sexual Reproduction and Multicellularity (page 428)

17. How did sexual reproduction speed up the evolutionary process? _____

_____

_____

_____

18. Is the following sentence true or false? Sexual reproduction
evolved after the first multicellular organisms appeared.

_____

Reading Skill Practice

When you read a section that contains new or difficult material, identifying the
sentence that best expresses the main topic under each heading can help you focus
on the most important points. For each heading in Section 17–2, identify and copy
the sentence that best expresses the main topic under that heading. Do your work
on a separate sheet of paper.

Section 17–3 Evolution of Multicellular Life (pages 429–434)

*This section describes how multicellular life evolved from its earliest forms to
its present-day diversity.*

Precambrian Time (page 429)

1. Is the following sentence true or false? Almost 90 percent of Earth's

history occurred during the Precambrian. _____

2. Circle the letter of each sentence that is true about life in the Precambrian.

   a. Anaerobic and photosynthetic forms of life appeared.

   b. Aerobic forms of life evolved, and eukaryotes appeared.

   c. Multicellular life forms evolved.

   d. Life existed on the land and in the sea.

3. Why do few fossils exist from the Precambrian? _____
   _____

Paleozoic Era (pages 429–431)

4. The first part of the Paleozoic Era is the _____ Period.

5. Is the following sentence true or false? Life was not very diverse during the Cambrian Period. _____

6. Circle the letter of each sentence that is true about the Cambrian Period.

   a. Organisms with hard parts first appeared.

   b. Most animal phyla first evolved.

   c. Many animals lived on the land.

   d. Brachiopods and trilobites were common.

Match the periods of the Paleozoic Era with the evolutionary events that occurred during them.

Periods	Events
_____ 7. Ordovician and Silurian	a. Reptiles evolved from amphibians, and winged insects evolved into many forms.
_____ 8. Devonian	b. The first vertebrates evolved, and insects first appeared.
_____ 9. Carboniferous and Permian	c. Many groups of fishes were present in the oceans, and the first amphibians evolved.

10. Animals first begin to invade the land during the _____ Period.

11. Where does the Carboniferous Period get its name? _____
    _____
    _____
    _____

12. When many types of living things become extinct at the same time, it is called a(an) _____.

13. Is the following sentence true or false? The mass extinction at the end of the Paleozoic affected only land animals.

    _____

Chapter 17, The History of Life (continued)

Mesozoic Era (pages 431–432)

14. Complete the compare-and-contrast table.

PERIODS OF THE MESOZOIC ERA

Period	Evolutionary Event
	First mammals
	First birds
	First flowering plants

15. The Mesozoic Era is called the Age of _____.

16. The first dinosaurs appeared in the _____ Period.

17. Is the following sentence true or false? The mammals of the Triassic Period were very small. _____

18. Is the following sentence true or false? Many paleontologists now think that dinosaurs are close relatives of birds.

_____

19. The dominant vertebrates throughout the Cretaceous Period were

_____.

20. What advantage do flowering plants have over conifers? _____

_____

_____

21. Describe the mass extinction that occurred at the end of the Cretaceous Period. _____

_____

_____

Cenozoic Era (pages 433–434)

22. Is the following sentence true or false? During the Cenozoic Era, mammals evolved adaptations that allowed them to live on land, in water, and in the air. _____

23. The Cenozoic Era is called the Age of _____.

24. What were Earth's climates like during the Tertiary Period? _____

_____

_____

25. How did Earth's climate change during the Quaternary Period? _____

_____

_____

26. Is the following sentence true or false? The very earliest ancestors of our species appeared about 100,000 years ago. _____

Section 17–4 Patterns of Evolution (pages 435–440)

This section describes six important patterns of large-scale, long-term evolutionary change.

Introduction (page 435)

1. The large-scale evolutionary changes that take place over long periods of time are referred to as _____.

2. Complete the concept map.

```
                                    ( Mass extinctions )

                                    (               )

( Patterns of Macroevolution )—include—<  (               )

                                    (               )

                                    (               )

                                    ( Changes in developmental genes )
```

Mass Extinctions (page 435)

3. What are possible causes of mass extinctions? _____

_____

_____

4. What effects have mass extinctions had on the history of life? _____

_____

_____

_____

Adaptive Radiation (page 436)

5. The process of a single species or a small group of species evolving into several different forms that live in different ways is called _____.

Chapter 17, The History of Life *(continued)*

6. What led to the adaptive radiation of mammals? _____

_____

_____

Convergent Evolution (pages 436–437)

7. The process by which unrelated organisms come to resemble one

   another is called _____.

8. Circle the letter of each choice that is an example of convergent
   evolution.

   a. Bird's wing and fish's fin

   b. Shark's fin and dolphin's limb

   c. Human's arm and bird's wing

   d. Human's leg and dolphin's limb

Coevolution (pages 437–438)

9. The process by which two species evolve in response to changes

   in each other over time is called _____.

10. How have plants and plant-eating insects coevolved? _____

_____

_____

Punctuated Equilibrium (page 439)

11. The idea that evolution occurs at a slow, steady rate is called

    _____.

12. What are some reasons rapid evolution may occur after long

    periods of equilibrium? _____

_____

_____

13. The pattern of long, stable periods interrupted by brief periods of

    more rapid change is called _____.

14. Is the following sentence true or false? Evolution has often
    proceeded at different rates for different organisms.

    _____

Developmental Genes and Body Plans (page 440)

15. How can hox genes help reveal how evolution occurred? _____

_____

_____

_____

16. Is the following sentence true or false? Changes in the timing of genetic control during embryonic development can contribute to the variation involved in natural selection. _____

WordWise

Match each definition in the left column with the correct term in the right column. Then, write the number of each term in the box below on the line under the appropriate letter. When you have filled in all the boxes, add up the numbers in each column, row, and two diagonals. All the sums should be the same.

Definition

A. Scientist who studies fossils

B. Term used to refer to a species that has ceased to exist

C. Process by which a single species evolves into many different forms

D. Microscopic fossil

E. Unit of time into which eras are subdivided

F. Length of time required for half of the radioactive atoms in a sample to decay

G. Method of determining the age of a fossil by comparing its placement with that of fossils in other layers of rock

H. Pattern of evolution in which long stable periods are interrupted by brief periods of more rapid change

I. One of several subdivisions of the time between the Precambrian and the present

Term

1. extinct

2. relative dating

3. half-life

4. era

5. period

6. paleontologist

7. microfossil

8. adaptive radiation

9. punctuated equilibrium

Classification

Section 18–1 Finding Order in Diversity (pages 447–450)

This section explains how living things are organized for study.

Why Classify? (page 447)

1. Why do biologists use a classification system to study the diversity
   of life? _____

   _____

2. The science of classifying organisms and assigning them
   universally accepted names is known as _____.

3. Is the following sentence true or false? In a good system of
   classification, organisms placed into a particular group are less
   similar to each other than they are to organisms in other groups.

   _____

Assigning Scientific Names (page 448)

4. Why is it confusing to refer to organisms by common names? _____

   _____

   _____

5. Circle the letter of each sentence that is true about early efforts at
   naming organisms.

   a. Names were usually in English.

   b. Names often described detailed physical characteristics of a
      species.

   c. Names could be very long.

   d. It was difficult to standardize the names.

6. The two-word naming system developed by Linnaeus is called

   _____.

7. Circle the letter of each sentence that is true about binomial
   nomenclature.

   a. The system is no longer in use today.

   b. Each species is assigned a two-part scientific name.

   c. The scientific name is always written in italics.

   d. The second part of the scientific name is capitalized.

8. What is the genus of the grizzly bear, *Ursus arctos*? _____

   _____

Linnaeus's System of Classification (pages 449–450)

9. A group or level of organization in taxonomy is called a taxonomic category, or _____.

10. The largest taxonomic category in Linnaeus's system of classification is the _____, and the smallest is the _____.

11. What two kingdoms did Linnaeus name? _____
_____

12. Fill in the name of each missing taxonomic category in the chart below.

Grizzly bear	Black bear	Giant panda	Red fox	Abert squirrel	Coral snake	Sea star	
							KINGDOM **Animalia**
							Chordata
							Mammalia
							Carnivora
							Ursidae
							Ursus
							SPECIES *Ursus arctos*

Reading Skill Practice

Taking notes can help you identify and remember the most important information when you read. Take notes on Section 18–1 by writing the main headings and under each heading listing the most important points. Include in your notes the bold-faced terms and sentences. Do your work on a separate sheet of paper.

Chapter 18, Classification *(continued)*

Section 18–2 Modern Evolutionary Classification (pages 451–455)

This section explains how evolutionary relationships are important in classification. It also describes how DNA and RNA can help scientists determine evolutionary relationships.

Introduction (page 451)

1. What traits did Linnaeus consider when classifying organisms? _____ _____ _____

Problems With Traditional Classification (page 451)

2. What problems are faced by taxonomists who rely on body

   structure comparisons? _____ _____ _____ _____

Evolutionary Classification (page 452)

3. Is the following sentence true or false? Darwin's theory of evolution changed the way biologists thought about classification.

   _____

4. How do biologists now group organisms into categories? _____ _____ _____

5. Is the following sentence true or false? Genera placed within a family should be less closely related to one another than to

   members of any other family. _____

6. The strategy of grouping organisms together based on their

   evolutionary history is called _____

   _____.

Classification Using Cladograms (page 453)

7. Circle the letter of each sentence that is true about cladistic analysis.

   a. It considers only traits that are evolutionary innovations.

   b. It considers all traits that can be measured.

   c. It considers only similarities in body structure.

   d. It is a method of evolutionary classification.

8. Characteristics that appear in recent parts of a lineage, but not in

   its older members, are called _____.

9. A diagram that shows the evolutionary relationships among a group of organisms is called a(an) _____.

10. Is the following sentence true or false? Derived characters are used to construct a cladogram. _____

Similarities in DNA and RNA (page 454)

11. Is the following sentence true or false? Some organisms do not have DNA or RNA. _____

12. How do similarities in genes show that humans and yeasts share a common ancestry? _____
_____
_____

Molecular Clocks (page 455)

13. A model that uses DNA comparisons to estimate the length of time that two species have been evolving independently is known as a(an) _____.

14. A molecular clock relies on the repeating process of _____.

15. Why are only neutral mutations useful for molecular clocks? _____
_____
_____

16. Is the following sentence true or false? The degree of dissimilarity in DNA sequences is an indication of how long ago two species shared a common ancestor. _____

17. Why are there many molecular clocks in a genome instead of just one? _____
_____

Section 18–3 Kingdoms and Domains (pages 457–461)

This section describes the six kingdoms of life as they are now identified. It also describes the three-domain system of classification.

The Tree of Life Evolves (pages 457–458)

1. Is the following sentence true or false? The scientific view of life was more complex in Linnaeus's time. _____

2. What fundamental traits did Linnaeus use to separate plants from animals? _____
_____

Chapter 18, Classification *(continued)*

3. What type of organisms were later placed in the kingdom Protista? _____
_____
_____

4. Mushrooms, yeast, and molds have been placed in their own
kingdom, which is called _____.

5. Why did scientists place bacteria in their own kingdom, the Monera? _____
_____
_____

6. List the two groups into which the Monera have been separated.

   a. _____

   b. _____

7. Complete the concept map.

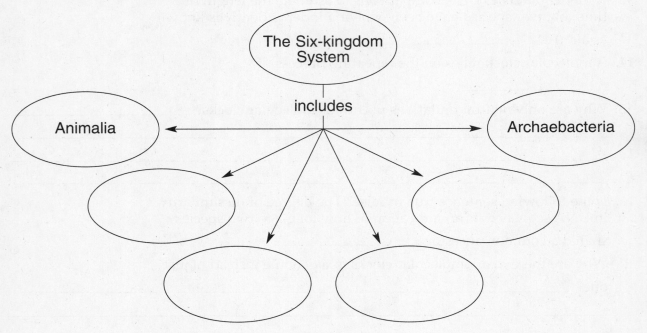

The Three-Domain System (page 458)

8. A more inclusive category than any other, including the kingdom,
is the _____.

9. What type of analyses have scientists used to group modern
organisms into domains? _____
_____

10. List the three domains.

   a. _____

   b. _____

   c. _____

11. Complete the chart below.

CLASSIFICATION OF LIVING THINGS

Domain	Kingdom	Examples
	Eubacteria	*Streptococcus, Escherichia coli*
Archaea		
	Protist	
		Mushrooms, yeasts
	Plantae	
		Sponges, worms, insects, fishes, mammals

Domain Bacteria (page 459)

12. Circle the letter of each sentence that is true about members of the domain Bacteria.

    a. They are multicellular.

    b. They are prokaryotes.

    c. They have rigid cell walls.

    d. The cell walls contain peptidoglycans.

13. Is the following sentence true or false? All members of the domain Bacteria are parasites. _____

Domain Archaea (page 459)

14. Circle the letter of each sentence that is true about members of the domain Archaea.

    a. They are unicellular.   **c.** They lack cell walls.

    b. They are eukaryotes.   **d.** They lack cell membranes.

15. Is the following sentence true or false? Many members of the domain Archaea can survive only in the absence of oxygen.

_____

Domain Eukarya (pages 460–461)

16. Circle the letter of each sentence that is true about all the members of the domain Eukarya.

    a. They have a nucleus.

    b. They are multicellular.

    c. They are heterotrophs.

    d. They have cell walls and chloroplasts.

Chapter 18, Classification (continued)

Match each kingdom with the description that applies to members of that kingdom.

Kingdom	Description
_____ 17. Protista	a. They have cell walls of chitin.
_____ 18. Fungi	b. They have no cell walls or chloroplasts.
_____ 19. Plantae	c. They include slime molds and giant kelp.
_____ 20. Animalia	d. They include mosses and ferns.

WordWise

Use the clues to help you identify the vocabulary terms from Chapter 18. Then, put the numbered letters in the right order to spell out the answer to the riddle.

Clues   **Vocabulary Terms**

Most inclusive taxonomic category   __ __ __ __ __ __
     1

Group of similar families   __ __ __ __ __
   2

Group of closely related classes   __ __ __ __ __ __
     3

Type of classification based on evolutionary history   __ __ __ __ __ __ __ __ __ __ __
  4

Group of closely related orders   __ __ __ __
  5

Group of closely related species   __ __ __ __
    6

Branching diagram showing evolutionary change   __ __ __ __ __ __ __ __ __
   7   8   9

One of two domains of unicellular prokaryotes   __ __ __ __ __ __ __
    10

Group of genera that share many characteristics   __ __ __ __ __ __
     11

Group into which organisms are classified   __ __ __ __ __
   12

The other domain of unicellular prokaryotes   __ __ __ __ __
   13

Domain of all organisms whose cells have nuclei   __ __ __ __ __ __
   14

Riddle: What kind of clock does a paleontologist use?

Answer: __ __ __ __ __ __ __ __ __   __ __ __ __ __
    1   2   3   4   5   6   7   8   9   10   11   12   13   14

Chapter 19

Bacteria and Viruses

Section 19–1 Prokaryotes (pages 471–476)

This section describes two groups of prokaryotes and explains how they differ. It also explains what factors are used to identify prokaryotes.

Introduction (page 471)

1. What are prokaryotes? _____

_____

2. Is the following sentence true or false? Prokaryotes are much smaller than most eukaryotic cells. _____

Classifying Prokaryotes (pages 471–472)

3. What are the two different groups of prokaryotes?

   a. _____   b. _____

4. Which is the larger of the two kingdoms of prokaryotes? _____

5. Where do eubacteria live? _____

_____

_____

6. What protects a prokaryotic cell from injury? _____

_____

7. Circle the letter of what is within the cell wall of a prokaryote.

   a. another cell wall   c. archaebacteria

   b. cell membrane   d. pili

8. What is peptidoglycan? _____

_____

9. Some eubacteria have a second, outer _____.

10. Circle the letter of each sentence that is true about archaebacteria.

    a. Their membrane lipids are different from those of eubacteria.

    b. They lack a cell wall.

    c. They lack peptidoglycan.

    d. They look very similar to eubacteria.

11. What is significant about the DNA sequences of key archaebacterial genes? _____

_____

12. How are archaebacteria related to eukaryotes? _____

_____

_____

Chapter 19, Bacteria and Viruses *(continued)*

13. What are methanogens, and where do they live? _____
_____
_____

14. Complete the illustration of a typical prokaryote by labeling the parts.

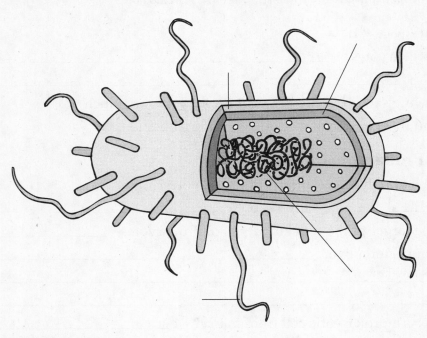

Identifying Prokaryotes *(page 473)*

15. What are four characteristics used to identify prokaryotes?

   a. _____

   b. _____

   c. _____

   d. _____

16. What are each of the differently shaped prokaryotes called?

   a. The rod-shaped are called _____.

   b. The spherical-shaped are called _____.

   c. The corkscrew-shaped are called _____.

17. A method of telling two different types of eubacteria apart by using dyes is called _____.

18. What colors are Gram-positive and Gram-negative bacteria under the microscope when treated with Gram stain? _____
_____

19. What are flagella? _____

20. Is the following sentence true or false? Many prokaryotes do not move at all. _____

Obtaining Energy (page 474)

21. Complete the table about prokaryotes classified by the way they obtain energy.

GROUPS OF PROKARYOTES

Group	Description
	Organism that carries out photosynthesis in a manner similar to plants
Chemoautotroph	
	Organism that takes in organic molecules and then breaks them down
Photoheterotroph	

22. Members of which group of photoautotrophs contain a bluish pigment and chlorophyll *a*? _____

23. How do the chemoautotrophs that live near hydrothermal vents on the ocean floor obtain energy? _____
_____

Releasing Energy (page 475)

24. Complete the table about prokaryotes classified by the way they carry out respiration.

GROUPS OF PROKARYOTES

Group	Description
	Organisms that require a constant supply of oxygen
Obligate anaerobes	
Facultative anaerobes	

25. How is botulism caused? _____
_____

26. Facultative anaerobes can switch between cellular respiration and
_____.

Growth and Reproduction (page 476)

27. What occurs in the process of binary fission? _____
_____
_____

Chapter 19, Bacteria and Viruses *(continued)*

28. What occurs during conjugation? _____

_____

29. Is the following sentence true or false? Most prokaryotes
reproduce by conjugation. _____

30. What is an endospore? _____

_____

_____

Section 19–2 Bacteria in Nature (pages 477–481)

This section describes ecological roles bacteria play in the environment. It also explains how bacteria cause disease.

Decomposers (page 477)

1. How do decomposers help the ecosystem recycle nutrients when
a tree dies? _____

_____

_____

2. What would happen to plants and animals if decomposers did
not recycle nutrients? _____

_____

Nitrogen Fixers (page 478)

3. Why do plants and animals need nitrogen? _____

_____

_____

4. How does nitrogen fixation help plants? _____

_____

5. What kind of relationship do many plants have with nitrogen-
fixing bacteria? _____

Bacteria and Disease (pages 479–480)

6. What are pathogens? _____

7. What are the two general ways that bacteria cause disease?

a. _____

_____

b. _____

_____

8. What kind of tissue do the bacteria that cause tuberculosis break
down? _____

9. What are most cases of food poisoning caused by? _____

_____

10. What are antibiotics? _____

_____

11. What is one of the major reasons for the dramatic increase in life
expectancy during the past two centuries? _____

_____

_____

Human Uses of Bacteria (page 480)

12. In the production of what foods are bacteria used? _____

_____

13. How can bacteria be used to clean up an oil spill? _____

_____

14. What have biotechnology companies begun to realize about
bacteria adapted to extreme environments? _____

_____

_____

Controlling Bacteria (page 481)

15. What is sterilization? _____

_____

16. A chemical solution that kills bacteria is called a(an)

_____.

17. Why will food stored at low temperatures keep longer? _____

_____

18. How can food be preserved through canning? _____

_____

19. What everyday chemicals can be used to inhibit the growth of
bacteria in food? _____

Reading Skill Practice

Writing a summary can help you remember the information you have read. When
you write a summary, write only the most important points. Write a summary of the
information under the blue heading *Decomposers*. Your summary should be shorter
than the text on which it is based. Do your work on a separate sheet of paper.

Chapter 19, Bacteria and Viruses *(continued)*

Section 19–3 Viruses (pages 482–487)

This section describes the structure of a virus. It also explains how viruses cause infection.

What Is a Virus? (pages 482–483)

1. What are viruses? _____
   _____

2. What do all viruses have in common? _____
   _____
   _____

3. Is the following sentence true or false? Most viruses are so small that they can be seen only with the aid of a powerful electron microscope. _____

4. What is the structure of a typical virus? _____
   _____

5. Circle the letter of what a virus's protein coat is called.

   a. capsid   **b.** envelope   **c.** head   **d.** lysis

6. How does a typical virus get inside a cell? _____
   _____
   _____

7. What occurs when viruses get inside of cells? _____
   _____
   _____
   _____

Viral Infection (pages 484–486)

8. Why are most viruses highly specific to the cells they infect? _____
   _____
   _____

9. What are bacteriophages? _____

10. Why is the process called a lytic infection? _____
    _____

11. Circle the letter of each sentence that is true about a lysogenic infection.

    a. The virus lyses the host cell immediately.

    b. The virus embeds its DNA into the host's DNA.

    c. The virus's DNA is replicated along with the host cell's DNA.

    d. A host cell makes copies of the virus indefinitely.

Name_____ Class_____ Date_____

12. Complete the flowchart about a lytic infection.

The bacteriophage attaches to the bacterium's _____.

↓

The bacteriophage injects its _____ into the cell.

↓

The cell makes mRNA from the bacteriophage's _____.

↓

The virus's genes wreck the cell, causing it to _____.

↓

The bursting of the cell releases new bacteriophage _____.

13. What is a prophage? _____
_____

Viruses and Disease (pages 486–487)

14. What are some human diseases that viruses cause? _____
_____
_____

15. What is a vaccine? _____
_____

16. How does a vaccine prevent a viral disease when injected into the
body? _____
_____

17. Cancer-causing viruses are known as
_____.

18. What are retroviruses? _____
_____

19. What happens when retroviruses infect a cell? _____
_____
_____

20. A disease-causing particle that contains only protein and not
DNA or RNA is called a(an) _____.

Chapter 19, Bacteria and Viruses *(continued)*

Are Viruses Alive? (page 487)

21. Circle the letter of each reason why biologists do not consider viruses to be alive.

   a. They can't infect living cells.

   b. They can't evolve.

   c. They can't regulate gene expression.

   d. They can't reproduce independently.

WordWise

Answer the questions by writing the correct vocabulary terms in the blanks. Use the circled letter in each word to find the hidden word. Then, write a definition for the hidden word.

What is the viral DNA that is embedded in a host's DNA?

__ __ __ Ⓞ __ __ __ __

What is a rod-shaped bacterium?

__ Ⓞ __ __ __ __ __ __

What is a compound that blocks the growth and reproduction of bacteria?

__ __ __ __ __ __ Ⓞ __ __ __

What is a virus that infects bacteria?

__ __ __ __ __ __ __ __ Ⓞ __ __ __

What is a prokaryote that can capture sunlight for energy but also needs organic compounds for nutrition?

__ __ __ Ⓞ __ __ __ __ __ __ __ __ __ __ __ __

What is the exchange of genetic information that occurs from one bacterium to another through a hollow bridge?

__ __ __ __ __ Ⓞ __ __ __ __ __ __

What is a virus that contains RNA as its genetic information?

__ Ⓞ __ __ __ __ __ __ __ __

What is the process in which nitrogen is converted into a form plants can use?

__ __ __ __ __ __ Ⓞ __ __ __ __ __ __ __ __

Hidden Word: __ __ __ __ __ __ __ __

Definition: _____

Chapter 20

Protists

Section 20–1 The Kingdom Protista (pages 495–496)

This section explains what protists are.

What Is a Protist? (page 495)

1. What is a protist? _____

_____

2. Circle the letter of each sentence that is true about protists.

   a. All are unicellular.

   b. All cells have a nucleus.

   c. All cells have membrane-bound organelles.

   d. All are multicellular.

3. Why are some organisms that consist of thousands of cells

   considered to be protists? _____

_____

Evolution of Protists (pages 495–496)

4. The first eukaryotic organisms on Earth were _____.

5. What is biologist Lynn Margulis's hypothesis about where the first

   protists came from? _____

_____

_____

_____

Classification of Protists (page 496)

6. Complete the table about protist classification.

GROUPS OF PROTISTS

Group	Method of Obtaining Food
	Consume other organisms
Plantlike protists	
Funguslike protists	

7. What don't categories of protists based on the way they obtain

   food reflect about these organisms? _____

_____

Chapter 20, Protists *(continued)*

Reading Skill Practice

By looking at illustrations in textbooks, you can help yourself remember better what you have read. Look carefully at Figure 20–1 on page 495. What important idea do these photographs communicate? Do your work on a separate sheet of paper.

Section 20–2 Animallike Protists: Protozoans (pages 497–503)

This section describes the distinguishing features of the major phyla of animallike protists. It also explains how animallike protists harm other living things.

Introduction

1. At one time, what were all animallike protists called?

   _____

2. How are the four phyla of animallike protists distinguished from

   one another? _____

   _____

Zooflagellates (page 497)

3. What kind of protists are classified in the phylum Zoomastigina? _____

   _____

4. How many flagella does a zooflagellate have? _____

   _____

5. Zooflagellates reproduce asexually by means of

   _____.

6. Is the following sentence true or false? Some zooflagellates have a

   sexual life cycle. _____

Sarcodines (page 498)

7. Sarcodines are members of the phylum _____.

8. What are pseudopods? _____

   _____

9. What do sarcodines use pseudopods for? _____

   _____

10. The best known sarcodines are the _____.

11. What is amoeboid movement? _____

   _____

12. What is a food vacuole? _____

13. How do amoebas capture and digest food? _____

_____

_____

14. Amoebas reproduce by means of _____.

15. Circle the letter of each example of a sarcodine.

   a. foraminiferan   **b.** paramecium   **c.** amoeba   **d.** heliozoan

Ciliates   (pages 499–500)

16. Ciliates are members of the phylum _____.

17. What are cilia? _____

18. What do ciliates use cilia for? _____

Match the ciliate structure with its description.

Structure	**Description**
_____ **19.** Trichocysts	**a.** Indentation on one side of a ciliate into which food is swept
_____ **20.** Macronucleus	**b.** Smaller nucleus containing a "reserve copy" of the cell's genes
_____ **21.** Micronucleus	**c.** Small, bottle-shaped structures used for defense
_____ **22.** Gullet	**d.** Region of cell membrane where waste-containing food vacuoles fuse
_____ **23.** Anal pore	**e.** Larger nucleus containing multiple copies of most of the cell's genes
_____ **24.** Contractile vacuole	**f.** Cavity in cytoplasm specialized to collect and pump out water

25. Label the illustration of a paramecium.

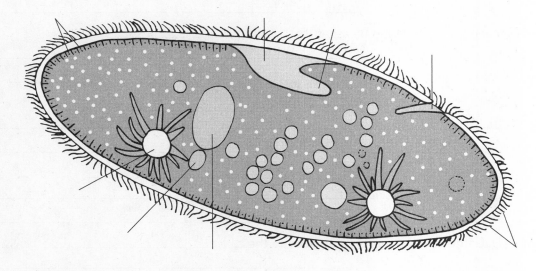

26. What is conjugation? _____

_____

Chapter 20, Protists *(continued)*

27. Within a large population, how does conjugation benefit ciliates? _____

_____

_____

Sporozoans (page 500)

28. Sporozoans are members of the phylum _____.

29. Circle the letter of each sentence that is true about sporozoans.

   a. They are parasitic.

   b. They do not move on their own.

   c. All have only one host.

   d. They reproduce by means of sporozoites.

Animallike Protists and Disease (pages 501–502)

30. What causes malaria? _____

_____

31. Complete the flowchart about the cycle of malarial infection.

> An infected *Anopheles* mosquito bites a human and deposits *Plasmodium* sporozoites into the _____.

> The sporozoites travel to the _____.

> Infected liver cells burst, releasing parasites that infect _____ cells.

> The red blood cells rupture, releasing _____.

> Toxins produce the chills and fever that are symptoms of _____.

> A mosquito bites the infected human and picks up the _____ cells.

Ecology of Animallike Protists (page 503)

32. Is the following sentence true or false? Some animallike protists recycle nutrients by breaking down dead organic matter.

_____

33. How does the zooflagellate *Trichonympha* make it possible for

termites to eat wood? _____

_____

_____

_____

Section 20–3 Plantlike Protists: Unicellular Algae (pages 505–509)

This section explains the function of chlorophyll and accessory pigments in algae. It also describes the distinguishing features of the major phyla of unicellular algae.

Introduction (page 505)

1. Plantlike protists are commonly called _____.

2. Is the following sentence true or false? Algae include only multicellular organisms. _____

Chlorophyll and Accessory Pigments (pages 505–506)

3. In the process of photosynthesis, what substances trap the energy of sunlight? _____

_____

4. How does water affect the sunlight that passes through it? _____

_____

5. Why does the dim blue light that penetrates deep into the sea contain little energy that chlorophyll *a* can use? _____

_____

6. How have various groups of algae adapted to conditions of limited light? _____

_____

7. What are accessory pigments? _____

_____

8. Why are algae such a wide range of colors? _____

_____

_____

Euglenophytes (page 506)

9. Euglenophytes are members of the phylum

_____.

Chapter 20, Protists *(continued)*

10. Circle the letter of each sentence that is true about euglenophytes.

    a. They are remarkably similar to zooflagellates.

    b. They possess chloroplasts.

    c. They have a cell wall.

    d. They have two flagella.

11. What is an eyespot, and what is its function? _____

_____

_____

12. Euglenas have a tough, intricate membrane called a(an)

_____.

13. How do euglenas reproduce? _____

14. Label the illustration of a euglena.

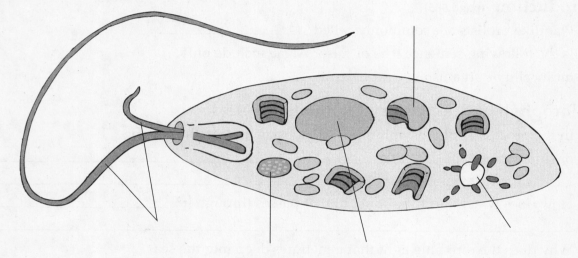

Dinoflagellates (page 507)

15. Dinoflagellates are members of the phylum _____.

16. How do dinoflagellates obtain nutrition? _____

_____

17. Circle the letter of each sentence that is true about dinoflagellates.

    a. They generally have one flagellum.

    b. Many species are luminescent.

    c. Most reproduce by binary fission.

    d. Their DNA is not tightly bound with histones.

Chrysophytes (page 507)

18. The yellow-green algae and the golden-brown algae are members
of the phylum _____.

19. What color are the chloroplasts of chrysophytes?

_____

20. Circle the letter of each sentence that is true about chrysophytes.

   a. The cell walls of some contain the carbohydrate pectin.

   b. They reproduce sexually but not asexually.

   c. They generally store food in the form of oil.

   d. Some form threadlike colonies.

Diatoms (page 507)

21. Diatoms are members of the phylum _____.

22. Circle the letter of each sentence that is true about diatoms.

   a. They are very rare in almost all environments.

   b. Their cell walls are rich in silicon.

   c. They are shaped like a petri dish or flat pillbox.

   d. They are among the most abundant organisms on Earth.

Ecology of Unicellular Algae (pages 508–509)

23. How do plantlike protists make much of the diversity of aquatic life possible? _____

24. What are phytoplankton? _____
_____

25. What are the benefits for both the corals and the intercellular dinoflagellates that some contain in this symbiotic relationship? _____

_____

_____

_____

26. What are algal blooms? _____

_____

27. How can an algal bloom be harmful? _____

_____

_____

_____

Section 20–4 Plantlike Protists: Red, Brown, and Green Algae (pages 510–515)

This section describes the distinguishing features of the major phyla of multicellular algae. It also explains how multicellular algae reproduce.

Introduction (page 510)

1. What are seaweeds? _____

Chapter 20, Protists *(continued)*

2. What are the most important differences among the three phyla of multicellular algae? _____

_____

Red Algae *(page 510)*

3. Red algae are members of the phylum _____.

4. Why are red algae able to live at great depths? _____

_____

5. What pigments do red algae contain? _____

_____

6. Which color of light are phycobilins especially good at absorbing?

    a. red   **b.** green   **c.** yellow   **d.** blue

7. Circle the letter of each sentence that is true about red algae.

    a. They can grow in the ocean at depths up to 260 meters.

    b. Most are unicellular.

    c. All are red or reddish-brown.

    d. Coralline algae play an important role in coral reef formation.

Brown Algae *(page 511)*

8. Brown algae are members of the phylum _____.

9. What pigments do brown algae contain? _____

_____

10. Where are brown algae commonly found growing? _____

_____

11. What is the largest known alga? _____

Match the Fucus structure with its description.

	Structure	Description
_____	**12.** Holdfast	**a.** Flattened stemlike structure
_____	**13.** Stipe	**b.** Gas-filled swelling
_____	**14.** Blade	**c.** Structure that attaches alga to the bottom
_____	**15.** Bladder	**d.** Leaflike structure

Green Algae *(pages 511–512)*

16. Green algae are members of the phylum _____.

17. What characteristics do green algae share with plants? _____

_____

_____

18. What is the connection that scientists think there is between mosses and green algae? _____

_____

19. The freshwater alga *Spirogyra* forms long threadlike colonies called _____.

20. How can the cells in a *Volvox* colony coordinate movement? _____

_____

21. "Sea lettuce" is the multicellular alga _____.

Reproduction in Green Algae (pages 512–514)

22. What occurs in the process known as alternation of generations? _____

_____

_____

23. The single-celled *Chlamydomonas* reproduces asexually by producing _____.

24. Circle the letter of each sentence that is true about sexual reproduction in *Chlamydomonas*.

   a. If conditions become unfavorable, cells release gametes.

   b. Paired gametes form a diploid zygote.

   c. A zygote quickly grows into an adult organism.

   d. The gametes are called male and female.

25. Complete the life cycle of *Ulva* by labeling the sporophyte, the male gametophyte, and the female gametophyte. Also, label the places where the processes of fertilization, mitosis, and meiosis occur.

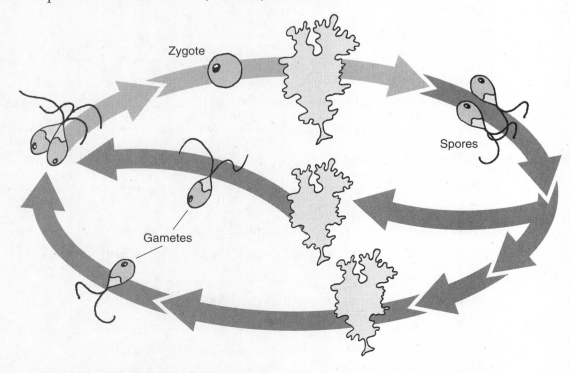

Zygote

Spores

Gametes

Chapter 20, Protists *(continued)*

26. Complete the table about the generations in an organism's life cycle.

GENERATIONS IN A LIFE CYCLE

Generation	Definition	Diploid or Haploid?
	Gamete-producing phase	
	Spore-producing phase	

Human Uses of Algae (page 515)

27. Why have algae been called the "grasses" of the sea? _____
_____

28. Through photosynthesis, algae produce much of Earth's

_____.

29. What is the compound agar derived from, and how is it used? _____
_____
_____
_____

Section 20–5 Funguslike Protists (pages 516–520)

This section explains the similarities and differences between funguslike protists and fungi. It also describes the defining characteristics of the slime molds and water molds.

Introduction (page 516)

1. How are funguslike protists like fungi? _____
_____

2. How are funguslike protists unlike most true fungi? _____
_____

Slime Molds (pages 516–518)

3. What are slime molds? _____
_____

4. Cellular slime molds belong to the phylum _____.

5. Is the following sentence true or false? Cellular slim molds spend most of their lives as free-living cells. _____

6. What do cellular slime molds form when their food supply is exhausted? _____
_____

7. What structure does a cellular slime mold colony produce, and what is that structure's function? _____

_____

_____

8. Acellular slime molds belong to the phylum _____.

9. What is a plasmodium? _____

_____

10. The plasmodium eventually produces sporangia, which in turn produce haploid _____.

Water Molds (pages 518–519)

11. Water molds, or oomycetes, are members of the phylum

_____.

12. Water molds produce thin filaments known as

_____.

13. What are zoosporangia? _____

_____

_____

14. Where are male and female nuclei produced in water mold sexual reproduction? _____

_____

_____

15. Fertilization in water molds occurs in the _____.

Ecology of Funguslike Protists (page 519)

16. Why aren't there bodies of dead animals and plants littering the woods and fields you walk through? _____

_____

_____

17. What are examples of plant diseases that water molds cause? _____

_____

Water Molds and the Potato Famine (page 520)

18. What produced the Great Potato Famine of 1846? _____

_____

_____

19. What did the Great Potato Famine lead to? _____

_____

_____

Chapter 20, Protists *(continued)*

WordWise

*Solve the clues by filling in the blanks with vocabulary terms from Chapter 20.
Then, write the numbered letters in the correct order to find the hidden message.*

Clues   **Vocabulary Terms**

Any organism that is not a plant, an animal,
a fungus, or a prokaryote
$\_\ \_\ \_\ \_\ \_\ \_\ \_$
$\overset{1}{}$

Very small, bottle-shaped structure on a
paramecium used for defense
$\_\ \_\ \_\ \_\ \_\ \_\ \_\ \_\ \_$
$\overset{2}{}\overset{3}{}\overset{4}{}$

Hairlike projection similar to a flagellum
$\_\ \_\ \_\ \_\ \_\ \_$
$\overset{5}{}$

Spore-producing organism
$\_\ \_\ \_\ \_\ \_\ \_\ \_\ \_\ \_$
$\overset{6}{}\overset{7}{}$

Cluster of red pigments on euglenas that
helps the organism find sunlight
$\_\ \_\ \_\ \_\ \_\ \_\ \_$
$\overset{8}{}$

Long, threadlike colony of green algae
$\_\ \_\ \_\ \_\ \_\ \_$
$\overset{9}{}$

Larger nucleus in a paramecium
$\_\ \_\ \_\ \_\ \_\ \_\ \_\ \_\ \_$
$\overset{10}{}\overset{11}{}$

Temporary projection of cytoplasm
$\_\ \_\ \_\ \_\ \_\ \_\ \_$
$\overset{12}{}\ \overset{13}{}$

Population of photosynthetic organisms
near the surface of the ocean
$\_\ \_\ \_\ \_\ \_\ \_\ \_\ \_\ \_\ \_\ \_\ \_$
$\overset{14}{}$

Thin filaments of water molds
$\_\ \_\ \_\ \_\ \_$
$\overset{15}{}$

Small nucleus of paramecium
$\_\ \_\ \_\ \_\ \_\ \_\ \_\ \_\ \_\ \_$
$\overset{16}{}$

Gamete-producing organism
$\_\ \_\ \_\ \_\ \_\ \_\ \_\ \_\ \_$
$\overset{17}{}$

Structure of water molds that produces
female nuclei
$\_\ \_\ \_\ \_\ \_\ \_\ \_$
$\overset{18}{}$

Indentation on one side of a ciliate
$\_\ \_\ \_\ \_\ \_\ \_$
$\overset{19}{}$

Tough, intricate cell membrane of euglenas
$\_\ \_\ \_\ \_\ \_\ \_\ \_\ \_$
$\overset{20}{}$

Structure with many nuclei formed by
acellular slime molds
$\_\ \_\ \_\ \_\ \_\ \_\ \_\ \_$
$\overset{21}{}$

Hidden Message:

$\overline{}\ \overline{}\ \overline{}\ \overline{}\ \overline{}\ \overline{}\ \overline{}\ \overline{}\ \ \ \overline{}\ \overline{}\ \overline{}$
$\ \,1\ \ \ 2\ \ \ 3\ \ \ 4\ \ \ 5\ \ \ 6\ \ \ 7\ \ \ 8\ \ \ \ \ \,9\ \ 10\ \ 11$

$\overline{}\ \overline{}\ \overline{}\ \overline{}\ \overline{}\ \overline{}\ \overline{}\ \overline{}\ \overline{}\ \overline{}$.
$12\ \ 13\ \ 14\ \ 15\ \ 16\ \ 17\ \ 18\ \ 19\ \ 20\ \ 21$

Fungi

Section 21–1 The Kingdom Fungi (pages 527–529)

This section describes the defining characteristics of fungi. It also describes the internal structure of a fungus and explains how fungi reproduce.

What Are Fungi? (page 527)

1. Circle the letter of each sentence that is true about fungi.

   a. They are heterotrophs.

   b. They have cell walls.

   c. They are photosynthetic.

   d. They are eukaryotic.

2. The cell walls of fungi are made of a complex carbohydrate called

   _____.

3. How do fungi digest their food? _____
   _____

4. Is the following sentence true or false? Some fungi are parasites.

   _____

Structure and Function of Fungi (pages 527–528)

5. Which group of fungi are not multicellular? _____

6. What are hyphae? _____
   _____

7. How thick is each hypha? _____

8. In some fungi, what divides the hyphae into cells containing one
   or two nuclei? _____

9. What is a mycelium? _____
   _____

10. Why is a mycelium well-suited to absorb food? _____
    _____
    _____

11. What is a fruiting body of a fungus? _____
    _____
    _____

12. What is a fairy ring, and why does it form? _____
    _____
    _____

Chapter 21, Fungi *(continued)*

13. Label the parts of the fungus.

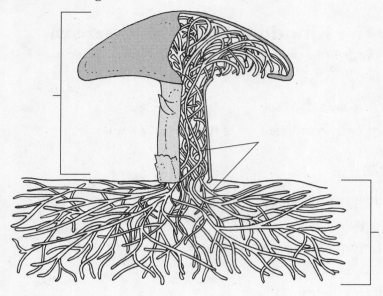

Reproduction in Fungi (pages 528–529)

14. Is the following sentence true or false? Most fungi can only reproduce asexually. _____

15. How does asexual reproduction occur in fungi? _____
_____
_____

16. In some fungi, spores are produced in structures called
_____.

17. Where are sporangia found in a fungus? _____
_____

18. Sexual reproduction in fungi usually involves two different
_____.

19. What is a gametangium? _____

20. How does a zygote form in fungal sexual reproduction? _____
_____
_____

21. Circle the letter of each sentence that is true about sexual reproduction in fungi.

    a. The zygote is often the only diploid cell in the fungus's entire life cycle.

    b. Mating types are called male and female.

    c. Gametes of both mating types are about the same size.

    d. One mating type is a "+" (plus) and the other is a "−" (minus).

How Fungi Spread (page 529)

22. Why do molds seem to spring up in any location that has the right combination of moisture and food? _____

_____

23. Is the following sentence true or false? The spores of many fungi scatter easily in the wind. _____

24. For a fungal spore to grow, where must it land? _____

_____

_____

Section 21–2 Classification of Fungi (pages 530–536)

This section describes the characteristics of the four main phyla of fungi.

Introduction (page 530)

1. Complete the concept map about the four main groups of fungi.

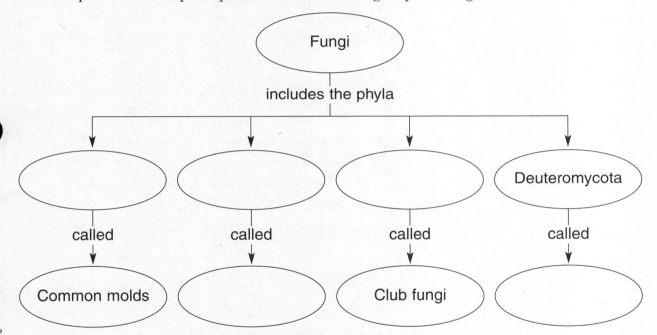

The Common Molds (pages 530–531)

2. What are zygomycetes? _____

_____

_____

3. The resting spore formed during the sexual phase of the mold's life cycle is called a(an) _____.

4. Is the following sentence true or false? The hyphae of zygomycetes are generally divided by cross walls. _____

5. What is the common name for *Rhizopus stolonifer*? _____

6. Complete the table about the kinds of hyphae of black bread mold.

KINDS OF HYPHAE

Kind of Hyphae	Description
Rhizoids	
Stolons	
	Hyphae that push up into the air and form sporangia at their tips.

7. Complete the flowchart about sexual reproduction in zygomycetes.

> Two hyphae from different mating types come together, forming _____.

↓

> Haploid gametes from the mating types fuse to form diploid zygotes, which make up a single _____.

↓

> The zygospore eventually germinates, and a(an) _____ emerges.

↓

> The sporangium reproduces asexually by releasing _____.

The Sac Fungi *(pages 532–533)*

8. What is an ascus? _____
_____

9. Is the following sentence true or false? Ascomycetes make up the largest phylum in the kingdom Fungi. _____

10. What occurs among sac fungi during asexual reproduction? _____
_____
_____
_____

11. Is the following sentence true or false? Yeasts are multicellular ascomycetes. _____

12. Why are yeasts classified as ascomycetes? _____
_____

13. Complete the flowchart about sexual reproduction in ascomycetes.

> Gametangia from two different mating types _____ together.

↓

> That fusion produces hyphae that contain haploid _____.

↓

> The N + N hyphae produce a fruiting body, inside of which the _____ forms.

↓

> Within the ascus, meiosis and mitosis occur to produce cells known as _____.

↓

> In a favorable environment, an ascospore germinates and grows into a haploid _____.

14. The common yeasts used for baking and brewing are members of the genus _____.

15. What process do yeasts carry out to obtain energy when they are in a nutrient mixture such as bread dough? _____

The Club Fungi (pages 534–536)

16. From what does the phylum Basidiomycota get its name? _____

_____

_____

17. Label the parts of a mushroom.

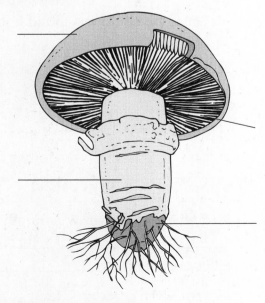

Chapter 21, Fungi *(continued)*

18. Where are basidia found on a basidiomycete? _____

_____

19. The cap of a basidiomycete is composed of tightly packed

_____.

20. Complete the flowchart about reproduction in basidiomycetes.

> A basidiospore germinates to produce a haploid primary _____.

↓

> The mycelia of different mating types fuse to produce a(an) _____.

↓

> A fruiting body pushes above ground, forming a(an) _____ at the soil's surface.

↓

> Two nuclei in each basidium fuse to form a diploid _____.

↓

> Each zygote undergoes meiosis, forming clusters of diploid _____.

21. Is the following sentence true or false? The remarkable growth of mushrooms overnight is caused by cell enlargement.

_____

22. Circle the letter of each example of basidiomycetes.

    a. puffballs   **b.** shelf fungi   **c.** rusts   **d.** yeasts

23. Why should you never pick or eat any mushrooms found in the wild? _____

_____

The Imperfect Fungi (page 536)

24. The phylum Deuteromycota is composed of what fungi? _____

_____

_____

25. What is *Penicillium notatum*, and where does it grow naturally? _____

_____

26. What is produced from *Penicillium notatum*? _____

_____

Reading Skill Practice

You can often increase your understanding of what you've read by making comparisons. A compare-and-contrast table helps you to do this. On a separate sheet of paper, make a table to compare the four main groups of fungi you read about in Section 21–2. For more information about compare-and-contrast tables, see Organizing Information in Appendix A of your textbook.

Section 21–3 Ecology of Fungi (pages 537–542)

This section explains what the main role of fungi is in natural ecosystems. It also describes problems that parasitic fungi cause and describes the kinds of symbiotic relationships that fungi form with other organisms.

All Fungi Are Heterotrophs (page 537)

1. Fungi cannot manufacture their own food because they are

   _____ .

2. What are saprobes? _____

   _____

3. Circle the letter of how the fungus *Pleurotus ostreatus* is classified.

   a. carnivorous   **c.** herbivorous

   b. omnivorous   **d.** detritivorous

Fungi as Decomposers (page 538)

4. Fungi recycle nutrients breaking down the bodies and wastes of

   other _____ .

5. How do fungi break down leaves, fruit, and other organic

   material into simple molecules? _____

   _____

Fungi as Parasites (pages 538–539)

6. Parasitic fungi cause serious plant and animal

   _____ .

7. Circle the letter of each example of a fungal plant disease.

   a. wheat rust   **b.** corn smut   **c.** thrush   **d.** mildews

8. Rusts are members of the phylum _____ .

9. What two kinds of plants do wheat rusts need to complete their

   life cycle? _____

   _____

10. One deuteromycete can infect the areas between the human toes,

    causing an infection known as _____ .

Chapter 21, Fungi *(continued)*

11. What happens when the fungus that causes athlete's foot infects other areas of the body? _____

Symbiotic Relationships (pages 540–542)

12. Lichens and mycorrhizae are both examples of what kind of symbiotic relationships? _____

13. What are lichens? _____

_____

14. What is the photosynthetic organism in a lichen? _____

_____

15. Where do lichens grow? _____

_____

16. What benefits do the fungus and the photosynthetic organism derive from the association in a lichen? _____

_____

_____

17. What are mycorrhizae? _____

18. Why is the presence of mycorrhizae essential for the growth of many plants? _____

_____

WordWise

Complete the sentences by using one of the scrambled words below.

Word Bank
yodb iiugntrf   chlnei   ziiohrd   roeaizrhcym   mmieulcy   sscua
iiausbdm   pyheah

1. A rootlike hypha of a zygomycete is a(an) _____.

2. A symbiotic association between a fungus and a photosynthetic organism is a(an)

_____.

3. The reproductive structure that develops from mycelia growing underground is a(an)

_____.

4. The body of a multicellular fungus composed of many hyphae tangled together into a thick mass is a(an) _____.

5. Associations of plant roots and fungi are _____.

6. A tough sac in ascomycetes that contains spores is a(an) _____.

7. The spore-bearing structure of basidiomycetes is a(an) _____.

8. Multicellular fungi are composed of tiny filaments called _____.

Plant Diversity

Section 22–1 Introduction to Plants (pages 551–555)

This section explains what a plant is and describes what plants need to survive. It also explains how the first plants evolved.

What Is a Plant? (page 551)

1. Circle the letter of each sentence that is true about plants.

   a. Plants are multicellular prokaryotes.

   b. Plants carry out photosynthesis.

   c. Plants have cell walls made of cellulose.

   d. Plants develop from multicellular embryos.

2. What pigments do plants use to carry out photosynthesis? _____

   _____

3. Is the following sentence true or false? All plants are autotrophs.

   _____

The Plant Life Cycle (page 552)

4. All plants have a life cycle that is characterized by alternation of

   _____.

5. Complete the table about plant generations.

PLANT GENERATIONS

Generation	Description	Haploid or Diploid?
	Gamete-producing plant	
	Spore-producing plant	

6. Complete the diagram of the plant life cycle by writing the name of the plant generation in the correct place. For each generation, indicate whether it is haploid or diploid by writing either *N* or *2N*.

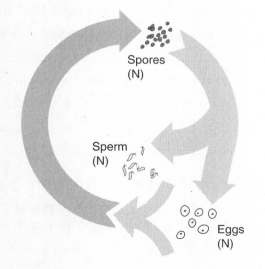

Spores (N)

Sperm (N)

Eggs (N)

Chapter 22, Plant Diversity *(continued)*

7. Seed plants have evolved reproductive cycles that are carried out
   independently of _____.

What Plants Need to Survive (page 552)

8. What are the four basic needs of plants? _____
   _____
   _____

9. Why are plant leaves typically broad and flat? _____
   _____

10. Circle the letter of each sentence that is true about the basic needs
    of plants.
    a. Plants require oxygen to support respiration.
    b. Plants must get rid of water as quickly as possible.
    c. Water is one of the raw materials of photosynthesis.
    d. Plants have specialized tissues to carry nutrients upward.

Early Plants (pages 553–554)

11. The history of plants can be understood in terms of the evolution
    of what kinds of structures? _____
    _____

12. What did the first plants evolve from? _____
    _____

13. Circle the letter of each sentence that is true about multicellular
    green algae.
    a. They have the same photosynthetic pigments as plants.
    b. They have the size, color, and appearance of plants.
    c. They are classified as early plants.
    d. They have reproductive cycles that are similar to early plants.

14. How were early plants similar to today's mosses? _____
    _____

15. From the first plants, at least two major groups of plants evolved.
    What did those groups develop into? _____
    _____
    _____

Overview of the Plant Kingdom (page 555)

16. Circle the letter of each of the important features that botanists
    use to divide the plant kingdom into four groups.
    a. seeds   b. water-conducting tissue   c. stems   d. flowers

17. What are the four main groups of living plants?

a. _____ c. _____

b. _____ d. _____

18. The great majority of plants alive today are _____

_____.

Reading Skill Practice

Finding the main ideas of a section can help you organize the important points you need to remember. Skim Section 22–1 to find the main ideas. Write them on the left-hand side of a separate sheet of paper. Then make a list of supporting details for each main idea on the right-hand side of the sheet.

Section 22–2 Bryophytes (pages 556–559)

This section identifies the adaptations that enable bryophytes—mosses and their relatives—to live on land. It also identifies three groups of bryophytes and describes how bryophytes reproduce.

Introduction (page 556)

1. Mosses and their relatives are generally called

_____.

2. Circle the letter of the substance that bryophyte life cycles are highly dependent on.

a. carbon dioxide   **b.** soil   **c.** oxygen   **d.** water

3. How does the lack of vascular tissue keep bryophytes small? _____

_____

_____

4. Why must bryophytes live in places where there is standing

water for at least part of the year? _____

_____

_____

Groups of Bryophytes (pages 556–557)

5. What are the three groups of plants that bryophytes include?

a. _____ b. _____ c. _____

6. Where would you expect to find mosses growing? _____

_____

_____

7. Why are mosses the most abundant plants in polar regions? _____

_____

Chapter 22, Plant Diversity *(continued)*

8. Why is the thin, upright shoot of a moss plant not considered to be a true stem? _____

9. Complete the illustration by identifying which part of a typical moss plant is the gametophyte and which part is the sporophyte.

10. What do the mature gametophytes of liverworts look like? _____
_____
_____

11. What are gemmae? _____
_____

12. How do liverworts reproduce asexually? _____
_____
_____

13. What does the hornwort sporophyte look like? _____
_____

14. In what sort of soil would liverworts and hornworts be expected to be found? _____
_____

Life Cycle of Bryophytes *(pages 558–559)*

15. In bryophytes, which stage of the life cycle carries out most of the plant's photosynthesis? _____

16. What fact of reproduction limits the distribution of bryophytes to habitats near water? _____
_____
_____

17. When a moss spore germinates, what does it grow into? _____
_____

18. Complete the table about bryophyte reproductive structures.

BRYOPHYTE REPRODUCTIVE STRUCTURES

Structure	Description	Structure Produces
	Male reproductive structure	
	Female reproductive structure	

19. What does the zygote depend on for water and nutrients? _____
_____

Human Use of Mosses (page 559)

20. In certain environments, the dead remains of sphagnum accumulate to form thick deposits of _____.

21. Why do gardeners add peat moss to soil? _____
_____

Section 22–3 Seedless Vascular Plants (pages 560–563)

This section explains how vascular tissue is important to ferns and their relatives. It also describes the characteristics of three phyla of spore-bearing plants and describes the stages in the life cycle of ferns.

Introduction (page 560)

1. What is vascular tissue? _____
_____

Evolution of Vascular Tissue (page 560)

2. What kind of cells did the first vascular plants have that were specialized to conduct water? _____

3. Circle the letter of each sentence that is true about tracheids.

    a. They are hollow cells.   **c.** Their thick cell walls resist pressure.

    b. They are connected end to end.   **d.** They are the key cells of phloem.

4. Complete the table about vascular tissue.

VASCULAR TISSUE

Type of Tissue	Function
Xylem	
Phloem	

Chapter 22, Plant Diversity *(continued)*

5. Is the following sentence true or false? Phloem and xylem cannot move water and nutrients against the force of gravity.

_____

Ferns and Their Relatives (pages 561–562)

6. Spore-bearing vascular plants include what three types of plants?

a. _____   b. _____   c. _____

7. Is the following sentence true or false? Vascular plants have true roots and stems. _____

8. Complete the table about plant structures.

PLANT STRUCTURES

Structure	Description
Roots	
Leaves	
Stems	

9. The fossilized remains of ancient forests of club mosses exist today as huge beds of _____.

10. Why is *Equisetum* called "horsetail"? _____

_____

11. Circle the letter of each structure a horsetail has.

a. stems   b. cones   c. leaves   d. roots

12. Ferns are members of phylum _____.

13. What are rhizomes? _____

14. The large leaves of ferns are called _____.

15. Fronds grow from what fern structures? _____

16. In what kind of habitats are ferns most abundant? _____

_____

_____

Life Cycle of Ferns (pages 562–563)

17. What is the dominant stage in the life cycle of ferns and other spore-bearing vascular plants? _____

_____

18. Fern sporophytes produce haploid spores on the underside of their fronds in tiny containers called _____.

19. What are sori? _____

20. Are the spores of ferns haploid or diploid? _____

21. Label each drawing of a fern as either the sporophyte or the gametophyte.

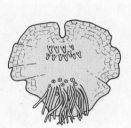

_____   _____

22. Where are the antheridia and archegonia found in ferns? _____
_____

23. Why does fertilization in ferns require at least a thin film of water? _____
_____

24. Circle the letter of each sentence that is true about the life cycle of ferns.

    a. The zygote grows into a new gametophyte.

    b. The sporophyte is a heart-shaped, green structure.

    c. Fern sporophytes often live several years.

    d. When spores germinate, they grow into haploid gametophytes.

Section 22–4 Seed Plants (pages 564–568)

This section explains what features allow seed plants to reproduce without standing water. It also describes the four groups of gymnosperms.

Introduction (page 564)

    1. Complete the table about seed plants.

SEED PLANTS

Type	Description	Examples
	Seed plants that bear seeds directly on the surfaces of cones	
	Seed plants that bear their seeds within a layer of protective tissue	

Chapter 22, Plant Diversity *(continued)*

Reproduction Free From Water (pages 564–565)

2. What are three features that allow seed plants to reproduce without water?

   a. _____

   b. _____

   c. _____

3. What are cones and flowers? _____

   _____

4. Why don't the gametophytes or the gametes of seed plants need standing water to function? _____

   _____

5. What is pollination? _____

   _____

Match the structure with its description.

	Structure	Description
_____	**6.** pollen grain	**a.** An embryo encased in a protective covering
_____	**7.** seed	**b.** Structure that surrounds and protects the plant embryo
_____	**8.** endosperm	**c.** Early developmental stage of sporophyte plant
_____	**9.** embryo	**d.** Male gametophyte of seed plants
_____	**10.** seed coat	**e.** Seed's food supply

11. What are examples of tissues or structures that seeds have that aid in their dispersal? _____

    _____

    _____

12. What is the strategy that allows seeds to survive long periods of bitter cold, extreme heat, or drought? _____

    _____

    _____

Evolution of Seed Plants (page 566)

13. How did conditions on Earth change during the Carboniferous and Devonian periods, and how did those changes affect plants? _____

    _____

    _____

14. What link do seed ferns represent in the fossil record? _____

15. What adaptations did seed plants have that allowed them to replace spore-bearing plants as continents became drier? _____

_____

Gymnosperms—Cone Bearers (pages 566–568)

16. Complete the concept map about gymnosperms.

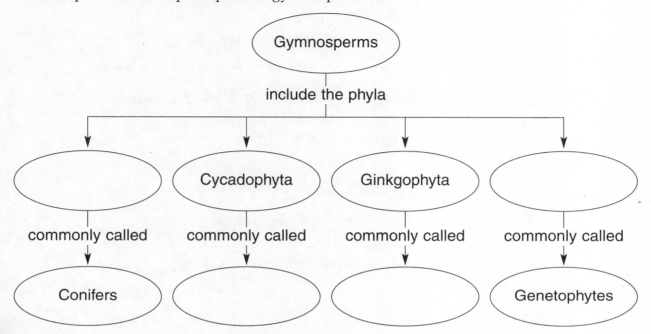

17. What kind of gymnosperm is *Ephedra*? _____

18. Where are the reproductive scales of gnetophytes found? _____

_____

19. What do cycads look like? _____

_____

20. In what kind of habitats can cycads be found growing naturally today? _____

21. Why is the ginkgo tree sometimes called a living fossil? _____

_____

22. What kinds of plants do conifers include? _____

_____

23. Why are the leaves of most conifers long and thin, such as pine needles? _____

_____

24. In addition to the shape of the leaves, what are two other adaptations that help conifers conserve water?

a. _____

b. _____

Chapter 22, Plant Diversity *(continued)*

25. Circle the letter of the reason why most conifers never become bare.

    a. They never lose their needles.

    b. The gametophyte supplies needles to the sporophyte.

    c. Older needles are gradually replaced by newer needles.

    d. The needles conserve water throughout the year.

26. How are larches and bald cypresses different from most other

    conifers? _____

Section 22–5 Angiosperms—Flowering Plants (pages 569–572)

This section identifies the characteristics of angiosperms. It also explains what monocots and dicots are and describes the three categories of plant life spans.

Introduction (page 569)

1. Angiosperms are members of the phylum _____.

2. Angiosperms have unique reproductive organs known as

   _____.

3. During which geologic period did flowering plants first appear? _____

   _____

Flowers and Fruits (page 569)

4. In flowering plants, the seed is encased in a(an)

   _____.

5. What is a fruit? _____

6. Why is using fruit to attract animals one of the reasons for the

   success of flowering plants? _____

   _____

   _____

   _____

Diversity of Angiosperms (pages 570–572)

7. The seed leaves of plant embryos are called _____.

8. Complete the table about classes of angiosperms.

CLASSES OF ANGIOSPERMS

Class	Common Name	Number of Seed Leaves	Examples
Monocotyledonae			
Dicotyledonae			

9. Circle the letter of each plant feature that is characteristic of dicots.

   a. Parallel leaf veins

   b. Floral parts in multiples of 4 or 5

   c. Roots include a taproot

   d. Vascular bundles scattered throughout stem

10. Classify each of the following plants as either woody or herbaceous by writing the correct term on the line.

    a. Rose shrubs _____

    b. Oaks _____

    c. Tomato plants _____

    d. Sunflowers _____

    e. Grape vines _____

    f. Dandelions _____

11. Woody plants are made primarily of what kind of cells? _____
    _____
    _____

12. What characteristics do the stems of herbaceous plants have? _____
    _____

13. Complete the table about plant life spans.

PLANT LIFE SPANS

Category	Definition	Examples
Annuals		
Biennials		
Perennials		

14. What structures do biennials produce in their first year of growth? _____
    _____

15. What happens to biennials once their flowers produce seeds? _____
    _____

16. Is the following sentence true or false? Most perennials have herbaceous stems. _____

Chapter 22, Plant Diversity *(continued)*

WordWise

Use the clues below to identify vocabulary terms from Chapter 22. Write the terms on the lines, putting one letter in each blank. When you finish, the word enclosed in the diagonal will reveal an important term related to plants.

Clues

1. Cluster of vascular tissue in a leaf
2. Female reproductive structure in mosses
3. Supporting structure that connects roots and leaves
4. Key cells in xylem
5. A thick wall of tissue surrounding angiosperm seed
6. Process by which pollen is carried to the female gametophyte
7. Photosynthetic organ that contains vascular tissue

8. Spore-producing plant
9. Bryophyte structure where sperm are produced
10. A long, thin cell that anchors a moss to the ground
11. Flowering plant
12. An embryo of a living plant that is encased in a protective covering
13. A cluster of sporangia
14. Creeping or underground stem in ferns

Vocabulary Terms

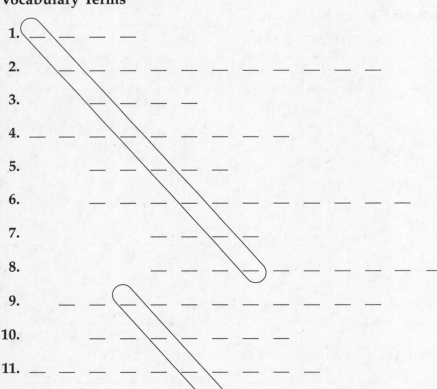

1. _ _ _ _
2. _ _ _ _ _ _ _ _ _ _
3. _ _ _ _ _
4. _ _ _ _ _
5. _ _ _ _
6. _ _ _ _ _ _ _ _ _
7. _ _ _ _
8. _ _ _ _ _ _ _ _
9. _ _ _ _ _ _
10. _ _ _ _ _ _
11. _ _ _ _ _ _ _ _ _
12. _ _ _ _
13. _ _ _ _
14. _ _ _ _ _ _ _

Roots, Stems, and Leaves

Section 23–1 Specialized Tissues in Plants (pages 579–583)

This section describes the principle organs and tissues of vascular plants. It also explains what specialized cells make up vascular tissue.

Structure of Seed Plants (pages 579–580)

1. What are the three principle organs of seed plants?

   a. _____ b. _____ c. _____

2. Circle the letter of each sentence that is true about a function that roots perform.

   a. They anchor plants in the ground.

   b. They compete with other plants for sunlight.

   c. They absorb water and nutrients from soil.

   d. They hold plants upright.

3. What does the vascular tissue of stems do? _____

   _____

   _____

4. The principal organs in which plants carry out photosynthesis are

   the _____.

5. What do the adjustable openings of leaves help conserve, and

   what do they allow to enter and leave a plant? _____

   _____

   _____

Tissue Systems (page 580)

6. What are the three tissue systems of plants?

   a. _____ c. _____

   b. _____

Meristematic Tissue (pages 580–581)

7. What do plants produce at their tips as long as they live? _____

   _____

8. The only plant tissue that produces new cells by mitosis is called

   _____.

9. What occurs as meristematic cells mature? _____

   _____

10. What is an apical meristem? _____

   _____

Chapter 23, Roots, Stems, and Leaves (continued)

11. Where else on many plants is there meristematic tissue other than at apical meristems? _____

_____

Dermal Tissue (page 581)

12. Dermal tissue typically consists of a single layer of

_____.

13. The layer of cells that covers a plant and protects it from disease and injury is called the _____.

14. What is cuticle, and what is its function? _____

_____

_____

15. What is the function of trichomes? _____

_____

16. What does dermal tissue consist of in roots, and what is its function? _____

_____

_____

Vascular Tissue (pages 582–583)

17. Complete the table about vascular tissue.

TYPES OF VASCULAR TISSUE

Type	Function	Cell Types Within Tissue
	Transports water	
	Transports food	

Match the vascular-tissue cells with their descriptions.

Vascular-tissue Cells

_____ **18.** Tracheids

_____ **19.** Vessel elements

_____ **20.** Sieve tube elements

_____ **21.** Companion cells

Description

a. The main phloem cells

b. Long, narrow xylem cells with walls that are impermeable to water

c. Phloem cells that control the activity of sieve tube elements

d. Xylem cells arranged end to end on top of one another

22. How can water move from one tracheid into a neighboring cell? _____

_____

_____

23. How can materials move from one sieve tube element into the next? _____

_____

_____

24. What cells control the activity of sieve tube elements? _____

Ground Tissue (page 583)

25. The cells that lie between dermal and vascular tissue make up

what kind of tissue? _____

26. Complete the table about ground-tissue cells.

GROUND-TISSUE CELLS

Type of Cell	Structure	Function
	Cells with thin cell walls and large central vacuoles	
	Cells with strong, flexible cell walls	
	Cells with extremely thick, rigid cell walls	

Section 23–2 Roots (pages 584–588)

This section describes the two main types of roots and the main tissues in a mature root. It also explains the different functions of roots.

Types of Roots (page 584)

1. How are primary roots and secondary roots different in some plants? _____

_____

2. Complete the table about types of roots.

TYPES OF ROOTS

Type of Root	Description	Mainly in Dicots or Monocots?	Examples
	Long and thick primary roots that grow deep into the soil		
	Roots that are usually shallow and consist of many thin roots		

Root Structure and Growth (page 585)

3. What is the structure of a mature root? _____

_____

_____

Chapter 23, Roots, Stems, and Leaves *(continued)*

4. Label the parts of a root on the illustration.

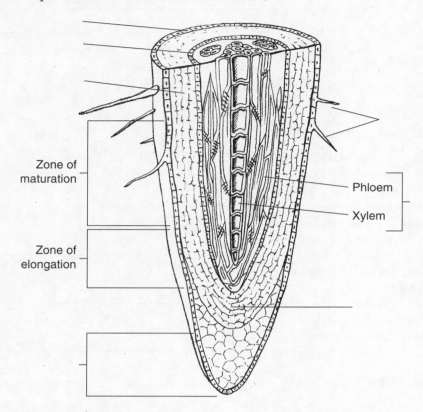

Zone of
maturation

Zone of
elongation

Phloem

Xylem

5. Water enters the plant through the large surface area provided by the _____.

6. What does the cortex of a root consist of? _____
_____

7. The vascular tissue in the central region of a root is called the _____
_____.

8. What protects the apical meristem of a root? _____

9. Where does most of the increase in root length occur? _____
_____

Root Functions (pages 586–588)

10. What are two functions of a plant's roots?

a. _____

b. _____

11. Is the following sentence true or false? The ingredients of a soil can determine what kinds of plants grow in it. _____

12. What role does calcium play in a plant? _____
_____

13. What is the result if a plant is deficient in nitrogen? _____

_____

14. Circle the letter of each sentence that is true about active transport of minerals in roots.

a. Water molecules move into the plant by active transport.

b. ATP is the source of energy used to pump mineral ions from the soil into the plant.

c. The cell membranes of root hairs contain active transport proteins.

d. Using active transport, a root actually pumps water into the plant.

15. What happens to the water and dissolved minerals after they move into the cortex? _____

_____

16. Each of the cells of a root's endodermis is surrounded on four sides by a waterproof strip called a(an) _____.

17. Why is there a one-way passage of materials into the vascular cylinder in plant roots? _____

_____

_____

Section 23–3 Stems (pages 589–594)

This section explains the two main functions of stems and how monocot and dicot stems differ. It also describes primary growth and secondary growth in stems.

Stem Structure and Function (page 589)

1. What are the two important functions of stems?

a. _____

b. _____

2. What three tissue systems compose a stem? _____

_____

Match the stem structure with its description.

	Structure	Description
_____	**3.** Node	**a.** A region between nodes
_____	**4.** Internode	**b.** Contains undeveloped tissue that can produce new stems and leaves
_____	**5.** Bud	**c.** Where leaves are attached

Monocot and Dicot Stems (page 590)

6. How does the arrangement of tissues in a stem differ among seed plants? _____

_____

_____

Chapter 23, Roots, Stems, and Leaves *(continued)*

7. In a monocot stem, what does each vascular bundle contain? _____
_____

8. What is the arrangement of vascular tissue in a monocot stem? _____
_____

9. What is the arrangement of vascular tissue in a dicot stem? _____
_____

10. The parenchyma cells inside the ring of vascular tissue in a dicot stem are known as _____.

11. What do the parenchyma cells outside the ring of vascular tissue form in a dicot stem? _____

Primary Growth of Stems (page 590)

12. What is primary growth in a plant? _____
_____
_____

13. Primary growth of stems is produced by cell division in the _____
_____.

14. Is the following sentence true or false? Only dicot plants undergo primary growth. _____

Secondary Growth of Stems (pages 591–594)

15. The pattern of growth in which stems increase in width is called _____
_____.

16. In conifers and dicots, where does secondary growth take place? _____
_____
_____

17. What type of lateral meristematic tissue produces vascular tissues and increases the thickness of stems over time? _____

18. What does cork cambium produce? _____

19. Circle the letter of each sentence that is true about the formation of vascular cambium.

   a. Vascular cambium forms between the xylem and phloem of individual vascular bundles.

   b. Divisions of vascular cambium give rise to new layers of xylem and phloem.

   c. Once secondary growth begins, vascular cambium appears as a thin layer.

   d. The production of new layers of xylem and phloem causes the stem to shrink when secondary growth begins.

20. Is the following sentence true or false? Most of what we call "wood" is actually layers of phloem. _____

21. What is heartwood? _____

_____

22. The wood that is active in fluid transport and therefore lighter in color is called _____.

23. The alternation of dark and light wood produces what we commonly call _____.

24. How can you estimate the age of a tree? _____

_____

25. On most trees, what does bark include? _____

_____

_____

26. Circle the letter of each sentence that is true about cork.

    a. Cork cells usually contain fats, oils, or waxes.

    b. Cork cells cause the loss of water from a stem.

    c. The outermost cork cells are usually dead.

    d. Cork cambium produces a thick, protective layer of cork.

27. Label the parts of the illustration of wood.

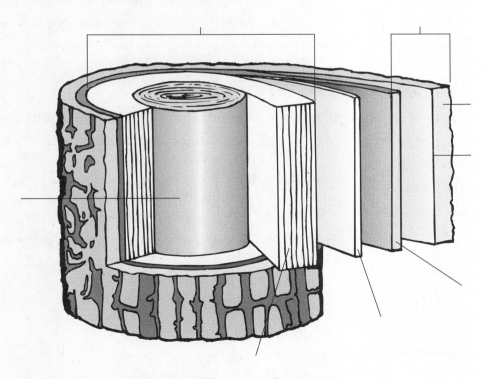

28. What are four kinds of modified stems that store food?

    a. _____   **c.** _____

    b. _____   **d.** _____

Chapter 23, Roots, Stems, and Leaves *(continued)*

Section 23–4 Leaves (pages 595–598)

This section explains how the structure of a leaf enables it to carry out photosynthesis. It also describes how gas exchange takes place in a leaf.

Leaf Structures (page 595)

1. The structure of a leaf is optimized for what purposes? _____
   _____

2. What is a leaf blade? _____

3. The blade is attached to the stem by a thin stalk called a(an)
   _____.

4. Circle the letter of the type of tissue that covers a leaf.
   a. vascular   **b.** dermal   **c.** ground   **d.** petiole

5. The vascular tissues of leaves are connected directly to the
   vascular tissues of _____.

Leaf Functions (pages 596–598)

6. The bulk of most leaves is composed of a specialized ground
   tissue known as _____.

7. How do the carbohydrates produced in photosynthesis get to the
   rest of the plant? _____
   _____

Match the leaf structure with its description.

	Structure	**Description**
_____	8. Palisade mesophyll	**a.** A bundle of xylem and phloem tissues
_____	9. Spongy mesophyll	**b.** Specialized cells that control the opening and closing of stomata
_____	10. Vein	**c.** A layer of mesophyll cells that absorb much of the light that enters the leaf
_____	11. Stomata	**d.** Openings in the underside of the leaf
_____	12. Guard cells	**e.** A loose tissue with many air spaces between its cells

13. How do the air spaces in the spongy mesophyll connect with the
    exterior of the leaf? _____
    _____

14. What is transpiration? _____
    _____

15. Why must a plant have its stomata open at least part of the time? _____
    _____
    _____

16. What would probably happen to a plant that kept its stomata open all the time? _____

_____

17. What is the balance plants maintain that prevents them from losing too much water? _____

_____

_____

18. Complete the flowchart about guard cells.

> Guard cells are forced in a curved shape when water pressure becomes _____.

↓

> The guard cells pull away from each other, opening the _____.

↓

> Guard cells straighten out when water pressure _____.

↓

> The guard cells pull together, closing the _____.

19. Is the following sentence true or false? In general, stomata are closed at night. _____

20. How is the structure of the leaves of a pine tree an adaptation to dry conditions? _____

_____

21. What are cactus leaves adapted for? _____

_____

22. Why must carnivorous plants rely on insects for their source of nitrogen? _____

_____

Reading Skill Practice

Writing a summary can help you remember the information that you have read. When you write a summary, write only the most important points. Write a summary of the information under the blue heading *Leaf Functions*. Your summary should be shorter than the text on which it is based. Do your work on a separate sheet of paper.

Chapter 23, Roots, Stems, and Leaves *(continued)*

Section 23–5 Transport in Plants (pages 599–602)

This section describes how water and the products of photosynthesis are transported throughout a plant.

Water Transport (pages 599–601)

1. What combination of factors provides enough force to move water through the xylem tissue of even the largest plant? _____

_____

_____

2. Complete the table about attraction between molecules.

ATTRACTION BETWEEN MOLECULES

Types of Attraction	Definition
Cohesion	
Adhesion	

3. The tendency of water to rise in a thin tube is called

_____ .

4. How does the thinness of a tube affect how high water will rise because of capillary action? Show your answer by drawing how high water would rise in each of the tubes on the illustration.

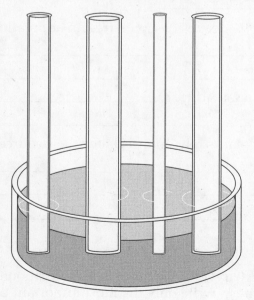

5. The tubelike structures of what two kinds of cells use capillary action to raise water above the level of ground?

a. _____ b. _____

Guided Reading and Study Workbook/Chapter 23

6. How do vessel elements form continuous tubes through which water can move freely? _____

_____

7. What causes the process known as transpiration pull? _____

_____

_____

_____

8. What normally keeps a plant's leaves and stems rigid? _____

_____

9. High transpiration rates can lead to water loss that is severe enough to cause _____.

10. How does the loss of osmotic pressure in leaves slow down the rate of transpiration? _____

_____

Nutrient Transport (pages 601–602)

11. The movement of sugars out of leaves and through stems to fruits takes place in what kind of vascular tissue? _____

12. Is the following sentence true or false? Many plants pump food down into their roots for winter storage. _____

13. The hypothesis that considers plants in terms of where they produce and use materials from photosynthesis is called the

_____.

14. Complete the flowchart about the pressure-flow hypothesis.

> Photosynthesis produces a high concentration of sugars in a cell, called the
>
> _____ cell.

↓

> Sugars move from the cell to phloem, and water also moves into the phloem by
>
> the process of _____.

↓

> Water moving into the phloem causes an increase in _____.

↓

> The pressure causes fluid to move through the phloem toward a cell where
>
> sugars are lower in concentration, called the _____ cell.

Chapter 23, Roots, Stems, and Leaves *(continued)*

WordWise

Use the clues to help you find the vocabulary terms from Chapter 23 hidden in the puzzle below. The words may occur vertically, horizontally, or diagonally.

1. Heartwood is surrounded by _____.

2. The parenchyma cells inside the ring of vascular tissue in dicot stems are known as
   _____.

3. Between the nodes on a stem are _____ regions.

4. A(an) _____ is a primary root that is longer and thicker than the
   secondary roots.

5. The bulk of most leaves is composed of _____.

6. Epidermal cells are often covered with a waxy layer called a(an) _____.

7. A(an) _____ contains undeveloped tissue that can produce a new stem
   or leaf.

8. The spongy layer of ground tissue just inside the epidermis of a root is known as the
   _____.

9. The thin, flattened section of a leaf is a(an) _____.

10. The place where a leaf is attached to a stem is a(an) _____.

11. The spongy layer of ground tissue that completely encloses vascular tissue in the
    central region of a root is _____.

12. At the end, or tip, of each growing stem and root is a group of undifferentiated cells
    called an apical _____.

```
e   n   d   o   d   e   r   m   i   s

c   p   p   i   t   h   b   a   q   n

u   n   m   w   a   i   p   u   m   o

t   c   s   a   p   w   o   o   d   d

i   n   t   e   r   n   o   d   e   e

c   m   e   s   o   p   h   y   l   l

l   y   a   p   o   b   l   a   d   e

e   c   o   r   t   e   x   w   m   l

k   n   m   e   r   i   s   t   e   m
```

Reproduction of Seed Plants

Section 24–1 Reproduction With Cones and Flowers (pages 609–616)

This section describes the reproductive structures of gymnosperms and angiosperms. It also explains how pollination and fertilization differ between angiosperms and gymnosperms.

Alternation of Generations (page 609)

1. Circle the letter of each sentence that is true about alternation of generations in plants.

   a. In all plants, the sporophyte generation is diploid.

   b. The gametophyte in seed plants is hidden within the sporophyte plant.

   c. The recognizable part of a seed-bearing plant is the gametophyte.

   d. In all plants, the gametophyte generation is haploid.

2. An important trend in plant evolution is the reduction in the size of the _____.

3. Where are the gametophytes found in gymnosperms and angiosperms? _____

_____

Life Cycle of Gymnosperms (pages 610–611)

4. Reproduction in gymnosperms takes place in _____.

5. Circle the letter of what produces cones in gymnosperms.

   a. mature sporophyte   c. pine trees

   b. mature gametophyte   d. pollen seeds

6. What kind of cone produces male gametophytes? _____

7. The male gametophytes of gymnosperms are called

   _____.

8. Circle the letter of each sentence that is true about seed cones.

   a. They produce pollen grains.

   b. They produce female gametophytes.

   c. They have two ovules at the base of each scale.

   d. They are generally much larger than pollen cones.

9. Is the following sentence true or false? Each mature female gametophyte contains hundreds of egg cells ready for fertilization. _____

10. How long does the gymnosperm life cycle typically take to complete? _____

Chapter 24, Reproduction of Seed Plants *(continued)*

11. In the gymnosperm life cycle, how do the pollen grains reach the female cones? _____

_____

_____

12. What ensures that pollen grains stay on the scales of a female cone? _____

_____

_____

13. A structure grown by a pollen grain that contains two sperm nuclei is called a(an) _____.

14. What happens to the two sperm cells once the pollen tube reaches the female gametophyte? _____

_____

_____

15. Circle the letter of what a gymnosperm embryo can be called.

   a. mature gametophyte   **c.** mature sporophyte

   b. new sporophyte   **d.** new gametophyte

16. What are the three generations of the gymnosperm life cycle that are contained in a gymnosperm seed? _____

_____

_____

_____

Structure of Flowers (pages 612–613)

17. What are the four kinds of specialized leaves that compose a flower?

   a. _____   **c.** _____

   b. _____   **d.** _____

Match the floral part with its description.

	Floral Part	Description
_____	**18.** Sepals	**a.** Stalk with the stigma at the top
_____	**19.** Petals	**b.** Structures where male gametophytes are produced
_____	**20.** Stamen	**c.** Flower part that contains one or more ovules
_____	**21.** Filament	**d.** Outermost, green floral parts
_____	**22.** Anthers	**e.** Long, thin structure that supports an anther
_____	**23.** Carpels	**f.** Innermost floral parts that produce female gametophytes
_____	**24.** Ovary	**g.** Sticky, top portion of style
_____	**25.** Style	**h.** Male structure made up of an anther and a filament
_____	**26.** Stigma	**i.** Brightly colored parts just inside the sepals

27. Label the parts of the flower on the illustration.

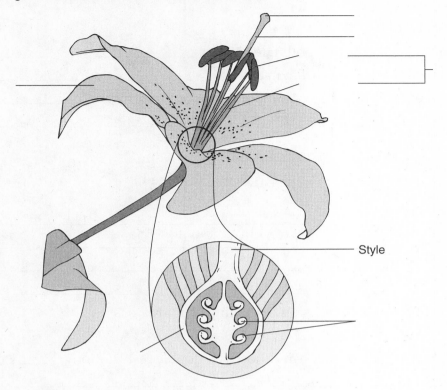

Style

28. What is a pistil? _____

_____

29. What are the separate male and female flowers on a corn plant? _____

_____

_____

Life Cycle of Angiosperms (pages 614–615)

30. Where does reproduction in angiosperms take place? _____

_____

31. Inside the anthers, each cell undergoes meiosis and produces

haploid cells called _____.

32. In angiosperms, the pollen grain is the entire

_____.

33. The female gametophyte of an angiosperm, contained within the

ovary, is called the _____.

34. Circle the letter of each sentence that is true about the life cycle of
angiosperms.

   a. The cycle begins when the mature sporophyte produces flowers.

   b. A pollen grain stops growing when it is released from the stigma.

   c. The female gametophyte develops in the ovule.

   d. The egg nucleus is one of the eight nuclei in the embryo sac.

Chapter 24, Reproduction of Seed Plants *(continued)*

Pollination (page 615)

35. How are most gymnosperms pollinated? _____

36. How are most angiosperms pollinated? _____

37. What are three kinds of animals that pollinate angiosperms? _____

_____

Fertilization in Angiosperms (page 616)

38. What are the two distinct fertilizations that take place in angiosperms?

  a. _____

_____

  b. _____

_____

39. The food-rich tissue that nourishes a seedling as it grows is

known as _____.

40. Why is fertilization in angiosperms known as double fertilization? _____

_____

_____

41. Use the information on pages 614 to 616 to complete the flowchart about the life cycle of angiosperms.

┌───┐
│ Inside the anthers, each cell undergoes _____ to produce four haploid spore cells. │
└───┘
                              ↓
┌───┐
│ Each spore cell becomes a(an) _____. │
└───┘
                              ↓
┌───┐
│ The nucleus of each pollen grain produces two haploid _____. │
└───┘
                              ↓
┌───┐
│ The pollen grain lands on a stigma and begins to grow a(an) _____ │
│ that eventually reaches the ovary and enters the _____. │
└───┘
                              ↓
┌───┐
│ One of the sperm nuclei fuses with the egg nucleus to produce a(an) _____, and │
│ the other sperm nuclei fuses with two other nuclei to form a cell that grows into the _____. │
└───┘

Reading Skill Practice

Outlining is a way you can help yourself understand better and remember what you have read. Write an outline for Section 24–1, *Reproduction With Cones and Flowers.* In your outline, use the blue headings for the first level and the green subheadings for the second level. Then list the details that support, or back up, the main ideas.

Section 24–2 Seed Development and Germination (pages 618–621)

This section explains how seeds develop and are dispersed. It also describes factors that influence the dormancy and germination of seeds.

Seed and Fruit Development (page 618)

1. What is a fruit? _____

_____

2. What happens as angiosperm seeds mature after fertilization is

complete? _____

_____

3. The outer layer of the seed that protects the embryo and its food

supply is called a(an) _____.

4. Is the following sentence true or false? Both cucumbers and

tomatoes are fruits. _____

5. Circle the letter of each sentence that is true about fruits.

   a. As seeds mature, the ovary walls thicken to form a fruit.

   b. Fruits can carry one seed or several seeds.

   c. A fruit is a ripened ovary that encloses a seed or seeds.

   d. The inner wall of the ovary never touches the seed.

Seed Dispersal (page 619)

6. Why are seeds that are dispersed by animals typically contained in

fleshy, nutritious fruits? _____

_____

_____

7. Circle the letter of why seeds dispersed by animals are covered
   with tough coatings.

   a. The seeds need to be able to float on water.

   b. The coatings enable the seeds to pass through an animal
      unharmed.

   c. The seeds need to be digested by the animal that eats them.

   d. The coatings prevent the seeds from being eaten by animals.

Chapter 24, Reproduction of Seed Plants *(continued)*

8. Why are seeds dispersed by wind or water typically lightweight? _____
_____
_____

9. How are the seeds of ash and maple trees dispersed large
distances from the parent plants? _____
_____
_____

10. What adaptation does a coconut seed have that helps its dispersal? _____
_____
_____
_____

Seed Dormancy (page 620)

11. What is dormancy? _____
_____

12. What are two environmental factors that can cause a seed to end
dormancy and germinate?

    a. _____   b. _____

13. What are two purposes served by seed dormancy?

    a. _____

    b. _____

14. Is the following sentence true or false? Some pine tree seeds remain
dormant until the high temperatures generated by a forest fire
cause cones to open and release the seeds. _____

Seed Germination (page 621)

15. What is seed germination? _____
_____

16. Complete the flowchart about seed germination.

> When a seed germinates, it absorbs _____.

↓

> The water causes the endosperm to swell, which cracks open the _____.

↓

> Through the cracked seed coat, the young _____ begins to grow.

17. Circle the letter of each sentence that is true about seed germination.

  a. In some dicots, the cotyledons protect the first foliage leaves.

  b. In most monocots, the cotyledon remains within the seed.

  c. In some dicots, the cotyledons remain below the soil and provide food for the seedling.

  d. In most monocots, the cotyledon emerges above ground to protect the leaves.

Section 24–3 Plant Propagation and Agriculture (pages 622–626)

This section describes how asexual reproduction occurs in plants. It also describes plant propagation and identifies which crops provide the major food supply for humans.

Vegetative Reproduction (pages 622–623)

1. The method of asexual reproduction used by many flowering plants is called _____.

2. What does vegetative reproduction enable a single plant that is well-adapted to the environment to do? _____

_____

_____

3. Vegetative reproduction includes the production of new plants from what three kinds of plant structures?

  a. _____

  b. _____

  c. _____

4. Why does vegetative reproduction enable plants to reproduce very quickly? _____

_____

5. What do spider plants produce that allow them to reproduce vegetatively? _____

_____

6. Is the following sentence true or false? New plants can grow from the leaves of a parent plant if the leaves fall to the ground and the conditions are right. _____

7. How do strawberry plants reproduce vegetatively? _____

_____

_____

8. How do bamboo plants reproduce asexually? _____

_____

_____

Chapter 24, Reproduction of Seed Plants *(continued)*

Plant Propagation (page 623)

9. What do horticulturists use plant propagation for? _____

_____

10. Why might a horticulturist not want a plant to reproduce sexually

by seeds? _____

_____

11. Circle the letter of what a cutting must have to form roots when
placed in a rooting mixture.

   a. Several stolons   **c.** Buds containing meristematic tissue

   b. A taproot   **d.** Buds without meristematic tissue

12. When a piece of stem or a lateral bud is cut from a parent and
attached to another plant, what are the cut piece and the plant to

   which it is attached called? _____

_____

13. When stems are used as scions, the process is called

   _____.

14. What is the process called when buds are used as scions? _____

15. In what kind of cases do growers use grafting and budding? _____

_____

_____

Agriculture (pages 624–626)

16. Circle the letter of when evidence suggests that agriculture
developed in many parts of the world.

   a. about 1–2 million years ago   **c.** about 10,000–12,000 years ago

   b. about 1000–2000 years ago   **d.** about 100,000 years ago

17. What are three crop plants that most people of the world depend
on for the bulk of their food supply?

   a. _____ **b.** _____ **c.** _____

18. The food taken from crops such as wheat, rice, and corn is stored

   in their _____.

19. What are the four crops that 80 percent of all U.S. cropland is

   used to grow? _____

_____

20. What important crops were unknown in Europe before they were

   introduced there from the Americas? _____

_____

21. What are two ways in which the efficiency of agriculture has been improved?

    a. _____

    b. _____

22. How has the use of pesticides and fertilizers affected crop yields? _____

_____

_____

WordWise

Answer the questions by writing the correct vocabulary terms in the blanks. Use the circled letter in each word to find the hidden word. Then, write a definition for the hidden word.

What is the process in which stems are used as scions?

— — — — — — — ◯

What are the flower parts that are brightly colored and are found just inside the sepals?

— ◯ — — — —

What are the floral parts called that produce the female gametophytes?

— —. ◯ — — —

What does an anther and a filament together make up?

— — — ◯ — —

What is the sticky portion of the style where pollen grains frequently land?

— — ◯ — — —

What is a period during which a plant embryo is alive but not growing?

— — — — ◯ — —

Which part of a flower is where haploid male gametophytes are produced?

◯ — — — — —

What is a long, trailing plant stem that produces roots when it touches the ground?

— ◯ — — — —

What is the process when buds are used as scions?

— — — — ◯ — —

In a flower, what part contains one or more ovules?

◯ — — — —

What is the food-rich tissue that nourishes a seedling as it grows?

— ◯ — — — — — — —

Hidden Word: — — — — — — — — — — — —

Definition: _____

Chapter 25

Plant Responses and Adaptations

Section 25–1 Hormones and Plant Growth (pages 633–638)

This section explains what plant hormones are. It also describes how hormones such as auxins, cytokinins, gibberellins, and ethylene affect plant growth.

Patterns of Plant Growth (page 633)

1. Is the following sentence true or false? Plant growth follows patterns that are the same for all species. _____

2. Circle the letter of each sentence that is true about plant growth.
   a. Chemicals direct, control, and regulate plant growth.
   b. Meristems are found at places where plants grow rapidly.
   c. Plants stop growing when they reach maturity.
   d. Even very old plants continue to grow.

Plant Hormones (page 634)

3. What is a hormone? _____

_____

_____

4. What are two ways in which plant hormones control plant growth?
   a. _____

   _____

   b. _____

   _____

5. What is a target cell? _____

_____

6. Circle the letter of each sentence that is true about hormones and plant growth.
   a. Plant hormones are produced in growing flowers and fruits.
   b. A single hormone may affect two different tissues in different ways.
   c. Hormones can activate the transcription of certain genes.
   d. All plant cells are affected by all plant hormones.

Auxins (pages 634–636)

7. What is phototropism? _____

_____

8. From their experiment with oak seedlings, what did the Darwins suspect about the seedlings? _____

_____

9. How do auxins affect plant cells? _____

_____

10. Where are auxins produced, and how are they distributed in a plant? _____

_____

_____

11. Complete the flowchart about phototropism.

When light hits one side of a stem, a higher concentration of auxins develops on the _____ side.

↓

The concentration of auxins stimulates cells on the shaded side to _____.

↓

As a result, the stem bends toward the _____.

12. What is gravitropism? _____

_____

13. Circle the letter of each sentence that is true about auxins.
   a. Auxins cause roots to grow downward.
   b. Auxins regulate cell division in meristems.
   c. Snipping off the tip of a plant removes the source of auxins.
   d. In roots, auxins stimulate cell elongation.

14. What is a lateral bud? _____

_____

15. The closer a bud is to the stem's tip, the more it is inhibited. What is this phenomenon called? _____

16. What are herbicides? _____

Cytokinins (page 636)

17. What are cytokinins? _____

_____

18. Circle the letter of each sentence that is true about cytokinins.
   a. They delay the aging of leaves.
   b. They stop cell division and the growth of lateral buds.
   c. They often produce effects opposite to those of auxins.
   d. They cause dormant seeds to sprout.

Chapter 25, Plant Responses and Adaptations *(continued)*

19. What are two examples of how cytokinins produce effects opposite those of auxins?

a. _____

_____

b. _____

_____

Gibberellins (page 637)

20. What are gibberellins? _____

_____

21. Particularly in stems and fruits, gibberellins produce dramatic

increases in _____.

Ethylene (page 638)

22. What do fruit tissues do in response to auxins? _____

_____

_____

23. Ethylene is a plant hormone that causes fruits to

_____.

Section 25–2 Plant Responses (pages 639–642)

This section explains what plant tropisms are. It also describes photoperiodism and explains how temperate plants prepare for winter.

Tropisms (page 639)

1. What are tropisms? _____

_____

2. What do tropisms demonstrate about plants? _____

_____

_____

3. Complete the table about plant tropisms.

PLANT TROPISMS

Tropism	Definition
Gravitropism	
Phototropism	
	The response of a plant to touch

4. Circle the letter of each sentence that is true about the effects of thigmotropism.

   a. The tendrils of a grapevine wrap tightly around any object they encounter.

   b. A plant that is touched regularly may be stunted in growth.

   c. The stems of climbing plants don't grow straight up.

   d. When the tip of a vine encounters an object, it breaks off.

Rapid Responses (page 640)

5. The folding together of mimosa leaflets when touched is the result of what changes in cells at the base of each leaflet? _____

   _____

6. What does a fly trigger in a Venus flytrap that causes the leaf to snap shut? _____

   _____

Photoperiodism (page 641)

7. Why are plants such as chrysanthemums and poinsettias called short-day plants? _____

8. What are long-day plants? _____

9. What is photoperiodism? _____

   _____

10. What is photoperiodism in plants responsible for? _____

    _____

    _____

11. What plant pigment is responsible for photoperiodism? _____

12. How does a phytochrome control photoperiodism? _____

    _____

    _____

    _____

Winter Dormancy (pages 641–642)

13. What is dormancy? _____

    _____

14. How do shorter days and lower temperatures affect photosynthesis? _____

    _____

15. As cold weather approaches, what happens to deciduous plants? _____

    _____

    _____

Chapter 25, Plant Responses and Adaptations *(continued)*

16. When days shorten at summer's end, what changes start a series of
    events that gradually shuts down the leaves of a flowering plant? _____

    _____

    _____

17. The layer of cells at the petiole that seals off a leaf from the
    vascular system is called the _____.

18. Why doesn't a tree's sap freeze during a cold winter? _____

    _____

    _____

    _____

Reading Skill Practice

A flowchart can help you remember the order in which events occur. On a separate
sheet of paper, create a flowchart that describes the steps that take place when
flowering plants lose their leaves as winter approaches. This process is explained in
the subsection *Winter Dormancy.* For more information about flowcharts, see
Organizing Information in Appendix A at the back of your textbook.

Section 25–3 Plant Adaptations (pages 643–646)

*This section describes how plants are adapted to different environments. It also
explains how plants obtain nutrients from sources other than photosynthesis.*

Aquatic Plants (page 643)

1. What adaptation do aquatic plants have that allows them to grow
   in mud that is saturated with water and nearly devoid of oxygen? _____

   _____

   _____

2. How do waterlilies get oxygen to their roots? _____

   _____

   _____

3. Circle the letter of each sentence that is true about the adaptations
   of aquatic plants.

   a. All aquatic plants grow very slowly after germination.

   b. In waterlilies, oxygen diffuses from open spaces in petioles
      into the roots.

   c. The knees of mangrove trees bring oxygen-rich air down to the
      roots.

   d. The seeds of some aquatic plants can float in water.

Salt-Tolerant Plants (page 644)

4. What adaptation do the leaves of salt-tolerant plants have that protects them against high salt concentration? _____
_____
_____

Desert Plants (pages 644–645)

5. What are three plant adaptations to a desert climate?

   a. _____
   b. _____
   c. _____

6. What are xerophytes? _____

7. Why do the roots of xerophytes have many hairs? _____
_____

8. Where is most of a desert plant's photosynthesis carried out? _____
_____

9. Why do cactuses have small leaves or no leaves at all? _____
_____

10. What is the advantage for many desert plants that have seeds that can remain dormant for years? _____
_____

Nutritional Specialists (page 645)

11. The Venus' flytrap is an example of what kind of nutritional specialist? _____

12. What nutrient do carnivorous plants need to obtain from insects that they can't otherwise get from the environment? _____

13. How does a Venus' flytrap obtain the nutrient it needs from an insect it catches? _____
_____

14. What common plant grows as a parasite on conifers in the western United States? _____

Epiphytes (page 645)

15. What are epiphytes? _____
_____

16. Why aren't epiphytes considered to be plant parasites? _____
_____
_____

Chapter 25, Plant Responses and Adaptations *(continued)*

17. Circle the letter of each example of an epiphyte.

    a. orchid   **b.** Spanish moss   **c.** pitcher plant   **d.** mistletoe

Chemical Defenses *(page 646)*

18. How do many plants defend themselves against insect attack? _____

_____

19. How does nicotine protect a tobacco plant from potential predators? _____

_____

_____

WordWise

Complete the sentences by using one of the scrambled words below.

Word Bank

eoormnh	iieehrbcd	otophmsiport	ynmrdoac	psmiort	xiuan
yhppieet	snniikoytc	preoiimsdoothp	somiptroghitm	tlrlaea dbu	
gmrsaivpiotr	oxretyeph	gttear lcel			

1. A compound that is toxic to a plant is a(an) _____.

2. The response of a plant to an environmental stimulus is a(an) _____.

3. A plant that grows directly on the body of another plant is a(an)

   _____.

4. The period during which an organism's growth and activity decrease or stop is

   _____.

5. A substance that is produced in one part of an organism and affects another part of the

   same individual is a(an) _____.

6. A substance produced in the apical meristem that stimulates cell elongation is a(an)

   _____.

7. The tendency of a plant to grow toward a source of light is _____.

8. Plant hormones that are produced in growing roots and in developing fruits and seeds

   are _____.

9. A plant's response to periods of light and darkness is _____.

10. The response of plants to touch is _____.

11. A meristematic area on the side of a stem that gives rise to side branches is a(an)

   _____.

12. The tendency of a plant to grow in a direction in response to the force of gravity is

   _____.

13. A desert plant is also called a(an) _____.

14. The portion of an organism affected by a particular hormone is known as its

   _____.

Chapter 26

Sponges and Cnidarians

Section 26–1 Introduction to the Animal Kingdom (pages 657–663)

This section describes characteristics that all animals share and the essential functions that animals carry out. It also explains the important trends in animal evolution.

What Is an Animal? (page 657)

1. Is the following sentence true or false? All animal cells are eukaryotic. _____

2. What characteristics do all animals share? _____
   _____

3. Complete the table about animals.

CATEGORIES OF ANIMALS

Category	Percentage of Species	Description	Examples
		Animals without backbones	
		Animals with backbones	

What Animals Do to Survive (pages 658–659)

4. What are seven essential functions that animals carry out?
   a. _____ d. _____ f. _____
   b. _____ e. _____ g. _____
   c. _____

5. Complete the table about feeding.

TYPES OF FEEDERS

Type of Feeder	Description
	Feeds on plants
Carnivore	
Filter feeder	
	Feeds on decaying plant and animal material

6. Explain the difference between a parasite and a host. _____
   _____
   _____

Chapter 26, Sponges and Cnidarians *(continued)*

7. What does an animal do when it respires? _____

_____

8. What does the excretory system of most animals do? _____

_____

_____

9. Animals respond to events in their environment using specialized

cells called _____.

10. What are receptors, and what is their function? _____

_____

11. What does it mean that an animal is motile? _____

_____

12. What enables motile animals to move around? _____

_____

13. Circle the letter of the process that helps a species maintain
genetic diversity.

   a. asexual reproduction   **c.** response

   b. movement   **d.** sexual reproduction

14. What does asexual reproduction allow animals to do? _____

_____

Trends in Animal Evolution (pages 660–663)

15. What are four characteristics that complex animals tend to have?

   a. _____

   b. _____

   c. _____

   d. _____

16. How have the cells of animals changed as animals have evolved? ___

_____

_____

17. Groups of specialized cells form _____, which

   form organs, which form _____.

18. Circle the letter of what a zygote forms after it undergoes a series
of divisions.

   a. blastopore   **b.** protostome   **c.** blastula   **d.** deuterostome

19. What is a protostome? _____

_____

20. What is a deuterostome? _____

_____

21. Is the following sentence true or false? Most invertebrates are deuterostomes. _____

22. In the development of a deuterostome, when is the mouth formed? _____
_____

23. Complete the table about germ layers.

GERM LAYERS

Germ Layer	Location	Develops Into These Body Structures
	Innermost layer	
	Middle layer	
	Outermost layer	

24. Complete the table about body symmetry.

BODY SYMMETRY

Type of Symmetry	Description	Examples
	Body parts that repeat around the center	
	A single plane divides the body into two equal halves	

25. In an animal with radial symmetry, how many imaginary planes can be drawn through the center of the animal that would divide the animal in half? _____

Match the term with its meaning.

Term	Meaning
_____ **26.** anterior	**a.** Upper side
_____ **27.** posterior	**b.** Back end
_____ **28.** dorsal	**c.** Front end
_____ **29.** ventral	**d.** Lower side

30. A body that is constructed of many repeated and similar parts, or segments, exhibits _____.

31. What is cephalization? _____
_____

32. How do animals with cephalization respond differently to the environment than animals without cephalization? _____
_____
_____

Chapter 26, Sponges and Cnidarians *(continued)*

33. What is a body cavity? _____

_____

34. Why is having a body cavity important? _____

_____

_____

Reading Skill Practice

An outline can help you remember the main points of a section. Write an outline of Section 26–1. Use the section's blue headings for the first level of your outline and the section's green headings for the second level. Support your headings with details from the section. Do your work on a separate sheet of paper.

Section 26–2 Sponges (pages 664–667)

This section explains what a sponge is. It also describes how sponges carry out essential functions.

What Is a Sponge? (page 664)

1. Sponges are placed in the phylum _____.

2. What are pores, and where are pores on a sponge's body? _____

_____

3. What does it mean that sponges are sessile? _____

_____

4. Why are sponges classified as animals? _____

_____

_____

Form and Function in Sponges (pages 664–667)

5. Is the following sentence true or false? Sponges have no tissues.

_____

6. What does the movement of water through a sponge provide? _____

_____

Match the body part with its description.

	Body Part	**Description**
_____	**7.** Choanocyte	**a.** Cells that make spicules
_____	**8.** Spicule	**b.** Cells that use flagella to move water through the sponge
_____	**9.** Osculum	**c.** A large hole at the top of the sponge
_____	**10.** Archaeocyte	**d.** A spike-shaped structure

11. Where does digestion take place in sponges? _____
_____

12. Circle the letter of each sentence that is true about sponges.

    a. Sponges are filter feeders.

    b. Sponges reproduce only asexually.

    c. Sponges rely on water movement to carry out body functions.

    d. Sponges do not have a nervous system.

13. How do many sponges protect themselves from predators? _____
_____
_____

14. An immature stage of an organism that looks different from the
adult form is called a(an) _____.

15. How is a sponge larva different from the adult form? _____
_____
_____

16. What are gemmules, and what is their role in sponge reproduction? _____
_____
_____
_____

Ecology of Sponges (page 667)

17. Why are many sponges colored green? _____
_____
_____

18. What adaptation may allow sponges to survive in a wide range of
habitats? _____
_____
_____

Section 26–3 Cnidarians (pages 669–675)

*This section explains what a cnidarian is and describes the two body plans that
exist in the cnidarian life cycle. It also identifies the three groups of cnidarians.*

Introduction (page 669)

    1. Cnidarians are members of the phylum _____.

What Is a Cnidarian? (page 669)

    2. What important features unite the cnidarians as a group? _____
_____
_____

Chapter 26, Sponges and Cnidarians *(continued)*

3. What are cnidocytes? _____

_____

4. A poison-filled, stinging structure within a cnidocyte that contains
a tightly coiled dart is called a(an) _____.

Form and Function in Cnidarians *(pages 670–672)*

5. Is the following sentence true or false? Cnidarians have bilateral
symmetry. _____

6. What are the two stages in the cnidarian life cycle?

   a. _____   **b.** _____

7. Write labels on each illustration below to identify the life-cycle
stage and to name the different body parts.

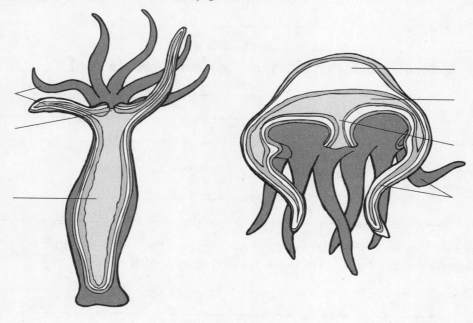

_____   _____

Match the cnidarian structure with its description.

Structure	Description
_____ **8.** Gastroderm	**a.** Digestive chamber with single opening
_____ **9.** Mesoglea	**b.** Sensory cells that help determine direction of gravity
_____ **10.** Gastrovascular cavity	**c.** Inner lining of the gastrovascular cavity
_____ **11.** Nerve net	**d.** Loosely organized network of nerve cells
_____ **12.** Statocysts	**e.** Layer that lies between gastroderm and epidermis
_____ **13.** Ocelli	**f.** Eyespots that detect light

14. Circle the letter of each sentence that is true about form and function in cnidarians.

    a. In a polyp, the mouth points downward.

    b. Materials that cannot be digested are passed out of the body through the mouth.

    c. Cnidarians respire by diffusion through their body walls.

    d. Most cnidarians reproduce sexually and asexually.

15. What does a cnidarian's hydrostatic skeleton consist of? _____

_____

_____

16. Cnidarian polyps can reproduce asexually by _____.

17. In the *Aurelia* life cycle, how is a medusa produced? _____

_____

Groups of Cnidarians (pages 672–674)

18. Complete the table about classes of cnidarians.

CLASSES OF CNIDARIANS

Class	Characteristics of Life Cycle	Examples
	Live lives primarily as medusas	
	Polyps of most grow in branching colonies; some lack a medusa stage	
	Have only the polyp stage	

19. What is bioluminescence, and for what do jellyfishes use it? _____

_____

_____

20. How do hydras differ from other cnidarians in the class

    Hydrozoa? _____

_____

21. Circle the letter of each sentence that is true about corals.

    a. Corals secrete an underlying skeleton of calcium carbonate.

    b. Corals are solitary polyps that live at all depths of the ocean.

    c. Coral colonies growing near one another produce coral reefs.

    d. Most corals are colonial.

22. Is the following sentence true or false? Sea anemones are solitary

    polyps. _____

Chapter 26, Sponges and Cnidarians *(continued)*

23. How are coral reefs produced? _____

_____

_____

Ecology of Corals (page 675)

24. What variables determine the worldwide distribution of corals?

a. _____ **b.** _____ **c.** _____

25. What do corals depend on to capture solar energy, recycle nutrients, and help lay down their skeletons? _____

_____

26. Circle the letter of each way that coral reefs can be harmed.

a. Sediments from logging can smother corals.

b. Overfishing can upset the ecological balance of coral reefs.

c. Algae can remove energy from corals.

d. Industrial pollutants can poison corals.

27. What is coral bleaching? _____

_____

_____

WordWise

Use the clues to help you identify the vocabulary terms from Chapter 26. Then, put the numbered letters in order to find the answer to the riddle.

Clues   **Vocabulary Terms**

A poison-filled, cnidarian stinging structure   __ __ __ __ __ __ __ __ __

                                                               1

An animal without a backbone   __ __ __ __ __ __ __ __ __ __ __ __

                                                         2

The innermost germ layer   __ __ __ __ __ __ __ __

                                                3

A large hole at the top of a sponge   __ __ __ __ __ __ __

                                                        4

An animal whose mouth is formed from   __ __ __ __ __ __ __ __ __

the blastopore   5

The concentration of sense organs and   __ __ __ __ __ __ __ __ __ __ __ __

nerve cells at the anterior end   6

Riddle: Which cnidarian stage is shaped like a bell?

Answer: __ __ __ __ __ __

          1 2 3 4 5 6

Worms and Mollusks

Section 27–1 Flatworms (pages 683–688)

This section describes the defining features of flatworms. It also describes the characteristics of the three groups of flatworms.

What Is a Flatworm? (page 683)

1. Flatworms make up the phylum _____.

2. What are the defining features of flatworms? _____

   _____

   _____

   _____

3. A fluid-filled body cavity that is lined with mesoderm is called

   a(an) _____.

4. Why are flatworms known as acoelomates? _____

   _____

5. Is the following sentence true or false? Flatworms are the simplest animals to have three germ layers. _____

Form and Function in Flatworms (pages 684–686)

6. Circle the letter of each sentence that is true about flatworms.

   a. Parasitic species are typically simpler in structure than free-living species.

   b. Free-living flatworms have organ systems for digestion, excretion, response, and reproduction.

   c. Free-living species probably evolved from parasitic ancestors.

   d. All flatworms rely on diffusion for some essential functions.

7. What do free-living flatworms feed on? _____

   _____

   _____

8. A muscular tube near the mouth at the end of the gastrovascular

   cavity is called a(an) _____.

9. What do flatworms use a pharynx to do? _____

   _____

   _____

10. What are flame cells, and what are their function? _____

    _____

    _____

    _____

Chapter 27, Worms and Mollusks *(continued)*

11. What are ganglia, and what do they do in flatworms? _____
_____
_____

12. A group of cells that can detect changes in the amount of light in
a flatworm's environment is called a(an) _____.

13. How do cilia and muscle cells help flatworms move in two ways? _____
_____
_____
_____

14. What is a hermaphrodite? _____
_____

15. What occurs during fission? _____
_____

16. Is the following sentence true or false? Free-living flatworms
often have complex life cycles that involve both sexual and
asexual reproduction. _____

Groups of Flatworms (pages 686–688)

17. Complete the table about the main groups of flatworms.

GROUPS OF FLATWORMS

Common Name	Class	Description
	Turbellaria	
		Parasitic flatworms that infect hosts' internal organs or outside parts
	Cestoda	

18. Circle the letter of each sentence that is true of turbellarians.

　a. Most live in marine or fresh water.

　b. Most are the same color, form, and size.

　c. Most are bottom dwellers.

　d. The most familiar are the planarians.

19. How does the blood fluke *Schistosoma mansoni* infect humans? _____
_____

20. In which host do blood flukes reproduce sexually, and in which
do they reproduce asexually? _____

21. On the illustration of the blood fluke's life cycle, label the primary host and the intermediate host.

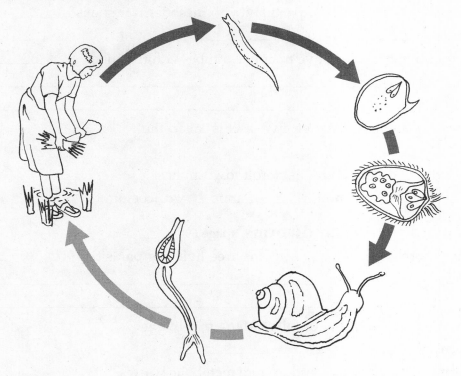

22. In what areas is schistosomiasis particularly widespread? _____
_____

23. The head of an adult tapeworm is called a(an) _____.

24. What does a tapeworm use its scolex for? _____
_____

25. What are proglottids? _____

26. Sperm are produced by male reproductive organs, called

_____.

27. Is the following sentence true or false? Sperm produced by a tapeworm's testes can fertilize the eggs of the same individual.

_____

Section 27–2 Roundworms (pages 689–693)

This section describes the defining features of roundworms. It also identifies which roundworms are important in human disease.

What Is a Roundworm? (page 689)

1. Circle the letter of each sentence that is true about roundworms.

  a. Parasitic roundworms live in plants and in animals.

  b. All roundworms are parasitic.

  c. Some roundworms are a meter in length.

  d. All roundworms develop from three germ layers.

Chapter 27, Worms and Mollusks *(continued)*

2. A body cavity that is lined only partially with mesoderm tissue is called a(an) _____.

3. How is a roundworm's digestive tract like a tube-within-a-tube? _____

_____

_____

4. The posterior opening of the digestive tract is called the

_____.

5. Circle the letter of each feature that a roundworm has.
   a. pseudocoelom   **b.** mouth   **c.** anus   **d.** coelom

Form and Function in Roundworms (page 690)

6. Which have more complex body systems, free-living or parasitic roundworms? _____

_____

7. Is the following sentence true or false? Many free-living roundworms are carnivores. _____

8. Roundworms exchange gases and excrete metabolic wastes through their _____.

9. What can roundworms' sense organs detect? _____

_____

10. Do roundworms reproduce sexually or asexually? _____

Roundworms and Human Disease (pages 690–692)

11. Complete the table about roundworms and human disease.

DISEASE-CAUSING ROUNDWORMS

Roundworm	Disease or Condition Caused	How Disease Is Spread
Trichinella		
	Elephantiasis	
Ascarid worms		
	Weakness and poor growth	

12. How do *Trichinella* roundworms cause pain in their hosts? _____

_____

_____

13. What is elephantiasis? _____

_____

_____

14. Circle the letter of each sentence that is true about the life cycle of *Ascaris*.

    a. Larvae in the lungs are coughed up and swallowed.

    b. The eggs develop into larvae in the lungs.

    c. Fertilized eggs leave the host's body in feces.

    d. The host ingests *Ascaris* eggs in contaminated food or water.

15. How are ascarid worms commonly spread? _____

_____

_____

16. Where do hookworm eggs hatch and develop? _____

_____

Research on *C. elegans* (page 693)

17. Circle the letter of each sentence that is true about *C. elegans*.

    a. It is a free-living roundworm.

    b. Its DNA was the first of any multicellular animal's to be sequenced completely.

    c. It feeds on rotting vegetation.

    d. Its DNA has 30 times the number of base pairs that human DNA has.

Section 27–3 Annelids (pages 694–699)

This section describes the defining features of annelids. It also describes the characteristics of the three classes of annelids.

Introduction (page 694)

1. What phylum are earthworms a member of? _____

2. What evidence is there that annelids are more closely related to clams and octopi than to flatworms or roundworms? _____

_____

What Is an Annelid? (page 694)

3. What is a septum? _____

_____

4. Attached to each annelid segment are bristles called

_____ .

5. Annelids are among the simplest animals to have a true

_____ .

Chapter 27, Worms and Mollusks *(continued)*

Form and Function in Annelids (pages 695–696)

6. How is the pharynx used differently in carnivorous species than in annelids that feed on decaying vegetation? _____
   _____
   _____
   _____

7. What is a closed circulatory system? _____
   _____

8. What is a gill? _____
   _____

9. How do aquatic annelids respire differently than land-dwelling annelids? _____
   _____

10. How do annelids keep their skins moist? _____
   _____

11. What are the two major groups of annelid body muscles called?
    a. _____   b. _____

12. Marine annelids have paddlelike appendages called
    _____.

13. What is a clitellum, and what is its function? _____
   _____
   _____

14. Write labels on the illustration of the annelid for each of the features pointed to.

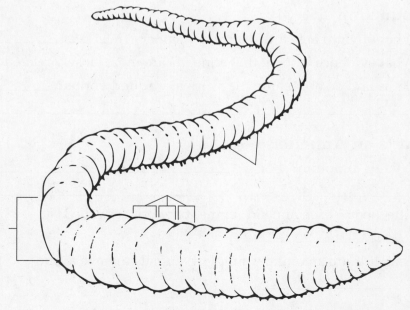

Groups of Annelids (pages 697–698)

15. Complete the table about common types of oligochaetes.

OLIGOCHAETES

Type of Oligochaete	Description	Habitat
	Long, pinkish-brown worms with few setae	
	Red, threadlike worms with few setae	

16. Circle the letter of each sentence that is true about leeches.

    a. They suck blood and body fluids from their hosts.

    b. Most live in moist, tropical habitats.

    c. They are typically external parasites.

    d. All are carnivores that feed on snails.

17. What annelids do polychaetes include? _____

_____

18. Circle the letter of each sentence that is true about polychaetes.

    a. They typically have only a few setae.

    b. They have paired, paddlelike appendages tipped with setae.

    c. They suck the blood of their host.

    d. They are marine annelids.

Ecology of Annelids (page 699)

19. How do the tunnels of earthworms affect other organisms? _____

_____

20. Circle the letter of each sentence that is true about annelids.

    a. Earthworms are important to the diet of birds.

    b. Annelids bring minerals from deep soil layers to the surface.

    c. Marine annelids spend their lives burrowing through soil.

    d. Annelid larvae form part of the animal plankton.

Reading Skill Practice

A flowchart can help you remember the order in which a process or series of events occurs. On a separate sheet of paper, make a flowchart for the process in earthworms of feeding and digestion, described on page 695. For more information about flowcharts, see Organizing Information in Appendix A of your textbook.

Chapter 27, Worms and Mollusks *(continued)*

Section 27–4 Mollusks (pages 701–708)

This section describes the defining features of mollusks. It also describes the basic mollusk body plan and the characteristics of the three main classes of mollusks.

What Is a Mollusk? (page 701)

1. Mollusks are members of the phylum _____.

2. Circle the letter of each sentence that is true about mollusks.

   a. They share similar developmental stages.

   b. They usually have an internal or external shell.

   c. They are the ancestors of annelids.

   d. They are soft-bodied animals.

3. What is a trochophore? _____

Form and Function in Mollusks (pages 702–704)

4. What are the four parts of the body plan of most mollusks?

   a. _____   **c.** _____

   b. _____   **d.** _____

5. What forms do the muscular mollusk foot take? _____

   _____

6. The thin layer of tissue that covers most of the mollusk's body is
   called the _____.

7. How is the mollusk shell made? _____

   _____

8. Snails and slugs feed using a tongue-shaped structure known as a(an)

   _____.

9. What is a siphon? _____

   _____

10. Why do land snails and slugs typically live only in moist places? _____

    _____

    _____

11. How does an open circulatory system carry blood to all parts of a
    mollusk's body? _____

    _____

    _____

12. A large saclike space in the body is called a(an) _____.

13. Ammonia is removed from the blood and released out of the body by tube-shaped _____.

14. Circle the letter of each sentence that is true about mollusk response.

    a. Clams have a simple nervous system.

    b. Octopi and their relatives have the most highly developed nervous system of all invertebrates.

    c. Clams have well-developed brains.

    d. Vertebrates are more intelligent than octopi.

15. Where does fertilization take place in tentacled mollusks and certain snails? _____

Groups of Mollusks (pages 705–707)

16. Complete the table about groups of mollusks.

GROUPS OF MOLLUSKS

Class	Common Name	Description of Shell	Examples
	Gastropods		
	Bivalves		
	Cephalopods		

17. How do gastropods move? _____

    _____

18. Circle the letter of each sentence that is true about bivalves.

    a. Mussels use sticky threads to attach themselves to rocks.

    b. Some bivalves feed on material deposited in sand or mud.

    c. Clams move by flapping their shells rapidly when threatened.

    d. Scallops sting predators with recycled cnidarian nematocysts.

19. The cephalopod head is attached to a single _____.

20. What is a cephalopod's foot divided into? _____

21. What allows squids to locate a wide variety of prey? _____

    _____

    _____

22. The only present-day cephalopods with external shells are

    _____.

Chapter 27, Worms and Mollusks (*continued*)

Ecology of Mollusks (page 708)

23. What allows mollusks to inhabit the extreme environment around deep-sea volcanic vents? _____

_____

_____

_____

24. Why can careful checks of bivalves warn public health officials of possible health problems to come? _____

_____

_____

WordWise

The block of letters below contains eight vocabulary terms from Chapter 27. Use the clues to identify the words you need to find. Then find the words across, down, or on the diagonal. Circle each word in the hidden-word puzzle.

Clues	Vocabulary Terms
The head of an adult tapeworm	_____
Where food is stored in an earthworm	_____
A fluid-filled body cavity that is lined with mesoderm	_____
A group of nerve cells	_____
A bristle attached to an annelid segment	_____
A filamentous organ specialized for the exchange of gases underwater	_____
A muscular tube near the mouth	_____
Asexual reproduction in which an animal splits in two	_____

```
f  x  y  m  h  a  c  r  o  p
i  n  o  q  t  m  h  r  c  h
s  i  t  e  l  m  g  n  p  a
s  a  s  b  v  o  i  x  n  r
i  o  c  c  o  e  l  o  m  y
o  p  g  a  n  g  l  i  o  n
n  u  e  i  s  c  o  l  e  x
```

Chapter 28

Arthropods and Echinoderms

Section 28–1 Introduction to the Arthropods (pages 715–719)

This section identifies the main features of arthropods. It also describes the important trends in arthropod evolution and explains how growth and development take place in arthropods.

What Is an Arthropod? (page 715)

1. What is the basic body plan of all arthropods? _____
_____

2. A tough body wall that protects and supports the body of arthropods is called a(an) _____.

3. What is chitin? _____
_____

4. Circle the letter of each sentence that is true about arthropod exoskeletons.

    a. The exoskeletons of many land-dwelling species have a waxy covering.

    b. All arthropod exoskeletons are the same shape.

    c. Lobster exoskeletons cannot be crushed by hand.

    d. An exoskeleton is an external covering.

5. What are appendages? _____
_____

6. Is the following sentence true or false? The appendages of arthropods are jointed. _____

Evolution of Arthropods (page 716)

7. Circle the letter of where the first arthropods appeared more than 600 million years ago.

    a. the land   **b.** the sea   **c.** the air   **d.** bodies of fresh water

8. What are two ways in which arthropods have evolved since they first appeared?

    a. _____

    b. _____

9. Circle the letter of each sentence that is true about arthropod evolution.

    a. Most primitive arthropods had only one or two body segments.

    b. Arthropod appendages evolved into different forms.

    c. The early body plan was modified gradually.

    d. Appendages of living arthropods include wings, flippers, and mouthparts.

Chapter 28, Arthropods and Echinoderms *(continued)*

Form and Function in Arthropods (pages 716–719)

10. Is the following sentence true or false? Arthropods include

herbivores, carnivores, and omnivores. _____

Match the arthropod structure with its function.

Structure

_____ **11.** Tracheal tubes

_____ **12.** Spiracles

_____ **13.** Book lungs

_____ **14.** Book gills

_____ **15.** Malpighian tubules

Description

a. Saclike organs that extract wastes from the blood and add them to feces

b. Network of branching tubes through which arthropods breathe

c. Organs through which horseshoe crabs respire

d. Layers of respiratory tissue stacked like the pages of a book through which spiders respire

e. Small openings on the side of the body through which air enters and leaves tracheal tubes

16. Complete the concept map about arthropod respiration.

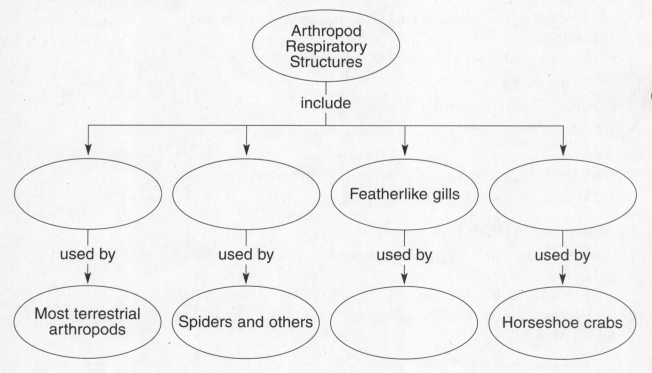

17. Circle the letter of each sentence that is true about the response to the environment by arthropods.

a. Most arthropods have sophisticated sense organs.

b. All arthropods have a brain.

c. Ganglia along a ventral nerve cord coordinate the movements of individual legs.

d. Very few arthropods have a well-developed nervous system.

18. How do aquatic arthropods carry out excretion? _____

_____

_____

19. How do arthropods move? _____

_____

20. Circle the letter of each sentence that is true about arthropod reproduction.

    a. Aquatic arthropods have only internal fertilization.

    b. In some species, males have an organ that places sperm inside females.

    c. Terrestrial arthropods may have internal or external fertilization.

    d. In some aquatic species, males shed sperm around eggs released into the environment.

Growth and Development in Arthropods (page 719)

21. When do arthropods undergo periods of molting? _____

_____

22. What occurs in arthropods during molting? _____

_____

_____

Section 28–2 Groups of Arthropods (pages 720–725)

This section explains how arthropods are classified. It also describes the distinguishing features of the three major groups of arthropods.

Introduction (page 720)

1. What characteristics do biologists use to classify arthropods? _____

_____

_____

2. What are the three major groups of arthropods?

    a. _____

    b. _____

    c. _____

Crustaceans (pages 720–721)

3. Circle the letter of each description of structures that crustaceans typically have.

    a. two pairs of branched antennae

    b. four or five body sections

    c. chewing mouthparts called mandibles

    d. two or three body sections

Chapter 28, Arthropods and Echinoderms *(continued)*

4. Label the two body sections of a typical crustacean.

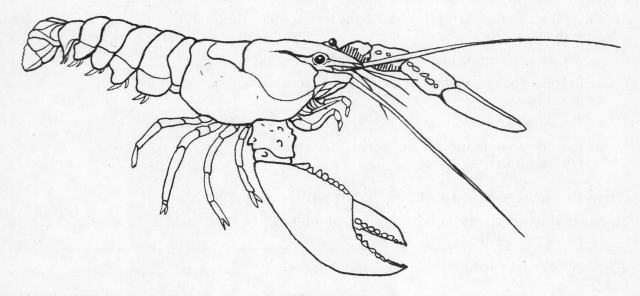

5. Complete the table about crustacean body parts.

CRUSTACEAN BODY PARTS

Body Part	Description
Thorax	
	Fusion of the head with the thorax
Abdomen	
	The part of the exoskeleton that covers the cephalothorax
Mandible	
	First pair of legs in decapods, which bear large claws
Swimmerets	

6. The largest group of crustaceans are the _____.

7. Circle the letter of each sentence that is true about barnacles.

   a. They are sessile.

   b. They have an outer, shell-like covering.

   c. They move backward by snapping a tail.

   d. They attach themselves to rocks and marine animals.

Spiders and Their Relatives (pages 722–724)

8. Horseshoe crabs, spiders, ticks, and scorpions are grouped as

_____ .

9. Circle the letter of each description of structures that chelicerates have.

   a. four or five pairs of legs

   b. three or four body sections

   c. two pairs of branched antennae

   d. mouthparts called chelicerae

10. What is the function of the chelicerae? _____

_____

_____

11. The appendages near the mouth that are usually modified to grab

prey are called _____ .

12. How do spiders respire? _____

_____

_____

13. What arthropods do arachnids include? _____

_____

14. How are horseshoe crabs like and unlike crabs? _____

_____

_____

15. Why must spiders liquify their food to swallow it? _____

_____

16. Circle the letter of each sentence that is true about spiders and silk.

   a. Spiders spin silk into cocoons for eggs.

   b. Spinning webs seems to be a programmed behavior.

   c. Spinnerets are organs that contain silk glands.

   d. Tarantulas cannot produce silk.

17. Is the following sentence true or false? Mites and ticks are usually

parasitic. _____

18. Scorpions have pedipalps that are enlarged into _____ .

19. How do ticks transmit Rocky Mountain spotted fever and Lyme

disease? _____

_____

Insects and Their Relatives (page 725)

20. Centipedes, millipedes, and insects are all grouped as

_____ .

Chapter 28, Arthropods and Echinoderms *(continued)*

21. Circle the letter of each description of structures that uniramians have.

    a. one pair of antennae

    b. unbranched appendages

    c. mouthparts called chelicerae

    d. jaws

22. Why are centipedes restricted to moist or humid areas? _____

    _____

    _____

23. How many pairs of legs does each body segment of centipedes

    and millipedes have? _____

    _____

    _____

Section 28–3 Insects (pages 726–733)

This section identifies the distinguishing features of insects. It also describes two types of development insects can undergo and explains what types of insects form societies.

Introduction (page 726)

1. What are three characteristics of insects that have contributed to their evolutionary success?

   a. _____

   b. _____

   c. _____

What Is an Insect? (pages 727–729)

2. Label the three body parts of an insect.

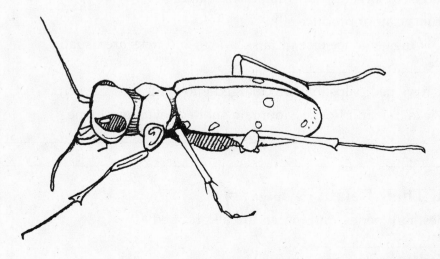

3. How many pairs of legs does an insect have, and where are they attached? _____

_____

4. Circle the letter of each sentence that is true about a typical insect.

   a. It has tracheal tubes used for respiration.

   b. It has a pair of compound eyes on the head.

   c. It has two pairs of wings on the abdomen.

   d. It has a pair of antennae on the head.

5. What is the multiple-lens structure of the compound eye better at detecting than the human eye? _____

6. Where do insects have chemical receptors for taste and smell? _____

_____

_____

7. Is the following sentence true or false? Many insects have well-developed ears. _____

8. Why do insect mouthparts take on a variety of shapes? _____

_____

9. How many pairs of wings does a flying insect typically have, and what are they made of? _____

_____

10. What has the evolution of flight allowed insects to do? _____

_____

_____

11. What is metamorphosis? _____

_____

12. What is the main difference between complete metamorphosis and incomplete metamorphosis? _____

_____

_____

13. The immature forms of an insect that undergo incomplete metamorphosis are called _____.

14. Circle the letter of each type of insect that undergoes complete metamorphosis.

   a. moths   **b.** bees   **c.** chinch bugs   **d.** beetles

15. What do the insects that undergo complete metamorphosis hatch into? _____

16. The stage in which an insect changes from larva to adult is called a(an) _____.

Chapter 28, Arthropods and Echinoderms *(continued)*

17. Circle the letter of each sentence that is true about complete metamorphosis.

    a. The nymphs gradually acquire adult structures.

    b. During the pupal stage, the body is completely remodeled inside and out.

    c. The larva molt a few times but change little in appearance.

    d. The adult that emerges seems like a completely different animal from the larva.

Insects and Humans **(page 730)**

18. Is the following sentence true or false? Only male mosquitoes bite humans and other animals to get a blood meal.

_____

19. How do insects contribute beneficially to agriculture? _____

_____

_____

Insect Communication **(page 731)**

20. Circle the letter of each sentence that is true about insect communication.

    a. To attract females, male crickets chirp.

    b. Much of an insect's communication involves finding a mate.

    c. Insects communicate using visual signals.

    d. Fireflies use sound cues to communicate with potential mates.

21. What are pheromones? _____

_____

_____

Insect Societies **(pages 732–733)**

22. What is a society? _____

_____

_____

23. Circle the letter of each sentence that is true about castes.

    a. Each caste has a body form specialized for its role.

    b. Most insect societies have multiple queens.

    c. Groups of individuals in a society are specialized to perform particular tasks.

    d. The queen is typically the largest individual in the colony.

24. What does a honeybee's round dance tell the other bees? _____
_____

25. What does a honeybee's waggle dance tell the other bees? _____
_____

Reading Skill Practice

By looking carefully at illustrations in textbooks, you can help yourself understand better what you have read. Look carefully at Figure 28–16 on page 728. What important idea do these illustrations communicate? Do your work on a separate sheet of paper.

Section 28–4 Echinoderms (pages 734–738)

This section identifies the distinguishing features of echinoderms. It also describes functions carried out by the water vascular system of echinoderms and describes the different classes of echinoderms.

Introduction (page 734)

1. An internal skeleton is called a(an) _____.

2. What forms an echinoderm's endoskeleton? _____
_____

3. In what environment do all echinoderms live? _____

What Is an Echinoderm? (page 734)

4. Is the following sentence true or false? The bodies of most echinoderms are two-sided. _____

5. What are five features that characterize echinoderms?

a. _____ d. _____

b. _____ e. _____

c. _____

6. What characteristic of echinoderms indicates that they are closely related to vertebrates? _____
_____

Form and Function in Echinoderms (pages 735–736)

7. What functions does the water vascular system carry out in echinoderms? _____
_____

8. The water vascular system opens to the outside through a sievelike structure called a(an) _____.

Chapter 28, Arthropods and Echinoderms *(continued)*

9. What is a tube foot? _____

_____

10. Is the following sentence true or false? Sea stars usually feed on

mollusks. _____

11. In most echinoderms, how are solid wastes released? _____

_____

12. What is the structure of the nervous system in most echinoderms? _____

_____

_____

13. What do most echinoderms use to move? _____

_____

_____

14. Is the following sentence true or false? Echinoderms reproduce by

internal fertilization. _____

Groups of Echinoderms **(pages 737–738)**

15. Complete the table about groups of echinoderms.

GROUPS OF ECHINODERMS

Group	Description of Feeding	Description of Body
		Disk-shaped
		Star-shaped with slender, flexible arms
		Look like warty, moving pickles
		Star-shaped
		Long, feathery arms and attached to the ocean bottom by a stalk

16. How do sand dollars defend themselves? _____

_____

17. When a brittle star is attacked, brittle stars shed one or more

arms. How does this help the echinoderm? _____

_____

_____

18. Where are herds of hundreds of thousands of sea cucumbers
found? _____

19. What happens if a sea star is pulled into pieces? _____

_____

_____

20. Where do many modern feather stars live? _____

_____

Ecology of Echinoderms (page 738)

21. What is the effect of a sudden rise or fall in the number of
echinoderms in a marine habitat? _____

_____

_____

22. Circle the letter of each sentence that is true about the ecology of
echinoderms.

   a. The crown-of-thorns sea star is a major threat to coral reefs.

   b. Sea urchins help control the distribution of algae.

   c. Echinoderms feed almost exclusively on coral.

   d. Sea stars help control the number of clams and corals.

WordWise

*Answer the questions by writing the correct vocabulary terms in the blanks.
Use the circled letter in each term to find the hidden word. Then write a
definition of the hidden word.*

What is it called when an arthropod sheds its
entire exoskeleton and manufactures a large one
to take its place?   _ _ _ ◯ _ _ _

What is the immature form of an insect called?   _ _ _ _ ◯

What is the structure called on an echinoderm
that operates much like a living suction cup?   _ _ _ _   _ ◯ _ _

What is a specific chemical messenger called that
affects the behavior or development of other
individuals of the same species?   _ _ _ ◯ _ _ _ _ _

What is a mouthpart adapted for biting and
grinding food called?   _ ◯ _ _ _ _ _ _

What is the tough external covering of an
arthropod called?   _ ◯ _ _ _ _ _ _ _ _ _

Hidden Word: _ _ _ _ _ _

Definition: _____

_____

Comparing Invertebrates

Section 29–1 Invertebrate Evolution (pages 745–750)

This section explains the origins of invertebrates. It also describes the major trends in invertebrate evolution.

Introduction (page 745)

1. What are three places where fossils have been found that shed light on the origins of invertebrates?

   a. _____

   b. _____

   c. _____

Origins of the Invertebrates (pages 745–747)

2. What are trace fossils? _____

_____

3. Circle the letter of how old the fossils of the Ediacaran fauna are.

   a. 700–600 years old   c. 60–75 million years old

   b. 6,500–7,500 years old   d. 610–570 million years old

4. Is the following sentence true or false? Most fossils of Ediacaran fauna show little evidence of cell specialization. _____

5. What is the best known site of Cambrian fossils? _____

_____

6. Circle the letter of each sentence that is true about animals of the Burgess Shale.

   a. They were ancestors of most modern animal phyla.

   b. They had features that are characteristic of most invertebrates living today.

   c. They had specialized cells, tissues, and organs.

   d. They were far less diverse than animals that lived earlier.

7. What features of the Burgess Shale animals made them so successful? _____

_____

_____

_____

Modern Evolutionary Relationships (page 747)

8. To which group of invertebrates are chordates most closely related to? _____

9. Number the features below according to the sequence in which they evolved. Number the first that evolved *1*.

_____ **a.** Deuterostome development

_____ **b.** Tissues

_____ **c.** Coelom

_____ **d.** Protostome development

Evolutionary Trends (pages 748–750)

10. What does the appearance of each phylum in the fossil record represent in terms of evolution? _____

_____

11. As larger and more complex animals evolved, in what ways did specialized cells join together? _____

_____

_____

12. Circle the letter of each animal group that has organ systems.

a. flatworms   **b.** cnidarians   **c.** mollusks   **d.** arthropods

13. What is cephalization? _____

_____

14. What body plan and lifestyle characterizes invertebrates that have evolved cephalization? _____

_____

15. What are the three germ layers that most invertebrates develop from? _____

16. What is a coelom? _____

17. Label each of the cross-sections according to whether it represents an acoelomate, a pseudocoelomate, or a coelomate.

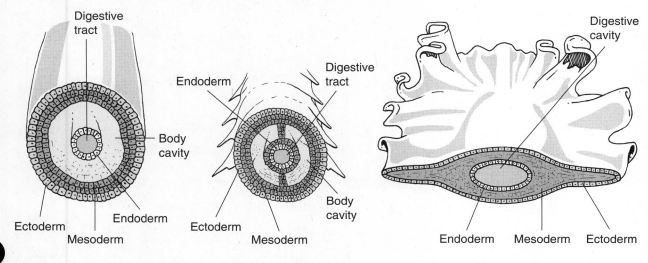

Chapter 29, Comparing Invertebrates *(continued)*

18. What does segmentation allow an animal to do with a minimum
    of new genetic material? _____

19. Most complex animal phyla have a true coelom that is lined
    completely with _____.

20. In most invertebrates, the zygote divides repeatedly to form a(an)

    _____.

21. What is the difference in early development between a
    protostome and a deuterostome? _____

    _____

22. Which groups of invertebrates are protostomes? _____

    _____

Reading Skill Practice

A good way to show similarities and differences between items is with a Venn
diagram, which consists of two or more circles that overlap. Create Venn diagrams
that compare these groups of invertebrates: (1) cnidarians and roundworms, (2)
annelids and mollusks, and (3) arthropods and echinoderms. Use the table in Figure
29–5 for the information to be contained in your diagrams. For more information
about Venn diagrams, see Organizing Information in Appendix A of your textbook.

Section 29–2 Form and Function in Invertebrates (pages 751–758)

*This section describes how different invertebrate phyla carry out their
essential functions.*

Introduction (page 751)

1. What are seven essential tasks all animals perform to survive? _____

   _____

2. Why aren't more complicated systems in living animals necessarily
   better than simpler systems in other living animals? _____

   _____

   _____

Feeding and Digestion (pages 751–752)

3. How is the digestion of food different in simple animals compared
   to that in more complex animals? _____

   _____

   _____

4. Complete the table about types of digestion.

TYPES OF DIGESTION

Type	Definition
	Digestion of food inside cells
Extracellular digestion	

5. Most complex animals digest food in a tube called a(an)

_____ .

Respiration (pages 752–753)

6. Why do respiratory organs have large surface areas? _____

_____

_____

7. Why are respiratory surfaces kept moist? _____

_____

8. What are gills? _____

_____

9. What are book lungs made of? _____

_____

Circulation (page 754)

10. How do the smallest and thinnest animals meet the requirement
of supplying oxygen and nutrients to cells and removing

metabolic wastes? _____

_____

_____

11. Most complex animals move fluid through their bodies using one

or more _____ .

12. Label each of the organisms below according to which has a closed
circulatory system and which has an open circulatory system.

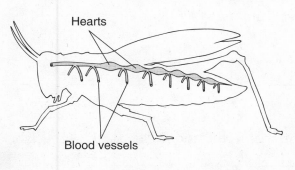

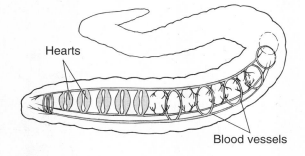

_____   _____

Chapter 29, Comparing Invertebrates *(continued)*

13. Closed circulatory systems are characteristic of what kind of animals? _____

Excretion (pages 754–755)

14. What does the excretory system of most animals do? _____

_____

_____

15. How do aquatic invertebrates rid their bodies of ammonia? _____

_____

_____

16. Circle the letter of each way that terrestrial invertebrates eliminate nitrogenous wastes from their bodies.

   a. Ammonia diffuses from body tissues into the surrounding water.

   b. They convert ammonia into urea.

   c. They convert ammonia into uric acid.

   d. They form a thick paste that leaves the body through the rectum.

Response (page 756)

17. What three trends do invertebrates show in the evolution of the nervous system?

   a. _____ **b.** _____ **c.** _____

18. Number the following groups of invertebrates according to how centralized their nervous system is. Number the simplest *1*.

   _____ **a.** Flatworms

   _____ **b.** Cnidarians

   _____ **c.** Arthropods

19. Is the following sentence true or false? The more complex an animal's nervous system, the more developed its sense organs are. _____

Movement and Support (pages 756–757)

20. What are the three main kinds of skeletal systems among invertebrates?

   a. _____ **b.** _____ **c.** _____

21. What invertebrates have endoskeletons? _____

Reproduction (pages 757–758)

22. What is the difference between external and internal fertilization? _____

_____

_____

23. Circle the letter of each sentence that is true about invertebrate reproduction.

   a. Most invertebrates reproduce sexually in one part of their life cycle.

   b. Asexual reproduction maintains genetic diversity in a population.

   c. Asexual reproduction includes budding and fragmentation.

   d. Most invertebrates have separate sexes.

WordWise

Match each definition in the left column with the correct term in the right column. Then, write the number of each term in the box below on the line under the appropriate letter. When you have filled in all the boxes, add up the numbers in each column, row, and diagonal. All the sums should be the same.

Definition

A. Fertilization in which eggs are fertilized inside the female's body

B. A body cavity completely lined with mesoderm

C. A body plan with mirror-image left and right sides

D. The concentration of sense organs and nerve cells in the front of the body

E. Skeletal system in which muscles surround and are supported by a water-filled body cavity

F. Fertilization in which eggs are fertilized outside the female's body

G. A hard body covering made of chitin

H. A body plan with body parts extending from the center of the body

I. A structural support located inside the body

Term

1. coelom

2. exoskeleton

3. external fertilization

4. endoskeleton

5. hydrostatic skeleton

6. internal fertilization

7. cephalization

8. bilateral symmetry

9. radial symmetry

A	B	C
_____	_____	_____
D	E	F
_____	_____	_____
G	H	I
_____	_____	_____

= _____

= _____

= _____

= _____

= _____   = _____   = _____

= _____

Chapter 30

Nonvertebrate Chordates, Fishes, and Amphibians

Section 30–1 The Chordates (pages 767–770)

This section describes the characteristics shared by all chordates. It also tells about the two groups of nonvertebrate chordates.

What Is a Chordate? (page 767)

1. List the four key characteristics of a chordate.

   a. _____

   b. _____

   c. _____

   d. _____

Use the diagram below to match the description of the chordate characteristic with its structure.

Structure

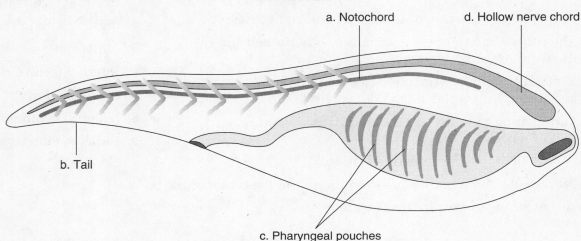

Description

_____ **2.** Connects nerves to internal organs, muscles, and sense organs

_____ **3.** Long supporting rod located just below the nerve cord

_____ **4.** Paired structures in the throat region

_____ **5.** Contains bone and muscle

Most Chordates Are Vertebrates (page 768)

6. What is a vertebrate? _____

7. Circle the letter of the chordate structure that becomes the spinal cord in vertebrates.

   a. hollow nerve cord   **c.** pharyngeal pouches

   b. notochord   **d.** tail

8. The backbone is made of individual segments called

_____ that enclose and protect the spinal cord.

9. Circle the letter of each sentence that is true about vertebrates.

   a. A vertebrate's backbone is part of an endoskeleton.

   b. The endoskeleton supports and protects the animal's body.

   c. The endoskeleton must be shed as the animal grows.

   d. The endoskeleton is made entirely of nonliving material.

Nonvertebrate Chordates (pages 769–770)

10. How are tunicates and lancelets similar to each other? _____

_____

_____

11. What evidence indicates that vertebrates and nonvertebrate

chordates evolved from a common ancestor? _____

_____

_____

_____

12. Circle the letter of each characteristic found only in tunicate
larvae and not in tunicate adults.

   a. tunic   c. hollow nerve cord

   b. tail   d. notochord

13. Is the following sentence true or false? Both larval and adult

tunicates are filter feeders. _____

14. Circle the letter of each characteristic found in lancelets.

   a. definite head region   c. notochord

   b. jaws   d. fins

15. Is the following sentence true or false? Lancelets use the pharynx

for feeding and gas exchange. _____

16. How is blood moved through the body of a lancelet? _____

_____

_____

Reading Skill Practice

A Venn diagram is a useful tool to compare and contrast two things. Construct a
Venn diagram to compare and contrast the characteristics of tunicates and lancelets.
See Appendix A for more information about Venn diagrams. Do your work on a
separate sheet of paper.

Chapter 30, Nonvertebrate Chordates, Fishes, and Amphibians *(continued)*

Section 30–2 Fishes (pages 771–781)

This section describes the basic characteristics of fishes, their evolutionary history, and how they are adapted for a life in water. It also tells about the three main groups of fishes.

What Is a Fish? (page 771)

1. Write the function of each characteristic of fishes.

   a. Paired fins _____

   b. Scales _____

   c. Gills _____

2. Is the following sentence true or false? The characteristics of living fishes are very uniform and almost no diversity exists among fishes.

   _____

Evolution of Fishes (pages 772–773)

3. Circle the letter of each sentence that is true about the evolution of fishes.

   a. Fishes were the first vertebrates to evolve.

   b. Fishes arose directly from tunicates and lancelets.

   c. Fishes changed little during the course of their evolution.

   d. Early fishes were jawless and covered with bony plates.

4. Circle the letter of the period known as the Age of Fishes.

   a. Cambrian   **c.** Silurian

   b. Ordovician   **d.** Devonian

5. Jawless fishes with little armor of the Devonian Period were the ancestors of modern _____ and

   _____.

6. Why were jaws an extremely useful adaptation? _____

   _____

   _____

7. A strong tissue that supports the body and is softer and more flexible than bone is _____.

8. Is the following sentence true or false? Paired fins gave fishes less control over their movement. _____

Form and Function in Fishes (pages 774–778)

9. Circle the letter of each mode of feeding seen in fishes.

   a. herbivore   **c.** parasite

   b. carnivore   **d.** filter feeder

10. Is the following sentence true or false? A single fish may exhibit only one mode of feeding. _____

● *Match the internal organ with its function.*

Function	**Internal Organ**
_____ **11.** Short tube connecting the fish's mouth to the stomach	**a.** Pyloric ceca
_____ **12.** Where food is first partially broken down	**b.** Intestine
_____ **13.** Fingerlike pouches in which food is processed and nutrients absorbed	**c.** Pancreas
_____ **14.** Adds digestive enzymes and other substances to food as it moves through the gut	**d.** Esophagus
_____ **15.** Completes the process of digestion and nutrient absorption	**e.** Anus
_____ **16.** Opening through which undigested material is eliminated	**f.** Stomach

17. What does the capillary network in each gill filament provide? _____

_____

_____

18. Describe how fishes with gills exchange gases. _____

_____

_____

_____

19. The protective bony cover over the gill slit from which water is pumped out of a fish's body is called a(an) _____.

20. How do lungfishes survive in oxygen-poor water? _____

_____

_____

21. Is the following sentence true or false? Fishes have an open circulatory system. _____

Match each chamber of the heart in fishes with its function.

Function	**Heart Chamber**
_____ **22.** Collects oxygen-poor blood from the veins	**a.** Ventricle
_____ **23.** Large muscular cavity that serves as a one-way compartment for blood entering the ventricle	**b.** Sinus venosus
_____ **24.** Thick-walled, muscular chamber that is the actual pumping portion of the heart	**c.** Bulbus arteriosus
_____ **25.** Large, muscular tube that connects to the ventricle and moves blood through the aorta toward the gills	**d.** Atrium

Chapter 30, Nonvertebrate Chordates, Fishes, and Amphibians *(continued)*

26. Circle the letter of the form of nitrogenous waste that most fishes excrete.

    a. urea   **c.** ammonia

    b. lactic acid   **d.** nitrate

27. How does the function of kidneys in saltwater fishes differ from their function in freshwater fishes? _____

_____

_____

Match the structures of the fish's brain with their functions.

      Function   **Structure**

_____ **28.** Controls the functioning of many internal organs   **a.** Olfactory bulb

_____ **29.** Primarily processes the sense of smell in fishes   **b.** Cerebrum

_____ **30.** Coordinates body movements   **c.** Optic lobe

_____ **31.** Involved with the sense of smell, or olfaction   **d.** Cerebellum

_____ **32.** Processes information from the eyes   **e.** Medulla oblongata

33. Circle the letter of each sentence that is true about the sense organs of fishes.

    a. Fishes have poorly developed sense organs.

    b. Many fishes have chemoreceptors that sense tastes and smells.

    c. Fishes have a lateral line system used for sensing sounds.

    d. Some fishes can sense low levels of electric current.

34. What are two ways that fins help fish to move?

    a. _____

    b. _____

35. The streamlined body shapes of most fishes help reduce the amount of _____ as they move through the water.

36. What is the function of the swim bladder? _____

_____

_____

37. Circle the letter of the mode of fish reproduction in which embryos develop inside the mother's body using the egg yolk for nourishment.

    a. oviparous   **c.** viviparous

    b. ovoviviparous   **d.** herbivorous

Groups of Fishes (pages 778–780)

38. Fishes are divided into groups according to _____ structure.

39. Complete the compare-and-contrast table of groups of fishes.

GROUPS OF FISHES

Type	Description	Examples
	No true teeth; skeletons made of fibers and cartilage; keep their notochord as adults	
		Sharks, rays, skates
		Ray-finned fishes, such as flounder, angelfish, and flying fish and lobe-finned fishes, such as lungfishes and the coelacanth

40. Is the following sentence true or false? Hagfishes are filter feeders as larvae and parasites as adults. _____

41. Circle the letter of each characteristic of a shark.

    a. torpedo-shaped body   **c.** many teeth

    b. secretes slime   **d.** winglike fins

42. Is the following sentence true or false? Lobe-finned fishes have fleshy fins supported by bones that are sometimes jointed.

_____

Ecology of Fishes (page 781)

43. Is the following sentence true or false? Anadromous fishes live in fresh water but migrate to the ocean to breed. _____

Section 30–3 Amphibians (pages 782–789)

This section describes the characteristics of amphibians and how they are adapted for life on land. It also tells about the main groups of living amphibians.

What Is an Amphibian? (page 782)

  1. Is the following sentence true or false? Amphibian adults are fishlike aquatic animals that respire using gills. _____

  2. Circle the letter of each characteristic of amphibians.

    a. scales   **b.** claws   **c.** moist skin   **d.** mucus glands

Chapter 30, Nonvertebrate Chordates, Fishes, and Amphibians *(continued)*

Evolution of Amphibians (pages 782–783)

3. List three challenges that had to be overcome by vertebrates colonizing land habitats.

a. _____

b. _____

c. _____

4. List three adaptations that evolved in amphibians that helped them live at least part of their lives out of water.

a. _____

b. _____

c. _____

5. Amphibians became the dominant form of animal life during the

_____ Period, also known as the Age of Amphibians.

6. Why did most amphibian groups become extinct by the end of the

Permian Period? _____

_____

7. What three orders of amphibians survive today?

a. _____

b. _____

c. _____

Form and Function in Amphibians (pages 784–787)

8. Circle the letter of each characteristic of a tadpole.

a. carnivore   **c.** long intestines

b. herbivore   **d.** short intestines

9. Circle the letter of each characteristic of an adult amphibian.

a. carnivore   **c.** sticky tongue

b. herbivore   **d.** long intestines

10. Briefly describe the path of food in a frog's digestive system.

_____

_____

_____

11. Circle the letter of each sentence that is true about respiration.

a. In tadpoles, gas exchange occurs only through the skin.

b. Lungs replace gills when an amphibian becomes an adult.

c. Gas exchange in adults can also occur through the skin.

d. All adult amphibians have lungs.

12. How is the first loop in the circulatory system of an adult amphibian different from the second loop? _____

_____

_____

13. Amphibians have _____ that filter wastes from the blood.

14. Complete the captions in the diagram about the stages in the life cycle of a frog.

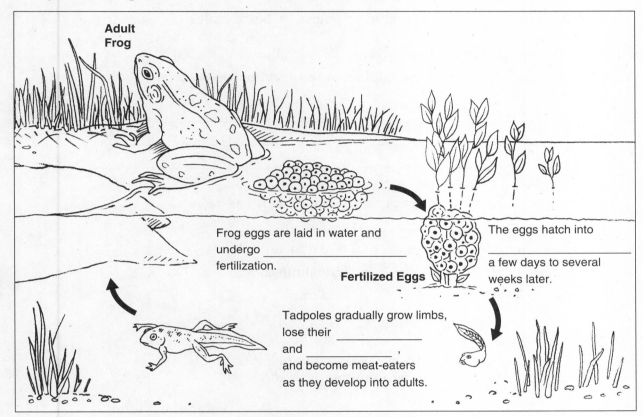

Adult Frog

Frog eggs are laid in water and undergo _____ fertilization.

Fertilized Eggs

The eggs hatch into _____ a few days to several weeks later.

Tadpoles gradually grow limbs, lose their _____ and _____ , and become meat-eaters as they develop into adults.

Match the type of amphibian with its method of movement.

Method of Movement

_____ **15.** Flattened tail for propulsion

_____ **16.** Well-developed hind limbs for jumping

_____ **17.** Legs push backward against the ground

Amphibian

a. Tadpoles

b. Adult salamanders

c. Frogs and toads

18. Circle the letter of each sentence that is true about response in amphibians.

a. An amphibian's brain is structured very differently from a fish's.

b. An amphibian's eye is protected from damage and kept moist by the nictitating membrane.

c. Frog's probably do not see color as well as fishes.

d. Amphibians hear through tympanic membranes, or eardrums.

Chapter 30, Nonvertebrate Chordates, Fishes, and Amphibians *(continued)*

Groups of Amphibians (page 788)

19. Circle the letter of each characteristic of salamanders.

a. tail **b.** carnivore **c.** herbivore **d.** short body

20. Circle the letter of each characteristic of frogs and toads.

a. tail **b.** no tail **c.** able to jump **d.** adults have gills

21. Circle the letter of each characteristic of caecilians.

a. legless **b.** long legs **c.** able to jump **d.** some scales

Ecology of Amphibians (page 789)

22. What are three ways in which amphibians protect themselves from predators?

a. _____

b. _____

c. _____

23. Is the following sentence true or false? For the past several decades the number of living species of amphibians has been growing. _____

24. Circle the letter of each environmental threat to amphibians.

a. decreasing habitat **c.** fungal infections

b. water pollution **d.** acid rain

WordWise

Use the clues to help you identify the vocabulary terms from Chapter 30. Then, put the numbered letters in order to answer the riddle.

Clues	Vocabulary Terms
It's at the end of the large intestine in amphibians.	— — — — — — 1
It often develops into the backbone.	— — — — — — — — — 2
It's an animal with a notochord.	— — — — — — — — 3
It's softer and more flexible than bone.	— — — — — — — — 4
It's responsible for all voluntary activities of the body.	— — — — — — — — 5
It's the amphibian membrane for hearing.	— — — — — — — — 6

Riddle: What heart chamber holds blood that will enter the ventricle?

Answer: __ __ __ __ __ __
     1 2 3 4 5 6

Reptiles and Birds

Section 31–1 Reptiles (pages 797–805)

This section describes the characteristics of reptiles and how reptiles are adapted to life on land. It also tells about the four orders of reptiles.

What Is a Reptile? (page 797)

1. List three characteristics shared by all reptiles.

   a. _____

   b. _____

   c. _____

2. What is the disadvantage of reptilian scaly skin? _____

_____

Evolution of Reptiles (pages 798–799)

3. Circle the letter of each sentence that is true about the evolution of reptiles.

   a. Reptiles evolved rapidly in the warm, humid climate of the Carboniferous Period.

   b. Mammal-like reptiles dominated many land habitats until they became extinct near the end of the Triassic Period.

   c. All dinosaurs were enormous.

   d. Some dinosaurs may have had feathers.

4. Is the following sentence true or false? The extinction of dinosaurs opened up new niches on land and in the sea, providing opportunities for other kinds of organisms to evolve. _____

Form and Function in Reptiles (pages 800–802)

5. How do ectotherms control their body temperature? _____

_____

6. Is the following sentence true or false? All reptiles are herbivores.

_____

7. Circle the letter of each adaptation reptiles have for respiration.

   a. lungs   b. moist skin   c. strong rib muscles   d. gill slits

8. Circle the letter of each sentence that is true about circulation in reptiles.

   a. Reptiles have a double-loop circulatory system.

   b. All reptile hearts have only one atrium.

   c. Most reptiles have one ventricle with partial internal walls.

   d. Crocodiles have the least developed heart of living reptiles.

Chapter 31, Reptiles and Birds *(continued)*

9. What is the advantage of uric acid to terrestrial reptiles? _____
_____
_____

10. Circle the letter of each sentence that is true about response in reptiles.

    a. The reptilian cerebrum is smaller than that of amphibians.

    b. Reptiles that are active during the day tend to have complex eyes.

    c. Reptiles do not have ears.

    d. Snakes sense vibrations in the ground through bones in their skulls.

11. Explain why reptiles are able to carry more body weight than

    amphibians. _____
    _____

12. All reptiles reproduce by _____ fertilization in which the male deposits sperm inside the body of the female.

13. In the diagram below, label the four membranes in the amniotic egg that surround the developing embryo.

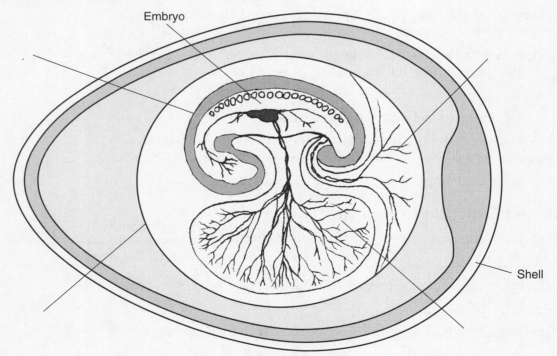

Embryo

Shell

Groups of Reptiles (pages 803–805)

14. List the four surviving orders of reptiles.

    a. _____

    b. _____

    c. _____

    d. _____

15. Is the following sentence true or false? Both snakes and lizards have scaly skin and clawed toes. _____

16. Circle the letter of each characteristic of crocodilians.

    a. long snout   **c.** herbivore

    b. long legs   **d.** protective of young

17. Members of the order Chelonia that live on land are referred to as

    _____.

18. How do most turtles and tortoises protect themselves? _____

_____

19. Circle the letter of each characteristic of turtles and tortoises.

    a. teeth   **c.** strong limbs

    b. strong jaws   **d.** long, broad snout

20. Describe how tuataras differ from lizards. _____

_____

_____

Ecology of Reptiles (page 805)

21. Circle the letter of each sentence that is true about the ecology of reptiles.

    a. Reptiles are in no danger of disappearing.

    b. Reptilian habitats have been expanding.

    c. Humans hunt reptiles for food, to sell as pets, and for their skins.

    d. Conservation programs are in place to help reptiles survive.

Reading Skill Practice

Flowcharts can help you to order the steps in a process or the stages in a series of events. Construct a flowchart that shows the stages in the evolution of reptiles, beginning at the end of the Carboniferous Period and ending with the extinction of dinosaurs at the end of the Cretaceous Period. See Appendix A for more information about flowcharts. Do your work on a separate sheet of paper.

Section 31–2 Birds (pages 806–814)

This section describes the characteristics of birds and how birds are adapted for flight.

What Is a Bird? (page 806)

1. Circle the letter of each characteristic of birds.

    a. feathers   **c.** wings

    b. four legs   **d.** scales

Chapter 31, Reptiles and Birds *(continued)*

2. The single most important characteristic that separates birds from all other living animals is _____ .

3. List two functions of feathers.

   a. _____

   b. _____

4. Identify each type of feather diagrammed below.

_____   _____

Evolution of Birds (page 807)

5. In what ways is the early bird *Archaeopteryx* different from modern birds? _____

_____

6. Is the following sentence true or false? Scientists know for certain that birds evolved directly from dinosaurs. _____

Form, Function, and Flight (pages 808–812)

7. What adaptations do birds have that enable them to fly? _____

_____

_____

8. For what two things do birds require energy?

   a. _____

   b. _____

9. Is the following sentence true or false? Birds have a low metabolic rate compared to reptiles. _____

Match the type of bird bill with the type of food it is adapted to eat.

	Bird Bill	Food
_____	10. Short and fine	a. Flower nectar
_____	11. Short and thick	b. Seeds
_____	12. Strong and hooked	c. Insects
_____	13. Long and thin	d. Animal prey

14. Circle the letter of each sentence that is true about bird adaptations.

    a. Birds break down food by chewing it with their teeth.

    b. Insect-eating birds have an expandable stomach in which large amounts of soft foods can be stored.

    c. Birds have a constant, one-way flow of oxygen-rich air in their respiratory system.

    d. In the bird's heart, oxygen-rich blood is completely separated from oxygen-poor blood.

15. Circle the letter of the form of nitrogenous waste excreted by birds.

    a. ammonia   **b.** urea   **c.** uric acid   **d.** nitrate

16. Circle the letter of each sentence that is true about response in birds.

    a. Birds have brains that quickly interpret and respond to signals.

    b. The cerebrum controls behaviors, such as nest building.

    c. The cerebellum in birds is much like that in reptiles.

    d. Birds can sense tastes and smells quite well.

17. What are two ways in which the skeleton of a flying bird is strengthened for flight?

    a. _____

    b. _____

18. How are the amniotic eggs of birds different from the eggs of reptiles? _____

19. Is the following sentence true or false? Bird parents do not ever care for their offspring. _____

Groups of Birds (pages 812–813)

Match the bird group with its characteristics. Use Figure 31–19 as a guide.

Characteristics	Bird Groups
_____ **20.** Largest order of birds, which includes songbirds	**a.** Birds of prey
_____ **21.** Fierce predators with hooked bills, large wingspans, and sharp talons	**b.** Ostriches and their relatives
_____ **22.** Flightless birds that move by running	**c.** Parrots
_____ **23.** Adapted to wading in aquatic habitats	**d.** Perching birds
_____ **24.** Colorful, noisy birds that use their feet to hold up food	**e.** Herons and their relatives

Ecology of Birds (page 814)

25. Circle the letter of each way in which birds interact with natural ecosystems.

    a. pollinate flowers   **c.** control insects

    b. disperse seeds   **d.** produce toxic wastes

Chapter 31, Reptiles and Birds *(continued)*

26. Is the following sentence true or false? Some species of migrating birds use stars and other celestial bodies as guides.

_____

27. Is the following sentence true or false? Birds are not affected by changes in the environment. _____

WordWise

Review vocabulary terms from Chapter 31 by solving the crossword puzzle.

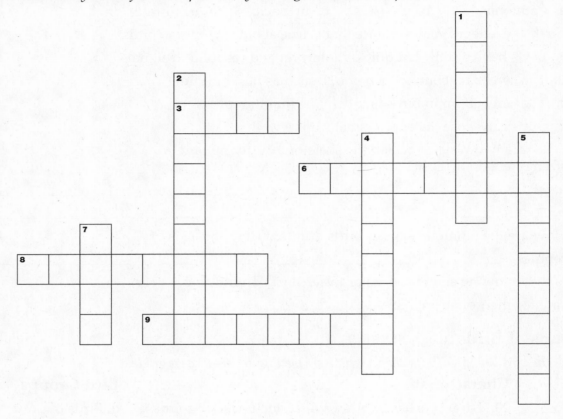

Clues down

1. Muscular organ in birds where food particles are crushed

2. An animal that relies on interactions with the environment to control body temperature

4. Dorsal part of a turtle shell

5. An animal that can generate its own body heat

7. In birds, inhaled air first enters large air _____ in the body cavity and bones.

Clues across

3. Organ located at the end of the esophagus in birds where food is stored and moistened

6. Ventral part of a turtle shell

8. The single most important characteristic that separates birds from all other living animals

9. Type of egg composed of a protective shell and membranes that surround the developing embryo

Chapter 32

Mammals

Section 32–1 Introduction to the Mammals (pages 821–827)

This section describes the characteristics common to all mammals, as well as how mammals carry out life functions. It also briefly tells about mammalian evolution.

Introduction (page 821)

1. List the two notable features of mammals.

   a. _____

   b. _____

2. Circle the letter of each characteristic of mammals.

   a. breathe air   **c.** ectotherm

   b. three-chambered heart   **d.** endotherm

Evolution of Mammals (page 821)

3. What three characteristics help scientists identify mammalian fossils?

   a. _____

   b. _____

   c. _____

4. The ancestors of mammals diverged from ancient _____ during the Permian Period.

5. Circle the letter of each sentence that is true about the evolution of mammals.

   a. The first true mammals were as large as dinosaurs.

   b. During the Cretaceous Period, mammals were probably nocturnal.

   c. After dinosaurs disappeared, mammals increased in size and filled many new niches.

   d. The Permian Period is usually called the Age of Mammals.

Form and Function in Mammals (pages 822–827)

6. Is the following sentence true or false? Mammals have a low rate of metabolism. _____

7. List two ways in which mammals conserve body heat.

   a. _____

   b. _____

8. Circle the letter of each way mammals are able to rid themselves of excess heat.

   a. fat   **b.** hair   **c.** sweat glands   **d.** panting

Chapter 32, Mammals *(continued)*

9. The ability of mammals to regulate their body heat from within is an example of _____.

10. Is the following sentence true or false? Cats and weasels are omnivores because they consume only meat. _____

11. As mammals evolved, the form and function of their _____ and _____ became adapted to eat foods other than insects.

12. List the four types of specialized teeth found in modern mammals.

   a. _____   c. _____

   b. _____   d. _____

13. Is the following sentence true or false? Carnivores have a shorter intestine than herbivores. _____

14. Complete the flowchart to show how cows digest their food.

   Newly swallowed food is stored and processed in the _____.

   ↓

   Symbiotic bacteria in the rumen digest the _____ of most plant tissues.

   ↓

   The cow _____ the food from the rumen into its mouth, and food is rechewed and mixed with saliva.

   ↓

   The food is swallowed again and moves through the rest of the _____ and _____.

15. How does the diaphragm work to help move air into and out of the lungs? _____

   _____

   _____

   _____

16. Is the following sentence true or false? Mammals have a four-chambered heart that pumps blood into two separate circuits around the body. _____

17. How do mammalian kidneys help to maintain homeostasis? _____

_____

_____

_____

Match each part of the mammalian brain with its function.

Function	Part of the brain
_____ **18.** Involved in thinking and learning	**a.** medulla oblongata
_____ **19.** Controls muscular coordination	**b.** cerebral cortex
_____ **20.** Regulates involuntary body functions	**c.** cerebrum
_____ **21.** Part of the cerebrum that is the center of thinking and other complex behaviors	**d.** cerebellum

22. Is the following sentence true or false? Mammals have a rigid backbone, as well as rigid shoulder and pelvic girdles for extra stability. _____

23. Mammals reproduce by _____ fertilization.

24. Is the following sentence true or false? All mammals are viviparous, or live-bearing. _____

25. What do young mammals learn from their parents? _____

_____

_____

Section 32–2 Diversity of Mammals (pages 828–832)

This section describes the characteristics of the three groups of living mammals. It also explains the role of convergent evolution in causing mammals on different continents to be similar in form and function.

Introduction (page 828)

1. List the three groups of living mammals.

a. _____ b. _____ c. _____

2. The three groups of mammals differ greatly in their means of _____ and development.

Monotremes and Marsupials (pages 828–829)

3. The mammals that lay eggs are _____. Those that bear live young that complete their development in a pouch are _____.

4. What two characteristics do monotremes share with reptiles?

a. _____

_____

b. _____

_____

Chapter 32, Mammals (*continued*)

5. How do monotremes differ from reptiles? _____

_____

_____

6. Circle the letter of each mammal that is a marsupial.

   a. koala   **c.** platypus

   b. echidna   **d.** kangaroo

7. Describe how marsupial embryos develop. _____

_____

_____

_____

_____

Placental Mammals (pages 829–831)

8. What is the placenta? _____

_____

_____

9. What four substances are exchanged between the embryo and the mother through the placenta?

   a. _____   **c.** _____

   b. _____   **d.** _____

10. Is the following sentence true or false? After birth, most placental mammals care for their young and provide them with

    nourishment by nursing. _____

Match the main order of placental mammal with its description. Use Figure 32–12 on pages 830–831.

Description	Order
_____ **11.** Hoofed mammal with an even number of digits on each foot	**a.** Insectivores
_____ **12.** Herbivores with two pairs of incisors in the upper jaw and hind legs adapted for leaping	**b.** Sirenians
_____ **13.** Herbivores that live in rivers, bays, and warm coastal waters	**c.** Chiropterans
_____ **14.** The only mammals capable of true flight	**d.** Artiodactyls
_____ **15.** Insect eaters with long, narrow snouts and sharp claws	**e.** Proboscideans
_____ **16.** Mammals that have trunks	**f.** Lagomorphs

Biogeography of Mammals (page 832)

17. Is the following sentence true or false? During the Paleozoic Era,

    the continents were one large landmass. _____

18. What effect on the evolution of mammals was caused when the continents drifted apart? _____

_____

_____

_____

Reading Skill Practice

A compare-and-contrast table is a useful tool for organizing similarities and differences. Make a table to compare the three groups of living mammals. Include information about the reproduction and development of each group. For more information about compare-and-contrast tables, look in Appendix A of your textbook. Do your work on a separate sheet of paper.

Section 32–3 Primates and Human Origins (pages 833–841)

This section describes the characteristics shared by all primates and the evolutionary history of primates. It also tells about the ancestors of humans.

What Is a Primate? (pages 833–834)

1. What characteristic distinguished the first primates from other mammals? _____

_____

2. List the four adaptations that are shared by primates.

a. _____

b. _____

c. _____

d. _____

3. Circle the letter of each sentence that is true about primates.

a. Primates are well adapted to a life of running on the ground.

b. Opposable digits allow primates to hold objects firmly in their hands.

c. A well-developed cerebrum enables primates to display elaborate social behaviors.

d. Because primates have a flat face, both eyes point to the sides.

4. What is binocular vision? _____

_____

_____

Chapter 32, Mammals *(continued)*

Evolution of Primates (pages 834–835)

5. Complete the concept map to show the evolution of primates.

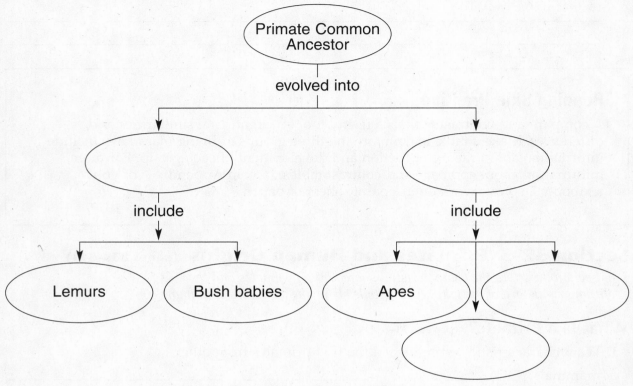

6. Circle the letter of each characteristic of prosimians.

　　a. nocturnal　　**b.** diurnal　　**c.** small in size　　**d.** small eyes

Match the characteristics to the anthropoid group. Each anthropoid group may be used more than once.

Characteristic	Anthropoid Group
_____ **7.** Found today in Central and South America	**a.** New World monkeys
_____ **8.** Found today in Africa and Asia	**b.** Old World monkeys
_____ **9.** Includes baboons and macaques	
_____ **10.** Includes squirrel monkeys and spider monkeys	
_____ **11.** Lack prehensile tails	
_____ **12.** Long, prehensile tails and long, flexible arms	

13. The anthropoid group that includes Old World monkeys also

includes the great apes, or _____.

What Is a Hominid? (pages 835–838)

14. What was the importance of bipedal locomotion that evolved in

the hominid family? _____

_____

15. The hominid hand evolved a(an) _____ thumb that enabled grasping objects and using tools.

16. Is the following sentence true or false? Hominids have a much larger brain than the other hominoids, such as chimpanzees.

_____

17. Is the following sentence true or false? Only one fossil species exists that links humans with their nonhuman primate ancestors.

_____

18. Circle the letter of each characteristic of the hominid genus *Australopithecus*.

a. bipedal apes   **c.** fruit eaters

b. never lived in trees   **d.** very large brains

19. Is the following sentence true or false? Fossil evidence shows that hominids walked bipedally long before they had large brains.

_____

20. Based on their teeth, what kind of diet did the known *Paranthropus* species probably eat? _____

_____

_____

21. Is the following sentence true or false? Currently, researchers completely understand the evolution of the hominid species.

_____

The Road to Modern Humans (page 839)

22. *Homo habilis* was found with tools made of _____.

Out of Africa—But Who and When? (page 840)

23. Describe the two hypotheses that explain how modern *Homo sapiens* might have evolved from earlier members of the genus *Homo*.

a. _____

_____

b. _____

_____

Modern *Homo sapiens* (page 841)

24. Circle the letter of each characteristic of Neanderthals.

a. stone tools   **c.** gave rise to *H. sapiens*

b. lived in social groups   **d.** made cave paintings

25. Is the following sentence true or false? Neanderthals and *Homo sapiens* lived side by side for around 50,000 years.

_____

Chapter 32, Mammals *(continued)*

26. What fundamental changes did some populations of *H. sapiens* make to their way of life around 50,000–40,000 years ago? _____

_____

_____

WordWise

Use the clues below to identify each vocabulary term from Chapter 32. Write the words on the line, putting one letter in each blank. When you finish, the word enclosed in the diagonal lines will reveal the name of one of the groups of primates.

Clues

1. The glands in mammals that produce milk to nourish the young are ____ glands.

2. The ability to merge visual images from both eyes is called ____ vision.

3. A mammal that lays eggs

4. A muscle that pulls the bottom of the chest cavity downward during inhalation

5. Part of the cerebrum that is the center of thinking is the cerebral ____.

6. This family includes modern humans and their closest relatives

7. An external pouch in which marsupial embryos complete their development

8. Anthropoid group that is also known as the great apes and includes gibbons, orangutans, gorillas, chimpanzees, and humans

9. A tail that can coil tightly around a branch

10. Locomotion that uses only two feet

Vocabulary Terms

1. __ __ __ __ __ __ __

2. __ __ __ __ __ __ __ __

3. __ __ __ __ __ __ __ __

4. __ __ __ __ __ __ __ __ __

5. __ __ __ __ __ __

6. __ __ __ __ __ __ __

7. __ __ __ __ __ __ __ __

8. __ __ __ __ __ __ __

9. __ __ __ __ __ __ __

10. __ __ __ __ __ __ __ __

Chapter 33

Comparing Chordates

Section 33–1 Chordate Evolution (pages 849–852)

This section describes how the different chordate groups are related. It also tells about the main trend in the evolution of chordates.

Chordate Origins (page 849)

1. Studies of embryos of living organisms suggest that the most ancient chordates were closely related to _____.

2. Why do scientists consider *Pikaia* to be an early chordate and not a worm? _____

_____

3. In the diagram below, label the notochord, head region, paired muscle blocks, tentacle, and tail fin of *Pikaia*.

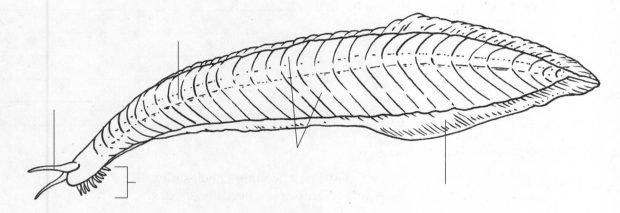

4. A flexible, supporting structure found only in chordates is a(an)

_____.

5. Is the following question true or false? Scientists study tunicate larvae to better understand the early evolution of chordates.

_____

The Chordate Family Tree (page 850)

6. Circle the letter of each sentence that is true about the chordate family tree. See Figure 33–2 on page 850.

   a. Vertebrates share a common invertebrate ancestor with tunicates and lancelets.

   b. Mammals and fishes share a more recent common ancestor than mammals and birds.

   c. Lungs evolved before paired appendages.

   d. Endothermy evolved after the amniotic egg.

Chapter 33, Comparing Chordates *(continued)*

Evolutionary Trends in Vertebrates (page 851)

7. What two things do scientists use to study the evolutionary trends in vertebrates?

    a. _____

    b. _____

8. What effect has the appearance of new adaptations had on the evolution of vertebrates? _____

    _____

    _____

    _____

9. What is convergent evolution? _____

    _____

    _____

10. When does convergent evolution occur? _____

    _____

    _____

11. What is one example of convergent evolution? _____

    _____

    _____

Chordate Diversity (pages 851–852)

12. Is the following sentence true or false? The chordate species alive today are a small fraction of the total number of chordate species that have existed over time. _____

13. List the six living chordate groups in order from largest to smallest. See Figure 33–4 on page 852.

    a. _____

    b. _____

    c. _____

    d. _____

    e. _____

    f. _____

Reading Skill Practice

By looking carefully at photographs and illustrations in textbooks, you can help yourself better understand what you have read. Look carefully at Figure 33–3 on page 851. What idea does the photograph communicate?

Section 33–2 Controlling Body Temperature (pages 854–856)

This section explains how controlling body temperature is important for maintaining homeostasis. It also describes the differences between ectotherms and endotherms.

Body Temperature and Homeostasis (pages 854–855)

1. Circle the letter of each sentence that is true about body temperature.

   a. Essential life functions in animals can be carried out most efficiently at any temperature.

   b. If muscles are too cold, they may contract slowly.

   c. If an animal gets too hot, its muscles will work more efficiently.

   d. The control of body temperature is important for maintaining homeostasis.

2. List three features that vertebrates need in order to control their body temperature.

   a. _____

   b. _____

   c. _____

Match each description with the method of controlling body heat. Methods may be used more than once.

Description	Method
_____ 3. An animal that is able to control its body temperature from within	a. Ectotherm
_____ 4. Examples include reptiles, fishes, and amphibians	b. Endotherm
_____ 5. Warm up by basking in the sun	
_____ 6. High metabolic rates that generate a significant amount of heat	
_____ 7. An animal whose body temperature is mainly determined by the temperature of its environment	
_____ 8. Have feathers, body fat, or hair for insulation	
_____ 9. Easily lose heat to the environment	
_____ 10. Low metabolic rate	
_____ 11. Cools off by panting or sweating	

Comparing Ectotherms and Endotherms (page 856)

12. Name one advantage and disadvantage of endothermy.

    Advantage: _____

    _____

    Disadvantage: _____

    _____

Chapter 33, Comparing Chordates *(continued)*

13. Is the following sentence true or false? Ectothermy is a more energy-efficient way to live in cold environments. _____

Evolution of Temperature Control (page 856)

14. Circle the letter of each sentence that is true about the evolution of temperature control.

   a. The first land vertebrates were ectotherms.

   b. Scientists know when endothermy evolved.

   c. Some biologists hypothesize that dinosaurs were endotherms.

   d. Evidence suggests that endothermy evolved more than once.

Section 33–3 Form and Function in Chordates (pages 857–864)

This section explains how the organ systems of the different chordate groups carry out essential life functions.

Feeding (pages 857–858)

1. Most tunicates, and all lancelets, are _____.
   They remove plankton from the water that passes through their

   _____.

2. Circle the letter of the vertebrates that are filter feeders.

   a. tunicates   b. flamingoes   c. manta rays   d. crocodiles

3. What adaptations do vertebrates have to feed on nectar? _____

   _____

4. Is the following sentence true or false? Mammals with sharp canine teeth and incisors are filter feeders. _____

5. Circle the letter of the vertebrates that typically have short digestive tracts that produce enzymes.

   a. herbivores   b. endotherms   c. carnivores   d. ectotherms

Respiration (pages 858–859)

6. Is the following sentence true or false? Generally, aquatic chordates use lungs for respiration. _____

7. List three examples of respiratory structures used by chordates in addition to gills and lungs.

   a. _____

   _____

   b. _____

   _____

   c. _____

   _____

8. Complete the flowchart that describes the path of water as it moves through a fish. See Figure 33–9 on page 859.

Water flows in through the fish's _____, where muscles pump the water across the _____ .

↓

As water passes over the gill filaments, _____ molecules diffuse into blood in the capillaries. At the same time, _____ diffuses from blood into water.

↓

Water and carbon dioxide are pumped out through the _____ .

9. Describe the basic process of breathing among land vertebrates. _____

_____

_____

_____

_____

10. Is the following sentence true or false? Mammals typically have more surface area in their lungs than amphibians.

_____

11. Bubblelike structures in the lungs that provide an enormous surface area for gas exchange are called _____ .

12. Why do mammals need large amounts of oxygen? _____

_____

_____

13. Why are the lungs of birds most efficient? _____

_____

_____

_____

Circulation (pages 860–861)

14. Is the following sentence true or false? Chordates that use gills for respiration have a single-loop circulatory system.

_____

15. Identify where the blood is carried in each loop of a double-loop circulatory system.

First loop: _____

Second loop: _____

Chapter 33, Comparing Chordates *(continued)*

16. Is the following sentence true or false? In a double-loop system, oxygen-poor blood from the heart is carried to the body.

_____

17. In vertebrates with gills, the heart consists of _____ chambers.

18. What is the advantage of the reptilian heart over the amphibian

heart? _____

_____

19. Why is a four-chambered heart sometimes described as a double

pump? _____

_____

Excretion (page 861)

20. In nonvertebrate chordates and fishes, _____ play an important role in excretion. However, most vertebrates rely on

_____.

21. Circle the letter of each chordate that eliminates nitrogenous wastes as urea.

a. tunicates   **b.** reptiles   **c.** birds   **d.** mammals

22. How do vertebrate kidneys help maintain homeostasis? _____

_____

_____

Response (page 862)

23. Is the following sentence true or false? Nonvertebrate chordates

have a complex brain with distinct regions. _____

24. Circle the letter of the part of the brain that controls the function of many internal organs.

a. medulla oblongata   **c.** olfactory bulbs

b. optic lobes   **d.** cerebrum

25. Is the following sentence true or false? The cerebrum and cerebellum

are most developed in birds and mammals. _____

Movement (page 863)

26. Although nonvertebrate chordates lack bones, they do have

_____.

27. What structures make it possible for vertebrates to control

movement? _____

_____

Reproduction (page 864)

28. Is the following sentence true or false? Vertebrate evolution shows a general trend from internal to external fertilization.

_____

29. Circle the letter of development in which the eggs develop internally and the embryos receive nutrients from the yolk surrounding them.

    a. oviparous   **c.** viviparous

    b. ovoviviparous   **d.** asexual

WordWise

Use the clues to identify vocabulary terms from Chapter 33. Write the words on the lines. Then, find the terms hidden in the puzzle and circle them.

Clues	Vocabulary Terms
An animal whose body temperature is mainly determined by the temperature of its environment	_____
A flexible, supporting structure that is found only in chordates	_____
Bubblelike structures in the lungs that provide an enormous surface area for gas exchange	_____
A rapid growth in the diversity of a group of organisms is a(an) _____ radiation.	_____
An animal that is able to control its body temperature from within	_____

```
e  c  o  r  m  w  l  e  u  r  d  w  p  l  m  o  h  t  a  r
a  p  k  m  n  g  t  n  t  e  w  u  n  k  m  e  t  h  d  p
r  l  p  o  e  r  h  d  e  a  t  h  m  l  e  f  t  a  a  b
k  e  v  m  a  e  o  o  n  o  t  o  c  h  o  r  d  b  p  a
a  l  m  e  k  o  r  t  g  r  e  a  v  k  l  h  y  o  t  l
c  t  h  r  o  g  w  h  f  c  e  r  t  a  n  y  l  k  i  v
p  u  r  g  t  l  v  e  t  e  r  h  b  s  w  u  k  h  v  m
h  e  f  g  a  l  i  r  t  s  h  k  b  g  c  h  i  o  e  i
a  s  l  o  m  b  r  m  t  m  r  e  h  t  o  t  c  e  l  a
s  e  t  h  d  v  a  l  t  i  p  e  c  t  b  w  r  p  j  m
```

Animal Behavior

Section 34–1 Elements of Behavior (pages 871–876)

This section explains what produces behavior in animals. It also describes innate behavior and the major types of learning.

Stimulus and Response (pages 871–872)

1. How do biologists define behavior? _____
_____
_____

2. Behaviors are usually performed when an animal reacts to a(an)
_____.

3. What is a response? _____
_____

4. Circle the letter of each response.
   a. alarm ringing   c. answering the phone
   b. hunger pangs   d. swimming toward moving prey

5. Circle the letter of each stimulus.
   a. light   b. sound   c. heat   d. odors

6. Is the following sentence true or false? All animals can detect all
types of stimuli. _____

7. What body systems interact to produce a behavior in response to
a stimulus? _____
_____

8. Is the following sentence true or false? Animals with more
complex nervous systems can respond to stimuli with more
complicated and precise behaviors. _____

Behavior and Evolution (page 872)

9. Is the following sentence true or false? Animal behaviors are not
influenced by genes. _____

10. Explain how natural selection works in the evolution of behaviors
in a population. _____
_____
_____
_____

Innate Behavior (page 873)

11. What is an innate behavior? _____
_____
_____
_____

12. What two things interact to cause innate behaviors?

a. _____

b. _____

Learned Behavior (pages 873–875)

13. What is learning? _____
_____

14. List the four major types of learning.

a. _____ c. _____

b. _____ d. _____

15. The process by which an animal decreases or stops its response to a repetitive stimulus that neither rewards nor harms the animal is called _____.

16. What is the advantage of habituation? _____
_____
_____

17. Identify the type of learning illustrated below. _____
What is the stimulus? _____ What is the reward or punishment that is associated with the stimulus? _____

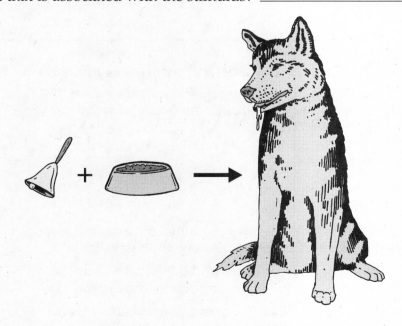

Chapter 34, Animal Behavior *(continued)*

18. What is operant conditioning? _____

_____

_____

19. How does a Skinner box work in operant conditioning? _____

_____

_____

20. When does insight learning occur? _____

_____

21. Is the following sentence true or false? Insight learning is
common among reptiles and amphibians. _____

Instinct and Learning Combined (page 876)

22. What is the purpose of imprinting? _____

_____

_____

23. Is the following sentence true or false? Imprinting can be changed
after it has occurred. _____

Reading Skill Practice

When you read a section, taking notes can help you organize and remember the information. As you read or review Section 34–1, take notes by writing each heading and listing the main points under each heading. Do your work on a separate sheet of paper.

Section 34–2 Patterns of Behavior (pages 878–882)

This section explains how environmental changes affect animal behavior. It also tells how behavior patterns, such as courtship and social behavior, increase an animal's evolutionary fitness.

Behavioral Cycles (page 878)

Match the behavioral cycle with its description.

Description	Behavioral Cycle
_____ **1.** A sleeplike state that allows an animal to survive periods when food or other resources may not be available	**a.** Dormancy
_____ **2.** Behavioral cycles that occur in daily patterns, such as sleeping at night and attending school during the day	**b.** Migration
_____ **3.** The periodic movement from one place to another and then back again to take advantage of favorable environmental conditions	**c.** Circadian rhythms

Courtship (page 879)

4. Circle the letter of each sentence that is true about courtship.

   a. Courtship behavior helps animals identify healthy mates.

   b. In courtship, an individual sends out stimuli to attract a member of the opposite sex.

   c. Fireflies have an elaborate dance to indicate their readiness to mate.

   d. Courtship rituals always involve a single behavior.

Social Behavior (page 880)

5. Is the following sentence true or false? Courtship is an example of a social behavior. _____

6. A group of closely related animals of the same species that work together for the benefit of the group is called a(an)

   _____.

7. What are the advantages of animal societies? _____

_____

_____

8. How does helping a relative survive improve an individual's evolutionary fitness? _____

_____

_____

_____

Competition and Aggression (page 881)

9. What is a territory? _____

_____

10. Circle the letter of each resource that animals need to survive and reproduce.

   a. odors   **b.** mates   **c.** nesting sites   **d.** water

11. When does competition occur? _____

_____

12. A threatening behavior that one animal uses to gain control over another is _____.

Communication (pages 881–882)

13. What is communication? _____

_____

14. Is the following sentence true or false? Animals with poor eyesight often use visual signals involving movement and color.

   _____

Chapter 34, Animal Behavior *(continued)*

15. Some animals communicate using _____,
a chemical messenger that affects the behavior of other
individuals of the same species.

16. Is the following sentence true or false? Some animals that use
sound to communicate, such as dolphins, might live in places

    where vision is not very useful. _____

WordWise

Answer the questions by writing the correct vocabulary terms in the blanks.
Use the circled letter from each term to find the hidden word. Then write a
definition for the hidden word.

1. What is any kind of signal that carries information that can be detected?

   _ _ _ _ _ Ⓞ _ _

2. What is a specific area that is occupied and protected by a group of animals?

   _ Ⓞ _ _ _ _ _ _ _ _

3. What is the way an organism reacts to changes in its internal condition or external
environment?

   _ _ _ Ⓞ _ _ _ _ _

4. What is the periodic movement from one place to another and then back again?

   _ _ _ Ⓞ _ _ _ _ _

5. What is the type of learning in which very young animals learn to recognize and follow
the first moving object that they see?

   _ _ _ _ _ Ⓞ _ _ _ _

6. In what type of behavior does an individual send out stimuli in order to attract a
member of the opposite sex?

   _ _ _ _ _ _ _ Ⓞ _

7. What behavior appears in fully functional form the first time it is performed?

   _ _ Ⓞ _ _ _   _ _ _ _ _ _ _ _

8. What is a system of communication that combines sounds, symbols, or gestures
according to a set of rules?

   _ _ _ Ⓞ _ _ _ _

Hidden Word: _ _ _ _ _ _ _ _

Definition: _____

_____

Nervous System

Section 35–1 Human Body Systems (pages 891–896)

This section describes human organ systems and explains how the body maintains homeostasis.

Organization of the Body (pages 891–894)

1. List the levels of organization in a multicellular organism, from smallest to largest.

   a. _____

   b. _____

   c. _____

   d. _____

Match the organ system with its function.

Organ System	Function
_____ 2. Nervous system	**a.** Stores mineral reserves and provides a site for blood cell formation
_____ 3. Skeletal system	**b.** Provides oxygen and removes carbon dioxide
_____ 4. Integumentary system	**c.** Coordinates the body's response to changes in its internal and external environments
_____ 5. Endocrine system	**d.** Helps produce voluntary movement, circulate blood, and move food
_____ 6. Lymphatic system	**e.** Controls growth, development, metabolism, and reproduction
_____ 7. Muscular system	**f.** Eliminates wastes and maintains homeostasis
_____ 8. Reproductive system	**g.** Serves as a barrier against infection and injury
_____ 9. Respiratory system	**h.** Converts food so it can be used by cells
_____ 10. Excretory system	**i.** Helps protect the body from disease
_____ 11. Circulatory system	**j.** Produces reproductive cells
_____ 12. Digestive system	**k.** Brings materials to cells, fights infection, and regulates body temperature

13. What are four types of tissues found in the human body? _____

    _____

    _____

14. The most abundant tissue in most animals is

    _____ tissue.

15. Circle the letter of the type of tissue that covers the surface of the body and lines internal organs.

    a. nervous   **c.** epithelial

    b. connective   **d.** muscle

Chapter 35, Nervous System *(continued)*

16. What is a gland? _____

_____

17. Circle the letter of the type of tissue that connects bones to muscles.

   a. nervous   **c.** epithelial

   b. connective   **d.** integumentary

Maintaining Homeostasis (pages 895–896)

18. The process of maintaining a controlled, stable internal environment is called _____.

19. The process by which the product of a system shuts down the system or limits its operation is referred to as

_____.

20. Fill in the missing labels in the diagram to show how a thermostat uses feedback inhibition to maintain a stable temperature in a house.

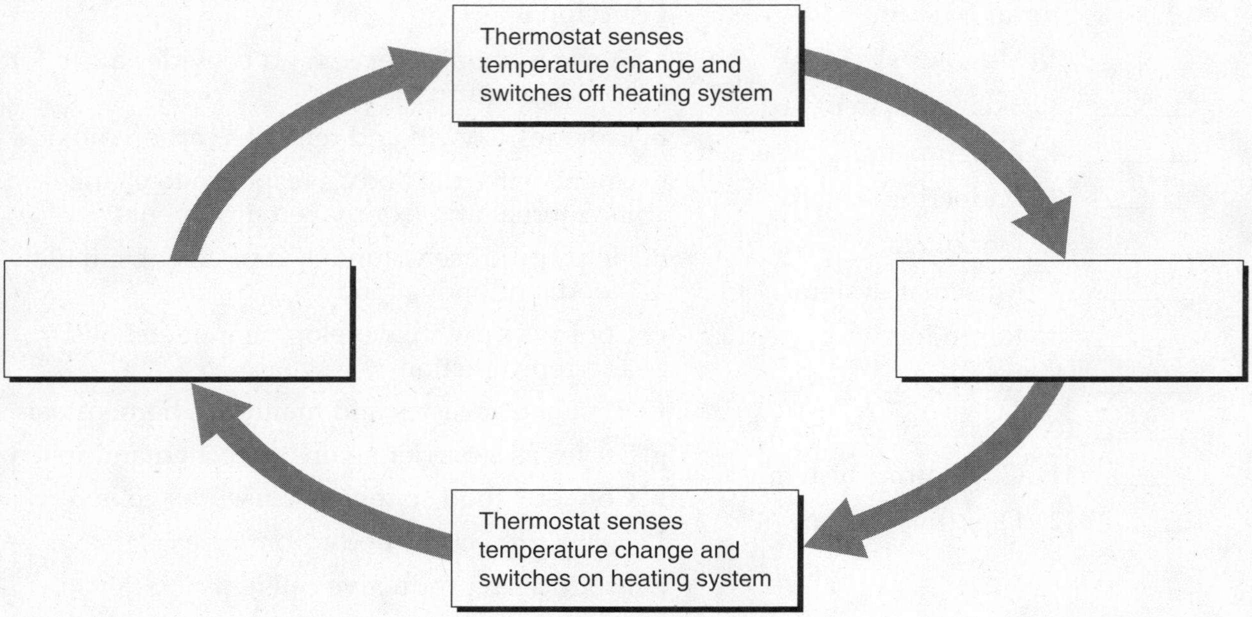

Thermostat senses temperature change and switches off heating system

Thermostat senses temperature change and switches on heating system

21. Is the following sentence true or false? The part of the brain that monitors and controls body temperature is the hypothalamus.

_____

22. What happens if nerve cells sense that the core body temperature has dropped below 37°C? _____

_____

_____

23. What happens if the body temperature rises too far above 37°C? _____

_____

_____

Section 35–2 The Nervous System (pages 897–900)

This section describes the nervous system and explains how a nerve impulse is transmitted.

Introduction (page 897)

1. What is the function of the nervous system? _____
_____
_____

2. What are three types of neurons?

   a. _____

   b. _____

   c. _____

Neurons (pages 897–898)

3. Is the following sentence true or false? Sensory neurons carry impulses from the brain and the spinal cord to muscles and glands.

   _____

4. Label the following features in the drawing of a neuron: cell body, dendrites, and axon.

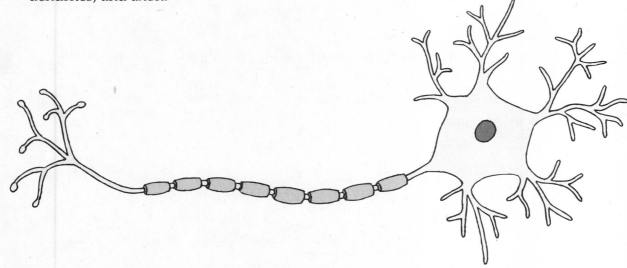

5. What is the function of the myelin sheath? _____
_____

The Nerve Impulse (pages 898–899)

6. Is the following sentence true or false? There are more sodium ions in the cytoplasm than in the fluid outside the cell.

   _____

7. The difference in electrical charge across the cell membrane of a resting neuron is called its _____.

Chapter 35, Nervous System *(continued)*

8. How does a nerve impulse begin? _____
_____
_____

9. Circle the letter of the choice that describes an action potential.

   a. Reversal of charges due to the flow of positive ions into a neuron

   b. Increase in negative ions in a neuron due to the flow of potassium out of the cell

   c. Change to a negative charge due to the flow of sodium ions out of a neuron

   d. Reversal of charges due to the flow of negative ions into a neuron

10. The minimum level of a stimulus that is required to activate a neuron is called the _____.

11. How does a nerve impulse follow the all-or-nothing principle? _____
_____
_____

The Synapse (page 900)

12. Circle the letter of the term that refers to the location at which a neuron can transfer an impulse to another cell.

    a. axon   **b.** dendrite   **c.** synapse   **d.** node

13. What are neurotransmitters? _____
_____
_____

14. Describe what happens when an action potential arrives at an axon terminal. _____
_____
_____
_____
_____

Reading Skill Practice

When you read about a complex process, representing the process with a diagram can help you understand it better. Make a diagram to show how a nerve impulse is transmitted from one cell to another. Do your work on a separate sheet of paper.

Name_____ Class_____ Date_____

Section 35–3 Divisions of the Nervous System (pages 901–905)

This section describes the major divisions of the nervous system and explains their functions.

Introduction (page 901)

1. What is the function of the central nervous system? _____

_____

The Central Nervous System (page 901)

2. The central nervous system consists of the _____ and the

_____.

3. Is the following sentence true or false? Three layers of connective tissue known as meninges protect the brain and spinal cord.

_____

4. The brain and spinal cord are bathed and protected by

_____.

The Brain (pages 902–903)

Match the part of the brain with its function.

Part of Brain	Function
_____ 5. Cerebrum	**a.** Coordinates and balances the actions of the muscles
_____ 6. Cerebellum	**b.** Regulates the flow of information between the brain and the rest of the body
_____ 7. Brain stem	**c.** Controls voluntary activities of the body
_____ 8. Thalamus	**d.** Controls hunger, thirst, fatigue, anger, and body temperature
_____ 9. Hypothalamus	**e.** Receives and relays messages from the sense organs

10. The two hemispheres of the brain are connected by a band of

tissue called the _____.

11. Identify the four lobes of the brain.

a. _____ c. _____

b. _____ d. _____

12. Is the following sentence true or false? The left hemisphere of the

cerebrum controls the body's left side. _____

13. Is the following sentence true or false? The outer surface of the

cerebrum is called the cerebral cortex. _____

14. What is gray matter, and where is it found? _____

_____

15. The two regions of the brain stem are the

_____ and the _____.

Chapter 35, Nervous System *(continued)*

The Spinal Cord (page 903)

16. Name two examples of a reflex. _____

17. What is the advantage of a reflex? _____

_____

_____

The Peripheral Nervous System (pages 903–904)

18. Circle the letter of each choice that is part of the peripheral nervous system.

    a. cranial nerves   **c.** ganglia

    b. spinal nerves   **d.** spinal cord

19. Complete the concept map.

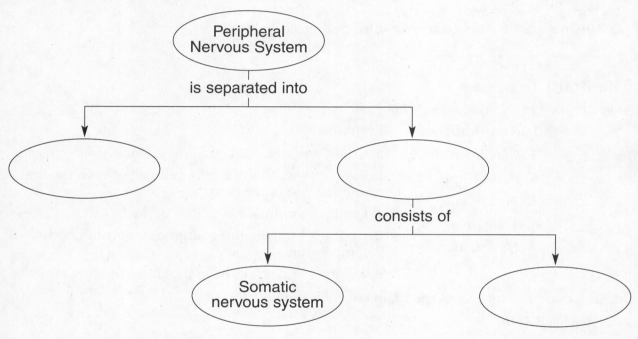

20. Circle the letter of each activity that is controlled by the somatic nervous system.

    a. Beating of the heart   **c.** Wiggling the toes

    b. Lifting a finger   **d.** Pulling foot away from tack

21. What does the autonomic nervous system regulate? _____

_____

_____

22. Why is it important to have two systems that control the same

organs? _____

_____

_____

Section 35–4 The Senses (pages 906–909)

This section explains how each of the five senses responds to stimuli from the environment.

Introduction (page 906)

1. What are sensory receptors? _____

_____

_____

2. List the five general categories of sensory receptors.

    a. _____

    b. _____

    c. _____

    d. _____

    e. _____

3. Which category of sensory receptors are sensitive to touch, sound, and motion? _____

_____

Vision (pages 906–907)

4. Circle the letter of each sentence that is true about the structures of the eye.

    a. Light enters the eye through the cornea.

    b. The anterior chamber is filled with vitreous humor.

    c. The pupil changes in size to let more or less light enter the eye.

    d. The lens focuses light on the retina.

5. Is the following sentence true or false? The function of the iris is to adjust the size of the pupil. _____

6. Where are the photoreceptors located in the eye? _____

_____

7. What do photoreceptors do? _____

_____

8. Is the following sentence true or false? Cones are extremely sensitive to light, but they do not distinguish different colors.

_____

9. How do impulses travel from the eyes to the brain? _____

_____

Hearing and Balance (pages 908–909)

10. List the two sensory functions of the ear.

    a. _____

    b. _____

Chapter 35, Nervous System *(continued)*

11. Label each of the following structures in the drawing of the ear:
    auditory canal, tympanum, semicircular canals, and cochlea.

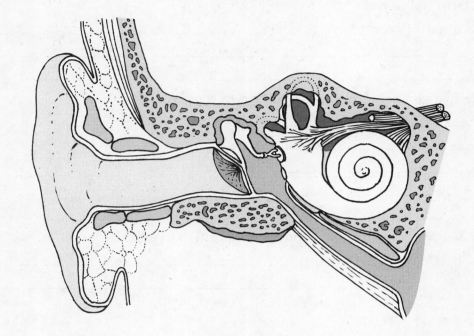

12. Is the following sentence true or false? The tympanum sends
    nerve impulses to the brain. _____

13. Complete the flowchart.

> Vibrations enter the ear through the _____.

> The vibrations cause the _____ to vibrate.

> These vibrations are picked up by three tiny bones, called the _____,
> _____, and _____.

> The last bone transmits the vibrations to the _____,
> creating pressure waves in the _____.

> Tiny hair cells inside the _____ produce nerve impulses that are sent
> to the brain through the _____ nerve.

14. What is the role of hair cells in the cochlea? _____

_____

_____

15. How do the semicircular canals help maintain balance? _____

_____

_____

Smell and Taste (page 909)

16. Is the following sentence true or false? Your sense of smell is actually an ability to detect pressure. _____

17. How does the body detect smell? _____

_____

_____

_____

18. Is the following sentence true or false? Much of what we commonly call the "taste" of food and drink is actually smell.

_____

19. The sense organs that detect taste are the _____.

20. List the four different categories of tastes.

   a. _____

   b. _____

   c. _____

   d. _____

Touch and Related Senses (page 909)

21. What is the largest sense organ? _____

_____

22. Is the following sentence true or false? The skin contains sensory receptors that respond to temperature, touch, and pain.

_____

23. Circle the letter of each choice that is true about the sense of touch.

   a. Unlike the other senses, the sense of touch is not found in one particular place.

   b. All parts of the body are equally sensitive to touch.

   c. The greatest density of touch receptors is found on the arms and legs.

   d. Touch is detected by mechanoreceptors.

24. Where is the greatest density of touch receptors found on the body? _____

_____

_____

Chapter 35, Nervous System *(continued)*

Section 35–5 Drugs and the Nervous System (pages 910–914)

This section describes how different types of drugs affect the nervous system.

Introduction (page 910)

1. Is the following sentence true or false? A drug is any illegal substance that changes the structure or function of the body.

   _____

2. Is the following sentence true or false? Among the most powerful drugs are the ones that cause changes in the nervous system, especially to the brain and the synapses between neurons.

   _____

3. How can drugs disrupt the functioning of the nervous system? _____

   _____

   _____

Drugs That Affect the Synapse (pages 910–914)

Match the drug or type of drug with one way that it can affect the body.

	Drug or Type of Drug	Effect on the Body
_____	4. Stimulant	a. Acts on pleasure centers of brain
_____	5. Depressant	b. Destroys liver cells
_____	6. Cocaine	c. Reduces pain
_____	7. Opiate	d. Decreases heart rate
_____	8. Marijuana	e. Increases blood pressure
_____	9. Alcohol	f. Causes lung damage

10. Circle the letter of each choice that is a stimulant drug.

    a. nicotine   b. cocaine   c. amphetamine   d. codeine

11. Circle the letter of each choice that is a depressant drug.

    a. alcohol   c. tranquilizer

    b. morphine   d. barbiturate

12. An uncontrollable craving for more of a drug is known as

    _____.

13. Cocaine causes the sudden release in the brain of a

    neurotransmitter called _____.

14. How does drug use increase the transmission of HIV, the virus that causes AIDS? _____

    _____

    _____

    _____

15. Complete the Venn diagram.

Cocaine _____   Opiate _____

Affects neurotransmitters

16. Is the following sentence true or false? The most widely abused illegal drug is marijuana. _____

17. Circle the letter of each choice that is a result of long-term use of marijuana.

    a. Loss of memory   **c.** Increase in testosterone

    b. Inability to concentrate   **d.** Cirrhosis of the liver

18. Is the following sentence true or false? Alcohol is the drug most commonly abused by teenagers. _____

19. What is fetal alcohol syndrome, or FAS? _____

_____

_____

20. People who have become addicted to alcohol suffer from a disease called _____.

21. How does long-term alcohol use affect the body? _____

_____

_____

Drug Abuse (page 914)

22. Using any drug in a way that most doctors could not approve is referred to as _____.

23. What is psychological dependence on a drug? _____

_____

24. When does physical dependence on a drug occur? _____

_____

_____

Chapter 35, Nervous System *(continued)*

WordWise

Solve the clues to determine which vocabulary terms from Chapter 35 are hidden in the puzzle. Then find and circle the terms in the puzzle. The terms may occur vertically, horizontally, or diagonally.

```
a  q  u  a  t  o  d  e  n  d  r  o  s
h  x  e  m  h  n  e  u  r  o  n  t  o
p  o  o  e  r  e  n  c  e  l  l  h  r
u  s  m  n  e  h  d  p  b  o  d  a  h
p  c  t  i  s  e  r  y  i  a  r  l  p
i  l  i  n  h  l  i  m  w  t  c  a  y
l  e  s  g  o  i  t  p  o  n  d  m  o
f  i  r  e  l  c  e  r  e  b  r  u  m
e  n  g  s  d  a  b  r  a  i  u  s  o
c  e  r  e  b  e  l  l  u  m  p  o  t
e  h  r  e  t  i  n  a  s  t  e  m  a
b  i  j  k  f  m  y  e  s  h  e  t  g
a  b  s  y  n  l  e  n  s  a  p  e  s
c  i  p  o  t  e  e  n  t  i  a  l  t
k  t  n  e  u  r  o  x  t  r  a  n  v
```

Clues	Hidden Words
Type of cell that carries messages throughout the nervous system	_____
Part of a neuron that carries impulses toward the cell body	_____
Part of a neuron that carries impulses away from the cell body	_____
Minimum level of a stimulus required to activate a neuron	_____
Three layers of tissue in which the brain and spinal cord are wrapped	_____
Area of the brain responsible for voluntary activities of the body	_____
Area of the brain that coordinates body movements	_____
Brain structure that receives messages from the sense organs	_____
Quick automatic response to a stimulus	_____
Part of the eye that focuses light on the retina	_____
Small opening in the iris of the eye	_____
Lining inside the eye that contains photoreceptors	_____

Chapter 36

Skeletal, Muscular, and Integumentary Systems

Section 36–1 The Skeletal System (pages 921–925)

This section describes the skeletal system and its functions.

Introduction (page 921)

1. What forms the skeletal system? _____

_____

The Skeleton (page 921)

2. List the functions of the skeletal system.

   a. _____   d. _____

   b. _____   e. _____

   c. _____

3. Is the following sentence true or false? Bones act like levers on which muscles act to produce movement. _____

4. Is the following sentence true or false? There are 106 bones in the adult human skeleton. _____

5. Complete the concept map.

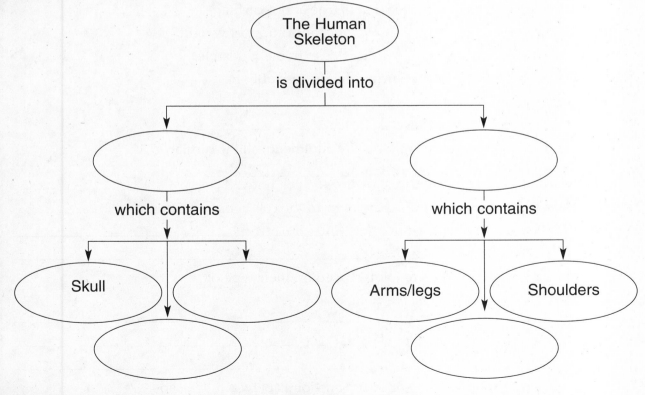

6. What is the general function of the axial skeleton? _____

_____

Chapter 36, Skeletal, Muscular, and Integumentary Systems *(continued)*

Structure of Bones (page 922)

7. The two minerals that make up most of the mass of bone are

_____ and _____.

8. Is the following sentence true or false? Bones are living tissue.

_____

Match each structure in a bone with its description.

Structure	Description
_____ **9.** Periosteum	**a.** Network of tubes running through bone
_____ **10.** Compact bone	**b.** Soft tissue contained in bone cavities
_____ **11.** Haversian canals	**c.** Tough layer of connective tissue surrounding bone
_____ **12.** Spongy bone	**d.** Thick layer of dense bone beneath the periosteum
_____ **13.** Bone marrow	**e.** Bone with a latticework structure

Development of Bones (pages 922–924)

14. The skeleton of a newborn baby is composed almost entirely of a

type of connective tissue called _____.

15. The network of fibers in cartilage is made from two proteins

called _____ and _____.

16. Circle the letter of each sentence that is true about cartilage.

a. It contains blood vessels.   **c.** It cannot support weight.

b. It is dense and fibrous.   **d.** It is extremely flexible.

17. Cartilage is replaced by bone during the process of bone

formation called _____.

18. Cells that create bone are called _____.

19. Is the following sentence true or false? By adulthood, all the cartilage

in the body has been replaced by bone. _____

Types of Joints (page 924)

20. What is a joint? _____

_____

21. List the three classifications of joints, based on their type of movement.

a. _____ **b.** _____ **c.** _____

22. What are examples of immovable joints? _____

_____

23. Is the following sentence true or false? The joints between the two bones of the lower leg are slightly movable joints.

_____

24. Identify the type of freely movable joint represented in each of the drawings below.

 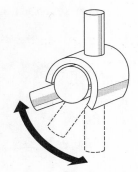 

_____   _____   _____

25. Is the following sentence true or false? Ball-and-socket joints permit the widest range of movement. _____

Structure of Joints (page 925)

26. Circle the letter of each sentence that is true about the structure of joints.

   a. Cartilage protects the ends of bones as they move against each other at joints.

   b. Ligaments hold bones together at joints.

   c. Synovial fluid prevents the ends of bones from slipping past each other at joints.

   d. A bursa is a swelling caused by inflammation of a joint.

27. A serious disorder that involves inflammation of one or more joints is _____.

Section 36–2 The Muscular System (pages 926–931)

This section describes types of muscles and explains how muscles contract.

Types of Muscle Tissue (pages 926–927)

   1. List the three different types of muscle tissue.

     a. _____ **b.** _____ **c.** _____

   2. Is the following sentence true or false? Each type of muscle has the same structure. _____

   3. Is the following sentence true or false? Skeletal muscles are usually attached to bones. _____

   4. Circle the letter of each sentence that is true about skeletal muscles.

     a. They have stripes.

     b. Most of them are controlled by the central nervous system.

     c. Their cells have just one nucleus.

     d. Their cells are long and slender.

Chapter 36, Skeletal, Muscular, and Integumentary Systems *(continued)*

5. Circle the letter of each sentence that is true about smooth muscle cells.

   a. They are spindle-shaped.

   b. They can function without nervous stimulation.

   c. They have two or more nuclei.

   d. They are connected by gap junctions.

6. What are three functions of smooth muscles? _____

   _____

   _____

7. Is the following sentence true or false? Cardiac muscle cells always have two nuclei. _____

8. Complete the table that compares and contrasts the three types of muscle tissue.

TYPES OF MUSCLE TISSUE

Muscle Tissue Type	Striated/Not Striated	What It Controls
Skeletal	Striated	
	Not striated	Involuntary movements
Cardiac		

Muscle Contraction (page 928)

9. Circle the letter of the choice that lists the muscle structures from largest to smallest.

   a. Myofibrils, filaments, muscle fibers

   b. Muscle fibers, myofibrils, filaments

   c. Muscle fibers, filaments, myofibrils

   d. Myofibrils, muscle fibers, filaments

Match each type of muscle filament with the protein it contains.

Type of Filament	Protein It Contains
_____ 10. thick	a. Actin
_____ 11. thin	b. Myosin

12. The filaments are arranged along the muscle fiber in units called

    _____.

13. Is the following sentence true or false? When a muscle is relaxed, there are only thin filaments in the center of a sarcomere.

    _____

14. How does a muscle contract according to the sliding-filament model of muscle contraction? _____
_____

15. The energy for muscle contraction is supplied by _____.

Control of Muscle Contraction (page 929)

16. Is the following sentence true or false? Impulses from motor neurons control the contraction of skeletal muscles. _____

17. The point of contact between a motor neuron and a skeletal muscle cell is a(an) _____.

18. Complete the flowchart to show the missing steps in the stimulation of a muscle cell by a neuron.

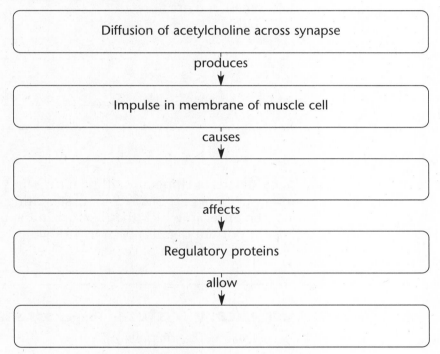

Diffusion of acetylcholine across synapse

produces

Impulse in membrane of muscle cell

causes

affects

Regulatory proteins

allow

19. What terminates a muscle contraction? _____
_____

20. Is the following sentence true or false? A single motor neuron can form synapses with just one muscle cell. _____

21. How can there be strong and weak muscle contractions if a single muscle fiber always contracts to its full extent? _____
_____

How Muscles and Bones Interact (pages 930–931)

22. Is the following sentence true or false? Individual muscles can pull in only one direction. _____

Chapter 36, Skeletal, Muscular, and Integumentary Systems *(continued)*

23. Circle the letter of the term that refers to the tough connective tissue joining skeletal muscle to bone.

    a. cartilage   **b.** ligament   **c.** tendon   **d.** bursa

24. If bones are like levers, what functions as a fulcrum? _____

25. What does it mean for muscles to "work in opposing pairs"? _____

_____

26. Which two opposing muscles allow the elbow joint to bend and

    extend? _____

_____

27. Is the following sentence true or false? Skeletal muscles generally remain in a state of total relaxation when you are at rest.

    _____

28. What is resting muscle tone? _____

_____

29. How can muscle tone be increased? _____

Reading Skill Practice

When you read a section with many details, writing an outline may help you organize and remember the material. Outline Section 36–2 by first writing the section headings as major topics in the order in which they appear in the book. Then, beneath each major topic, list important details about it. Title your outline *The Muscular System*. Do your work on a separate sheet of paper.

Section 36–3 The Integumentary System (pages 933–936)

This section describes the integumentary system and its functions.

Introduction (page 933)

1. Circle the letter of each choice that is part of the integumentary system.

    a. skin   **b.** bones   **c.** cartilage   **d.** nails

The Skin (pages 933–935)

2. The most important function of the skin is _____.

3. List the four functions of the integumentary system.

    a. _____

    b. _____

    c. _____

    d. _____

4. The largest component of the integumentary system is the

_____.

5. The outer layer of skin is called the _____.

6. Is the following sentence true or false? The inner layer of the epidermis is made up of dead cells. _____

Match each term with its definition.

	Term	Definition
_____	**7.** keratin	**a.** Tough, fibrous protein
_____	**8.** melanin	**b.** Inner layer of the skin
_____	**9.** dermis	**c.** Dark brown pigment

10. Circle the letter of each sentence that is true about melanocytes.

   a. Melanocytes are cells that produce melanin.

   b. Most people have roughly the same number of melanocytes in their skin.

   c. All melanocytes produce about the same amount of melanin.

   d. Most people have the same distribution of melanocytes in their skin.

11. Is the following sentence true or false? The epidermis contains blood vessels. _____

12. Circle the letter of each type of structure that is found in the dermis.

   a. blood vessels   **c.** glands

   b. nerve endings   **d.** hair follicles

13. How does the dermis help regulate body temperature? _____

_____

_____

_____

14. List the two types of glands contained in the dermis.

   a. _____   **b.** _____

15. How does sweat help keep you cool? _____

_____

16. What is the function of sebum? _____

_____

Hair and Nails (page 936)

17. The basic structure of human hair and nails is _____.

18. List the two functions of head hair.

   a. _____

   b. _____

19. How does hair in the nose and ears and around the eyes help protect the body? _____

_____

20. Hair is produced by cells called _____.

21. Is the following sentence true or false? Hair is composed of cells that have died. _____

22. What causes hair to grow? _____

_____

23. What is the nail root? _____

_____

WordWise

Test your knowledge of the vocabulary terms from Chapter 36 by solving the clues. Then, copy the numbered letters in order to complete the hidden message.

Clues

Place where one bone attaches to another

Tough layer surrounding a bone

Tough connective tissue that holds bones together

Inner layer of the skin

Type of junction where a motor neuron and a skeletal muscle cell have contact

Type of connective tissue making up the skeleton of a newborn baby

Replacement of cartilage by bone during the process of bone formation

Protein in thick filaments in muscle

Type of canal that runs through bone and contains blood vessels and nerves

Neurotransmitter that diffuses across a synapse to a muscle cell

Vocabulary Terms

_ _ _ _ _
 1   2

_ _ _ _ _ _ _ _ _ _
  3   4

_ _ _ _ _ _ _
     5   6

_ _ _ _ _ _
7   8

_ _ _ _ _ _ _ _ _ _ _ _
  9   10 11   12

_ _ _ _ _ _ _ _ _
              13

_ _ _ _ _ _ _ _ _ _ _
 14

_ _ _ _ _ _
15 16

_ _ _ _ _ _ _ _
   17 18

_ _ _ _ _ _ _ _ _ _ _
         19   20

Hidden Message: B _ _ _ _   _ _ _
                        1 2 3 4   5 6 7

_ _ _ _ _ _ _   _ _ _ _   _ _ u.
8 9 10 11 12 13 14 15 16 17 18 19 20

Chapter 37

Circulatory and Respiratory Systems

Section 37–1 The Circulatory System (pages 943–950)

This section describes the circulatory system and its functions.

Functions of the Circulatory System (page 943)

1. Why do large organisms require a circulatory system? _____
_____
_____

2. What is a closed circulatory system? _____
_____

3. List the three components of the circulatory system.
   a. _____ b. _____ c. _____

The Heart (pages 944–946)

4. Is the following sentence true or false? The heart is composed almost entirely of muscle. _____

Match each heart structure with its description.

	Structure	Description
_____	5. pericardium	a. Thick layer of muscle in the walls of the heart
_____	6. myocardium	b. Sac of tissue that encloses and protects the heart
_____	7. atrium	c. Upper chamber of the heart
_____	8. ventricle	d. Lower chamber of the heart

9. The heart pumps about _____ times per minute.

10. Dividing the right side of the heart from the left side is a wall called a(an) _____.

11. Is the following sentence true or false? The heart functions as four separate pumps. _____

12. Complete the compare/contrast table.

THE CIRCULATORY SYSTEM

Name of Circulatory Pathway	Side of Heart Involved	Route Blood Follows
Pulmonary circulation		From heart to lungs
	Left side	

13. What happens to blood when it reaches the lungs? _____
_____

Chapter 37, Circulatory and Respiratory Systems *(continued)*

14. Why is the blood that enters the heart from the systemic circulation oxygen-poor? _____

_____

_____

15. Circle the letter of each sentence that is true about blood flow through the heart.

    a. Blood enters the heart through the right and left atria.

    b. Blood enters the heart through the right and left ventricles.

    c. Blood flows from the ventricles to the atria.

    d. Blood flows out of the heart through the right and left atria.

16. Flaps of connective tissue called _____ prevent blood from flowing backward in the heart.

17. Each heart contraction begins in a small group of cardiac muscle cells called the _____ node.

18. Cells that set the pace for the beating of the heart as a whole are called the _____.

Blood Vessels (pages 946–947)

19. Complete the concept map.

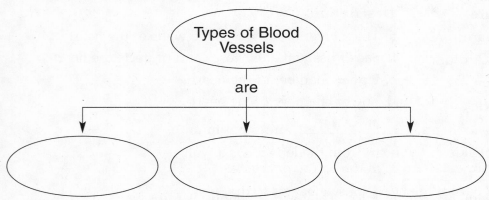

20. Circle the letter of each sentence that is true about arteries.

    a. Most carry oxygen-poor blood.   **c.** They have thin walls.

    b. They can expand under pressure.   **d.** The largest is the aorta.

21. Is the following sentence true or false? The smallest of the blood vessels are the capillaries. _____

22. What work is done in the capillaries? _____

_____

23. What keeps blood flowing toward the heart in the largest veins? _____

_____

Blood Pressure (pages 948–949)

24. The force of blood on the walls of arteries is known as

_____.

25. Is the following sentence true or false? Blood pressure increases

when the heart relaxes. _____

Match each type of blood pressure with the force it measures.

Type of Pressure	Force It Measures
_____ **26.** systolic	**a.** Force of the blood when the ventricles relax
_____ **27.** diastolic	**b.** Force of the blood when the ventricles contract

28. Is the following sentence true or false? An average adult's blood

pressure is 140/80. _____

29. How does the autonomic nervous system regulate blood

pressure? _____

_____

_____

30. How do the kidneys regulate blood pressure? _____

_____

_____

Disorders of the Circulatory System (pages 949–950)

31. A condition in which fatty deposits build up on the walls of

arteries is called _____.

32. High blood pressure also is called _____.

33. Is the following sentence true or false? High blood pressure

increases the risk of heart attack and stroke. _____

34. Circle the letter of each sentence that is true about heart attack.

a. It is caused by atherosclerosis in the coronary arteries.

b. It occurs when part of the heart muscle begins to die.

c. Its symptoms include nausea and chest pain.

d. It requires immediate medical attention.

35. Is the following sentence true or false? A stroke may be caused by

a clot in a blood vessel leading to the brain. _____

36. List the four keys to avoiding cardiovascular disorders.

a. _____

b. _____

c. _____

d. _____

Chapter 37, Circulatory and Respiratory Systems *(continued)*

Section 37–2 Blood and the Lymphatic System (pages 951–955)

This section describes the functions of the different components of blood. It also outlines the role of the lymphatic system.

Blood Plasma (page 951)

1. The straw-colored fluid portion of blood is called

   _____.

2. Circle the letter of each sentence that is true about plasma.

   a. It makes up 90 percent of the volume of blood.

   b. It is about 55 percent water.

   c. It contains only dissolved gases and salts.

   d. It contains both nutrients and enzymes.

Match each type of plasma protein with its function.

	Type of Protein	Function
_____	3. albumin	a. Helps blood clot
_____	4. globulin	b. Transports substances
_____	5. fibrinogen	c. Fights infections

Blood Cells (pages 952–954)

6. List the three types of blood cells.

   a. _____ b. _____ c. _____

7. Circle the letter of each sentence that is true about red blood cells.

   a. They are the least numerous cells in the blood.

   b. Their role is to transport oxygen.

   c. They contain hemoglobin.

   d. They are produced in the bone marrow.

8. Is the following sentence true or false? Mature red blood cells have two nuclei. _____

9. Circle the letter of each sentence that is true about white blood cells.

   a. They contain a nucleus.

   b. They attack foreign substances.

   c. They contain hemoglobin.

   d. They are also called leukocytes.

10. Is the following sentence true or false? Most white blood cells live for an average of 120 days. _____

11. White blood cells that engulf and digest foreign cells are called

    _____.

Match the type of white blood cell with its function.

Cell Type	Function
_____ **12.** eosinophils	**a.** Produce antibodies
_____ **13.** basophils	**b.** Attack parasites
_____ **14.** lymphocytes	**c.** Release histamines

15. What does a sudden increase in the number of white cells tell a

physician? _____

16. List the two components of blood that make clotting possible.

a. _____ **b.** _____

17. Number the drawings below to show the correct sequence in
which a blood clot forms when a blood vessel is injured.

_____   _____   _____

18. A genetic disorder that results from a defective protein in the

clotting pathway is _____.

The Lymphatic System (pages 954–955)

19. What is the lymphatic system? _____

_____

20. The fluid lost by blood is called _____.

21. Circle the letter of each choice that is a function of lymph nodes.

a. Trapping bacteria   **c.** Preventing backward flow of lymph

b. Helping blood to clot   **d.** Producing lymphocytes

Reading Skill Practice

When you read a section with difficult material, writing a summary can help you
identify and remember the main ideas and supporting details. Write a concise
paragraph summing up the material under each heading in Section 37–2. Each of
your paragraphs should be much shorter than the text under that heading in your
book. Include each of the boldfaced vocabulary terms in your summary. Do your
work on a separate sheet of paper.

Chapter 37, Circulatory and Respiratory Systems *(continued)*

Section 37–3 The Respiratory System (pages 956–963)

This section identifies the structures of the respiratory system and explains how we breathe. It also describes how smoking affects the respiratory system.

What Is Respiration? (page 956)

1. The process by which oxygen and carbon dioxide are exchanged between cells, the blood, and air in the lungs is known as

_____.

The Human Respiratory System (pages 956–958)

2. What is the basic job performed by the human respiratory system? _____

_____

_____

3. Label each of the following structures in the drawing of the human respiratory system: nose, pharynx, larynx, trachea, bronchus, and lung.

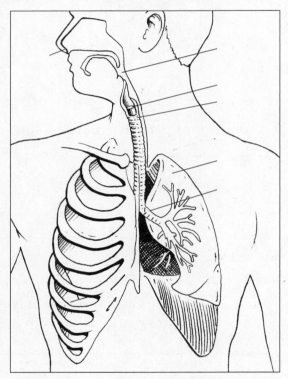

4. Circle the letter of the choice that lists the respiratory structures from largest to smallest.

a. Alveoli, bronchioles, bronchi   c. Bronchi, bronchioles, alveoli

b. Bronchioles, bronchi, alveoli   d. Bronchi, alveoli, bronchioles

5. What prevents food from entering your trachea? _____

_____

_____

Match each structure of the respiratory system with its description.

Structure	Description
_____ **6.** pharynx	**a.** Tiny air sacs where gas exchange occurs
_____ **7.** trachea	**b.** Tiny projections that sweep trapped particles and mucus away from the lungs
_____ **8.** cilia	**c.** Tube that serves as a passageway for both air and food
_____ **9.** larynx	**d.** Large passageways in the chest that lead to the lungs
_____ **10.** bronchi	**e.** Structure at the top of the trachea that contains the vocal cords
_____ **11.** alveoli	**f.** Passageway between the pharynx and bronchi

Gas Exchange (page 958)

12. Gas exchange occurs in the _____.

13. Describe the process of gas exchange. _____

_____

_____

_____

14. Circle the letter of each sentence that is true about gas exchange.

   a. It is a very efficient process.

   b. Exhaled air usually contains no oxygen.

   c. The lungs remove about half of the oxygen of inhaled air.

   d. The lungs increase the carbon dioxide content of inhaled air by a factor of 100.

15. Why is hemoglobin needed? _____

_____

_____

Breathing (pages 959–960)

16. The movement of air into and out of the lungs is called

_____.

17. The large, flat muscle at the bottom of the chest cavity is the

_____.

18. Is the following sentence true or false? The force that drives air

into the lungs comes from air pressure. _____

19. What happens when you inhale? _____

_____

_____

20. Circle the letter of the choice that describes what happens when pressure in the chest cavity becomes greater than atmospheric pressure.

   a. Air rushes into the lungs.   **c.** The diaphragm contracts.

   b. Air cannot escape from the lungs.   **d.** Air rushes out of the lungs.

Chapter 37, Circulatory and Respiratory Systems *(continued)*

How Breathing Is Controlled (pages 960–961)

21. The brain controls breathing in a center located in the

_____.

22. Is the following sentence true or false? Cells in the breathing center
monitor the amount of oxygen in the blood. _____

23. Why do airplane passengers in emergency situations often have
to be told to begin breathing pressurized oxygen? _____

_____

_____

Tobacco and the Respiratory System (pages 961–963)

24. List three of the most dangerous substances in tobacco smoke.

a. _____ **b.** _____ **c.** _____

25. Is the following sentence true or false? Nicotine is a stimulant drug
that increases pulse rate and blood pressure. _____

26. Why is carbon monoxide dangerous? _____

_____

_____

27. List three respiratory diseases caused by smoking.

a. _____ **b.** _____ **c.** _____

28. Circle the letter of each sentence that is true about chronic bronchitis.

a. It is characterized by swollen bronchi.

b. It occurs only in heavy smokers.

c. It can make stair climbing and similar activities difficult.

d. It is unrelated to smoking.

29. What is emphysema? _____

30. Circle the letter of each sentence that is true about lung cancer.

a. Its most important cause is smoking.

b. It is often deadly.

c. It cannot spread to other parts of the body.

d. It is usually detected early enough for a cure.

31. Circle the letter of each way that smoking affects the
cardiovascular system.

a. It constricts the blood vessels.

b. It causes blood pressure to rise.

c. It makes the heart work harder.

d. It causes heart disease.

32. Inhaling the smoke of others is called _____.

33. Why is passive smoking particularly harmful to young children? _____

_____

34. Why is it so hard to quit smoking? _____

_____

35. What is the best solution for dealing with tobacco? _____

_____

WordWise

Match each definition in the left column with the correct term in the right column. Then, write the number of each term in the box below on the line under the appropriate letter. When you have filled in all the boxes, add up the numbers in each column, row, and two diagonals. All the sums should be the same.

Definition	Term
A. Fluid lost by the blood into surrounding tissue	**1.** myocardium
B. Thick layer of muscle in walls of heart	**2.** ventricle
C. Stimulant drug in tobacco smoke	**3.** pacemaker
D. Passageway leading from the trachea to a lung	**4.** atherosclerosis
E. Protein in red blood cells	**5.** hemoglobin
F. Small group of heart cells that set the pace for the heartbeat	**6.** lymph
G. Lower chamber of the heart	**7.** bronchus
H. Disease in which tissues of the lungs lose elasticity	**8.** nicotine
I. Condition in which fatty deposits build up on the walls of arteries	**9.** emphysema

```
                                              = _____

┌──────────┬──────────┬──────────┐
│    A     │    B     │    C     │   = _____
│  ____    │  ____    │  ____    │
├──────────┼──────────┼──────────┤
│    D     │    E     │    F     │
│  ____    │  ____    │  ____    │   = _____
├──────────┼──────────┼──────────┤
│    G     │    H     │    I     │
│  ____    │  ____    │  ____    │   = _____
└──────────┴──────────┴──────────┘
     =          =          =
   ____       ____       ____        = _____
```

Digestive and Excretory Systems

Section 38–1 Food and Nutrition (pages 971–977)

This section identifies the nutrients your body needs and explains why water is such an important nutrient.

Food and Energy (page 971)

1. Cells convert the chemical energy in glucose and other molecules into _____.

2. The energy stored in food is measured in units called

   _____.

3. Is the following sentence true or false? The energy needs of an average-sized teenager are about 3000 Calories.

   _____

4. Is the following sentence true or false? Your body can extract energy from almost any type of food. _____

5. Besides supplying fuel, what are other important functions of food? _____

   _____

   _____

6. What is the science of nutrition? _____

   _____

Nutrients (pages 972–975)

7. Substances in food that supply the energy and raw materials your body uses for growth, repair, and maintenance are called

   _____.

8. List the six nutrients that the body needs.

   a. _____   c. _____   e. _____

   b. _____   d. _____   f. _____

9. Circle the letter of each sentence that is true about water as a nutrient.

   a. Water is the most important of all nutrients.

   b. Every cell in the human body needs water.

   c. Many of the body's processes take place in water.

   d. Water makes up the bulk of bodily fluids including blood.

10. How is water lost from the body? _____

    _____

11. If enough water is not taken in to replace what is lost,

    _____ can result.

12. Complete the concept map.

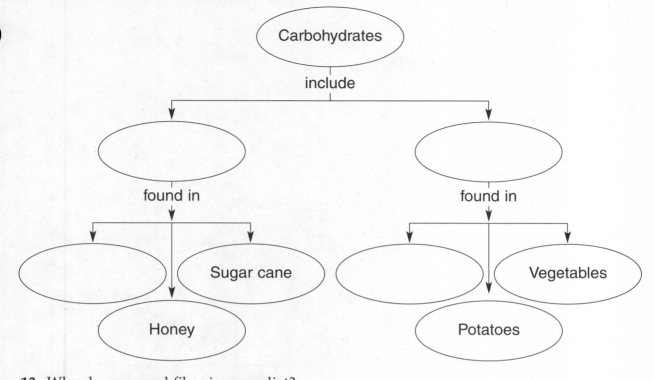

13. Why do you need fiber in your diet? _____

_____

14. Circle the letter of each choice that is a function of fat.

    a. Protecting body organs   **c.** Storing energy

    b. Insulating the body   **d.** Transporting oxygen

15. List four increased health risks associated with a diet high in fat.

    a. _____   **c.** _____

    b. _____   **d.** _____

16. Circle the letter of each choice that is a function of protein.

    a. Supplying raw materials for growth and repair

    b. Making up enzymes

    c. Helping the body absorb certain vitamins

    d. Producing cell membranes

17. The eight amino acids that the body is unable to produce are called

    _____ amino acids.

Match each vitamin with its function.

	Vitamin	Function
_____	**18.** A	**a.** Preventing cellular damage
_____	**19.** D	**b.** Promoting bone growth
_____	**20.** E	**c.** Repairing tissues and healing wounds
_____	**21.** C	**d.** Promoting growth of skin cells

Chapter 38, Digestive and Excretory Systems (continued)

Match each mineral with a food that supplies it.

Mineral	Food
_____ 22. calcium	**a.** Table salt
_____ 23. zinc	**b.** Dairy products
_____ 24. chlorine	**c.** Eggs
_____ 25. iron	**d.** Seafood

Balancing the Diet (pages 976–977)

26. Label the missing food groups in the Food Guide Pyramid.

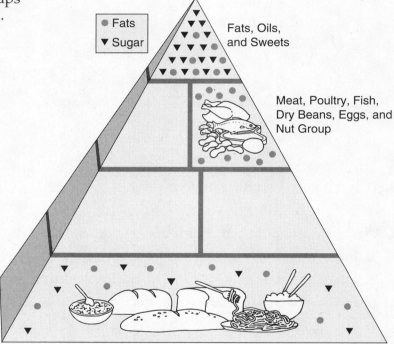

Bread, Cereal, Rice, and Pasta Group

Section 38–2 The Process of Digestion (pages 978–984)

This section describes the organs of the digestive system and explains their functions.

The Mouth (pages 978–979)

1. What is the function of the organs of the digestive system? _____

_____

_____

2. The physical breakdown of large pieces of food into smaller

    pieces is referred to as _____ digestion.

3. The breakdown of large food molecules into smaller molecules
   that can be absorbed into the bloodstream is called

    _____ digestion.

4. Label the drawing of the digestive system with the following structures: mouth, esophagus, stomach, liver, small intestine, and large intestine.

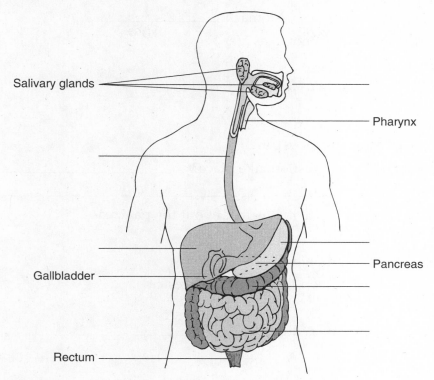

Salivary glands

Pharynx

Gallbladder

Pancreas

Rectum

5. What is the role of teeth in digestion? _____

_____

_____

The Esophagus (page 980)

Match each term with its definition.

Term	Definition
_____ **6.** bolus	**a.** Contractions of smooth muscle that aid in swallowing
_____ **7.** esophagus	**b.** Clump of chewed food
_____ **8.** peristalsis	**c.** Food tube connecting the mouth and stomach

9. Is the following sentence true or false? The pyloric valve prevents the contents of the stomach from moving back up into the

esophagus. _____

The Stomach (pages 980–981)

10. Circle the letter of each sentence that is true about the stomach.

a. It produces hydrochloric acid.

b. It produces trypsin.

c. It helps in the mechanical digestion of food.

d. It produces amylase.

Chapter 38, Digestive and Excretory Systems *(continued)*

11. Is the following sentence true or false? Pepsin cannot work under the acidic conditions present in the stomach. _____

12. A hole in the stomach wall is known as a(an)

_____.

13. A mixture of stomach fluids and food is referred to as

_____.

The Pancreas and Liver (pages 981–982)

14. Where does most chemical digestion take place? _____

_____

15. Circle the letter of each sentence that is true about the pancreas.

   a. It produces amylase.

   b. It produces sodium bicarbonate.

   c. Its enzymes help break down lipids and nucleic acids.

   d. It produces lactase.

16. What role does the liver play in digestion? _____

_____

_____

17. Bile is stored in a small pouchlike organ called the

_____.

The Small Intestine (page 983)

18. Name the two parts of the small intestine where nutrients are absorbed.

   a. _____   **b.** _____

19. Projections that cover the folds of the small intestine are called

_____.

20. Is the following sentence true or false? Molecules of undigested fat and some fatty acids are absorbed by lymph vessels called

lacteals. _____

The Large Intestine (page 984)

21. What is the primary job of the large intestine? _____

_____

22. Is the following sentence true or false? The appendix plays an

important role in human digestion. _____

23. When something happens that interferes with the removal of water by the large intestine, a condition known as

_____ results.

Reading Skill Practice

When you read about a complex process, representing the process with a flowchart can help you better understand and remember it. Make a flowchart to show how food travels through the digestive system and is broken down into simpler molecules that the body can use. For more information on flowcharts, see Appendix A of your textbook. Do your work on a separate sheet of paper.

Section 38–3 The Excretory System (pages 985–989)

This section identifies the organs of the excretory system. It also explains how the kidneys maintain homeostasis.

Excretion (page 985)

1. The process by which metabolic wastes are eliminated is called

   _____.

2. List the three organs that make up the excretory system.

   a. _____ b. _____ c. _____

The Kidneys (pages 985–988)

3. Circle the letter of each sentence that is true about the kidneys.

   a. They are the main organs of the excretory system.

   b. They are located on either side of the spinal column.

   c. They remove excess water and waste products from the urine.

   d. They receive blood through the renal vein.

Match each term with its definition.

Term	Definition
_____ 4. ureter	a. Saclike organ where urine is stored
_____ 5. urinary bladder	b. Functional unit of the kidney
_____ 6. renal medulla	c. Outer part of the kidney
_____ 7. renal cortex	d. Tube that carries urine from the kidney to the urinary bladder
_____ 8. nephron	e. Inner part of the kidney

9. Is the following sentence true or false? Nephrons are located in

   the renal medulla. _____

10. What ends up in the collecting duct? _____

    _____

    _____

11. List the three processes involved in blood purification.

    a. _____ b. _____ c. _____

Chapter 38, Digestive and Excretory Systems *(continued)*

12. The small network of capillaries in the upper end of the nephron is referred to as the _____.

13. The glomerulus is enclosed by a cup-shaped structure called

   _____.

14. Complete the Venn diagram.

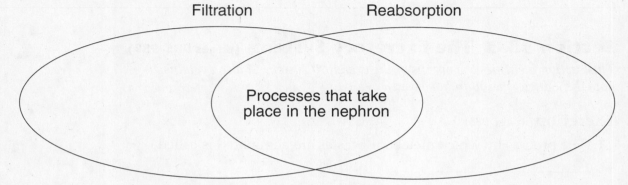

Filtration   Reabsorption

Processes that take place in the nephron

15. The materials that are filtered from the blood are collectively called the _____.

16. List six materials that are filtered from blood.

   a. _____   c. _____   e. _____

   b. _____   d. _____   f. _____

17. Which substances are removed from the filtrate and reabsorbed by the capillaries? _____

   _____

18. What happens during the process of secretion? _____

   _____

19. Circle the letter of each sentence that is true about urine.

   a. It is the material that remains after reabsorption.

   b. It contains only urea and water.

   c. It is concentrated in the loop of Henle.

   d. It is released from the body through the urethra.

Control of Kidney Function (page 988)

20. List three ways that the kidneys help maintain homeostasis.

   a. _____

   b. _____

   c. _____

21. How are the activities of the kidneys controlled? _____

   _____

   _____

22. Is the following sentence true or false? As the amount of water in the blood increases, the rate of water reabsorption in the kidneys increases. _____

Homeostasis by Machine (pages 988–989)

23. Is the following sentence true or false? Humans cannot survive with only one kidney. _____

24. The removal of wastes from blood using a machine is called _____ .

WordWise

Test your knowledge of vocabulary terms from Chapter 38 by completing this crossword puzzle.

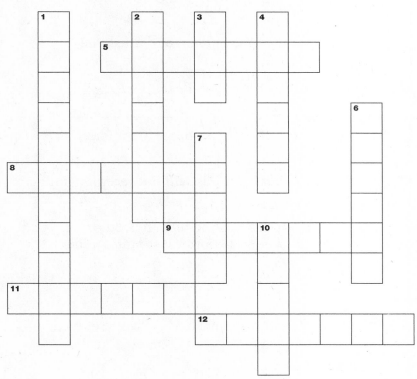

Clues down:

1. Muscular contractions of the esophagus
2. Inorganic nutrient needed in small amounts
3. Lipid
4. Main organ of excretion
6. Tube that carries fluid from kidney to bladder
7. Mixture of stomach fluids and food
10. Gland that produces bile

Clues across:

5. Organic molecule that helps regulate body processes
8. Large muscular sac important in digestion
9. Enzyme in saliva that helps digest starch
11. Projection from the wall of the small intestine
12. Tube through which urine is released from the body

Chapter 39

Endocrine and Reproductive Systems

Section 39–1 The Endocrine System (pages 997–1002)

This section describes the function of the endocrine system and explains how it maintains homeostasis.

Introduction (page 997)

1. What makes up the endocrine system? _____
   _____

2. What do the products of the endocrine system do? _____
   _____

Hormones (page 997)

3. Chemicals that travel through the bloodstream and affect the activities of other cells are called _____.

4. How do hormones affect the activities of other cells? _____
   _____

5. Cells that have receptors for a particular hormone are referred to as _____.

6. Is the following sentence true or false? Cells without receptors are not affected by hormones. _____

7. Is the following sentence true or false? Generally, the body's responses to hormones are quicker and shorter lasting than the responses to nerve impulses. _____

Glands (page 998)

8. An organ that produces and releases a substance, or a secretion, is called a(an) _____.

9. Complete the Venn diagram by adding titles.

   _____   _____

   Releases secretions into ducts   Releases secretions   Releases secretions into blood

10. What is the function of the parathyroid glands? _____
    _____

Match the endocrine gland with the hormone it produces.

Endocrine Gland	**Hormone It Produces**
_____ 11. Pineal	**a.** Glucagon
_____ 12. Thyroid	**b.** Melatonin
_____ 13. Pancreas	**c.** Epinephrine
_____ 14. Thymus	**d.** Thyroxine
_____ 15. Adrenal	**e.** Thymosin
_____ 16. Ovary	**f.** Testosterone
_____ 17. Testis	**g.** Estrogen

18. The hormone that regulates metabolism is _____.

Hormone Action (page 999)

19. List the two general groups into which hormones fall.

    a. _____   **b.** _____

20. Circle the letter of each sentence that is true about steroid hormones.

    a. They are lipids.

    b. They cannot cross cell membranes.

    c. They regulate gene expression.

    d. They can enter the nucleus.

21. Is the following sentence true or false? Steroid hormones are produced from cholesterol. _____

22. Circle the letter of each sentence that is true about nonsteroid hormones.

    a. They are proteins, peptides, or amino acids.

    b. They can cross cell membranes.

    c. They rely on secondary messengers.

    d. They cannot enter the nucleus.

23. Is the following sentence true or false? Secondary messengers may include calcium, cAMP, nucleotides, and fatty acids.

    _____

Prostaglandins (page 1000)

24. Hormonelike substances produced by other kinds of cells and tissues are called _____.

25. Why are prostaglandins known as "local hormones"? _____

    _____

26. Is the following sentence true or false? Some prostaglandins cause smooth muscles to contract. _____

Chapter 39, Endocrine and Reproductive Systems *(continued)*

Control of the Endocrine System (pages 1000–1001)

27. When does feedback inhibition occur? _____

_____

_____

28. Fill in the missing labels in the diagram to show how the thyroid gland is regulated by feedback controls.

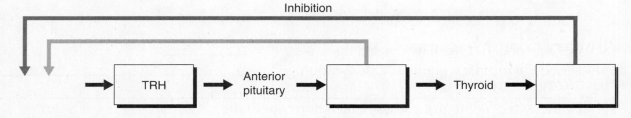

29. Circle the letter of each event that occurs when core body temperature begins to drop.

    a. The hypothalamus produces less TRH.

    b. More TSH is released.

    c. Less thyroxine is released.

    d. Metabolic activity increases.

30. Is the following sentence true or false? As you lose water, the concentration of dissolved materials in the blood falls.

    _____

Complementary Hormone Action (page 1002)

31. What is complementary hormone action? _____

_____

_____

32. Is the following sentence true or false? Calcitonin increases the concentration of calcium in the blood. _____

33. If calcium levels drop too low, the parathyroid glands release

    _____.

34. How does PTH increase calcium levels? _____

_____

_____

_____

35. Why is the regulation of calcium levels so important? _____

_____

_____

Section 39–2 Human Endocrine Glands (pages 1003–1008)

This section describes the functions of the major endocrine glands.

Introduction (page 1003)

1. List the seven major glands of the endocrine system.

   a. _____   e. _____

   b. _____   f. _____

   c. _____   g. _____

   d. _____

Pituitary Gland (page 1003)

2. Describe the pituitary gland and its location. _____

   _____

   _____

3. List the two parts of the pituitary gland.

   a. _____   b. _____

4. In general, what is the role of pituitary gland hormones? _____

   _____

   _____

Hypothalamus (page 1004)

5. Is the following sentence true or false? The hypothalamus controls
   the secretions of the pituitary gland. _____

6. What influences the activity of the hypothalamus? _____

   _____

   _____

7. In what way is the posterior pituitary an extension of the
   hypothalamus? _____

   _____

   _____

8. Is the following sentence true or false? The hypothalamus has
   direct control of the anterior pituitary. _____

Match each pituitary hormone with its action.

	Hormone	Action
_____	9. ADH	a. Stimulates ovaries and testes
_____	10. FSH	b. Stimulates production of eggs and sperm
_____	11. LH	c. Stimulates release of hormones from adrenal cortex
_____	12. GH	d. Stimulates protein synthesis and growth in cells
_____	13. ACTH	e. Stimulates the kidneys to reabsorb water

Chapter 39, Endocrine and Reproductive Systems (continued)

14. What are releasing hormones, and what do they do? _____

_____

_____

_____

Thyroid Gland (page 1005)

15. Where is the thyroid gland located? _____

_____

16. Is the following sentence true or false? The thyroid gland
regulates reproduction. _____

17. List the two hormones produced by the thyroid.

a. _____   **b.** _____

18. What does thyroxine do in the body? _____

_____

19. Production of too much thyroxine leads to a condition called

_____.

20. Circle the letter of each choice that is a symptom of too much
thyroxine.

a. nervousness   **b.** weight loss   **c.** lack of energy   **d.** goiter

21. An enlargement of the thyroid gland is called a(an)

_____.

22. Infants who lack enough iodine to produce normal amounts of
thyroxine suffer from a condition called _____.

23. How can cretinism usually be prevented? _____

_____

_____

Parathyroid Glands (page 1005)

24. How does parathyroid hormone regulate calcium levels in the blood? _____

_____

_____

Adrenal Glands (page 1006)

25. What is the general role of the adrenal glands? _____

_____

26. The outer part of the adrenal gland is called the

_____, and the inner part is called the

_____.

Name_____ Class_____ Date_____

27. Complete the compare-and-contrast table.

HORMONES OF THE ADRENAL GLAND

Part of Adrenal Gland	Hormones It Produces	Role of the Hormones
	Corticosteroids	Regulating minerals, metabolism
Adrenal medulla		

28. Is the following sentence true or false? The release of hormones from the adrenal medulla is regulated by the sympathetic nervous system. _____

Pancreas (pages 1007–1008)

29. Is the following sentence true or false? The pancreas is both an endocrine gland and an exocrine gland. _____

30. What is the role of insulin and glucagon? _____

31. When the pancreas produces too little insulin, a condition known as _____ occurs.

32. Is the following sentence true or false? Type I diabetes most commonly develops in people before the age of 15.

_____

33. Circle the letter of each sentence that is true about Type II diabetes.
   a. It most commonly develops before age 40.
   b. It is not due to lack of insulin.
   c. It is also called juvenile-onset diabetes.
   d. It requires daily insulin injections.

Reproductive Glands (page 1008)

34. List the two important functions served by the gonads.
   a. _____   **b.** _____

35. The female gonads are the _____, and the male gonads are the _____.

Reading Skill Practice

Taking notes can help you identify and remember the most important information in a section. Take notes on Section 39–2 by writing the main headings and under each heading listing the most important points. Do your work on a separate sheet of paper.

Chapter 39, Endocrine and Reproductive Systems *(continued)*

Section 39–3 The Reproductive System (pages 1009–1015)

This section explains the roles of the male and female reproductive systems. It also describes the four phases of the menstrual cycle.

Sexual Development (pages 1009–1010)

1. Circle the letter of each sentence that is true about sexual development before birth.

   a. Testes and ovaries begin to develop during the first six weeks.

   b. Male and female reproductive organs develop from the same tissues in the embryo.

   c. The testes produce androgens, and the ovaries produce estrogen.

   d. Hormones determine whether the embryo will develop into a male or a female.

2. What is puberty? _____

   _____

   _____

3. How does the hypothalamus begin puberty? _____

   _____

   _____

The Male Reproductive System (pages 1010–1011)

4. Is the following sentence true or false? The release of FSH and LH stimulates cells in the testes to produce testosterone.

   _____

5. List three secondary sex characteristics that appear in males at puberty.

   a. _____

   b. _____

   c. _____

6. Circle the letter of each term that refers to a structure of the male reproductive system.

   a. testes   **c.** vas deferens

   b. Fallopian tube   **d.** urethra

7. The testes are contained in a sac called the _____.

8. Why do the testes remain outside the body cavity? _____

   _____

   _____

9. Is the following sentence true or false? Sperm are produced in the vas deferens. _____

10. Label the drawing of a sperm with the following structures: head, nucleus, midpiece, and tail.

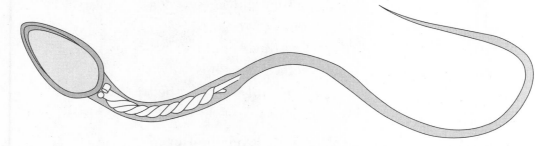

11. The structure in which sperm fully mature and are stored is the

_____.

12. The tube that leads to the outside of the body through the penis is

the _____.

13. A nutrient-rich fluid called seminal fluid, when combined with

sperm, forms _____.

The Female Reproductive System (pages 1012–1013)

14. List three secondary sex characteristics that develop in females at puberty.

a. _____

b. _____

c. _____

15. Circle the letter of each choice that is a structure of the female reproductive system.

a. ovary   **b.** epididymis   **c.** uterus   **d.** vagina

16. Is the following sentence true or false? The ovaries usually

produce only one mature ovum each month. _____

17. Clusters of cells surrounding a single egg are called primary

_____.

18. The hormone that stimulates a follicle to grow and mature each

month is _____.

19. Is the following sentence true or false? Fertilization takes place in

the uterus. _____

The Menstrual Cycle (pages 1013–1015)

20. Circle the letter of each sentence that is true about the menstrual cycle.

a. It lasts an average of 3 to 7 days.

b. It is controlled by hormones.

c. It prepares the uterus to receive an egg.

d. It has four phases.

Chapter 39, Endocrine and Reproductive Systems *(continued)*

Match each phase of the menstrual cycle with the event that occurs then.

Menstrual Phase	Event
_____ **21.** Follicular phase	**a.** Egg travels through Fallopian tube.
_____ **22.** Ovulation	**b.** Follicle develops.
_____ **23.** Luteal phase	**c.** Lining of uterus is shed.
_____ **24.** Menstruation	**d.** Egg is released from ovary.

25. Is the following sentence true or false? The level of estrogen falls during the follicular phase of the menstrual cycle.

_____

26. During the luteal phase, the follicle turns yellow and is now

known as the _____.

27. Is the following sentence true or false? The chances that an egg will be fertilized are the greatest during the first two days of the

luteal phase. _____

28. What triggers menstruation to occur? _____

_____

29. Is the following sentence true or false? A new cycle begins with

the last day of menstruation. _____

Section 39–4 Fertilization and Development (pages 1016–1022)

This section describes fertilization and explains the function of the placenta.

Fertilization (page 1016)

1. The process of a sperm joining an egg is called _____.

2. Is the following sentence true or false? A fertilized egg is known

as a zygote. _____.

3. After a fertilized egg divides to form two cells, it is called a(an)

_____.

Early Development (pages 1017–1019)

Match each term with its definition.

Term	Definition
_____ **4.** Morula	**a.** Organ that nourishes the embryo
_____ **5.** Blastocyst	**b.** Name of embryo when it is a solid ball of about 50 cells
_____ **6.** Implantation	**c.** Name of embryo when it is a hollow ball of cells
_____ **7.** Gastrulation	**d.** Membrane that surrounds and protects the embryo
_____ **8.** Amnion	**e.** Process in which the blastocyst attaches to the wall of the uterus
_____ **9.** Placenta	**f.** Process of cell migration that produces three cell layers

10. Is the following sentence true or false? The first few cell divisions take place in the Fallopian tube. _____

11. After eight weeks of development, the embryo is called a(an) _____.

12. Is the following sentence true or false? Most of the major organs and tissues are fully formed by the end of three months of development. _____

Later Development (page 1019)

13. What changes occur during the last three months of fetal development? _____

_____

_____

Childbirth (pages 1020–1021)

14. Is the following sentence true or false? The process of childbirth begins when the hormone calcitonin is released from the posterior pituitary gland. _____

15. The series of rhythmic contractions of the uterine wall that force the baby out through the vagina is known as _____.

16. What stimulates the production of milk in the breast tissues of the mother? _____

Early Years (pages 1021–1022)

17. Is the following sentence true or false? A baby's birth weight generally triples within 12 months of birth. _____

18. Is the following sentence true or false? Infancy refers to the first year of life. _____

19. Circle the letter of each development that occurs during infancy.

   a. Crawling   **c.** Appearance of first teeth

   b. Walking   **d.** First use of language

20. Childhood lasts from infancy until the onset of _____.

21. Is the following sentence true or false? Reasoning skills are not developed until adolescence. _____

22. Adolescence begins with puberty and ends with _____.

23. What produces the growth spurt that starts at puberty? _____

_____

_____

Chapter 39, Endocrine and Reproductive Systems (*continued*)

Adulthood (page 1022)

24. Is the following sentence true or false? Adults reach their highest levels of physical strength and development between the ages of 25 and 35. _____

25. When do the first signs of physiological aging appear in most individuals? _____

WordWise

Use the clues to help you identify the vocabulary terms from Chapter 39. Then, put the numbered letters in the right order to spell out the answer to the riddle.

Clues	Vocabulary Terms
Tube through which urine and semen are released from the body	_ _ _ _ _ _ _ 1
Fertilized egg cell	_ _ _ _ _ _ 2
Hormonelike substance that affects only nearby cells and tissues	_ _ _ _ _ _ _ _ _ _ _ 3
Cluster of cells surrounding an egg in the ovary	_ _ _ _ _ _ _ _ 4
Male gonad that produces sperm	_ _ _ _ _ _ 5
Chemicals that travel through the bloodstream and affect the activities of other cells	_ _ _ _ _ _ _ 6
Female gonad that produces eggs	_ _ _ _ _ 7
Organ that nourishes the embryo	_ _ _ _ _ _ _ 8 9
Process in which a blastocyst attaches to the wall of the uterus	_ _ _ _ _ _ _ _ _ _ _ _ 10
Name given to the human embryo after eight weeks of development	_ _ _ _ 11 12

Riddle: What controls the pituitary gland?

Answer: _ _ _ _ _ _ _ _ _ _ _ _
        1   2   3   4   5   6   7   8   9 10 11 12

Chapter 40

The Immune System and Disease

Section 40–1 Infectious Disease (pages 1029–1033)

This section describes the causes of disease and explains how infectious diseases are transmitted.

Introduction (page 1029)

1. Any change, other than an injury, that disrupts the normal functions of the body, is a(an) _____.

2. What are three ways diseases can come about? _____
_____
_____

3. Disease-causing organisms are called _____.

The Germ Theory of Disease (pages 1029–1030)

4. State the germ theory of disease. _____
_____

5. Circle the letter of each scientist whose work led to the germ theory of disease.

   a. Koch   **b.** Steere   **c.** Pasteur   **d.** Burgdorfer

6. Is the following sentence true or false? Lyme disease is caused by bacteria. _____

7. Circle the letter of the type of organism that spreads Lyme disease.

   a. mosquito   **b.** deer tick   **c.** deer fly   **d.** horse fly

Koch's Postulates (page 1030)

8. What are scientists trying to identify when they use Koch's postulates? _____
_____
_____

9. Number the steps in the flowchart below so they show how to apply Koch's postulates.

Pathogen identified	Pathogen injected into healthy lab mouse	Pathogen grown in pure culture	Healthy mouse becomes sick	Pathogen identified

_____   _____   _____   _____   _____

Chapter 40, The Immune System and Disease *(continued)*

Agents of Disease (page 1031)

10. Is the following sentence true or false? Most of the bacteria and yeast that are found in the body are harmful and cause disease.

_____

11. List two ways that bacteria can produce illness.

a. _____ **b.** _____

12. Poisons that produce illness by disrupting body functions are

called _____.

13. How does a virus reproduce inside a host cell? _____

_____

_____

14. Pathogens that live and feed inside infected organisms are called

_____.

Match each type of pathogen with a disease caused by that type.

Type of Pathogen	Disease
_____ **15.** Virus	**a.** Athlete's foot
_____ **16.** Bacterium	**b.** Tetanus
_____ **17.** Protist	**c.** Tapeworm
_____ **18.** Worm	**d.** Influenza
_____ **19.** Fungus	**e.** Malaria

How Diseases Are Spread (page 1032)

20. List three ways that infectious diseases are spread.

a. _____

b. _____

c. _____

21. Animals that carry disease-causing organisms from person to

person are called _____.

22. Is the following sentence true or false? Thorough handwashing does not help prevent the spread of many pathogens.

_____

23. Is the following sentence true or false? Some of the most dangerous disease-causing organisms are spread from one

person to another by sexual contact. _____

24. Circle the letter of each choice that is a sexually transmitted disease.

a. syphilis **b.** gonorrhea **c.** AIDS **d.** malaria

Fighting Infectious Diseases (page 1033)

25. Compounds that kill bacteria without harming the cells of

humans or animals are called _____.

26. Circle the letter of each sentence that is true about antibiotics.

    a. They work by interfering with the cellular processes of
microorganisms.

    b. Many of them are produced by living organisms.

    c. They were first discovered in the 1940s.

    d. They are effective against viruses.

27. How do antiviral drugs fight viral diseases? _____

_____

Section 40–2 The Immune System (pages 1034–1040)

*This section describes the body's defenses against disease-causing organisms
and explains what immunity is.*

Nonspecific Defenses (pages 1034–1035)

    1. The body's primary defense against pathogens is the

_____.

Match the type of defense with its role in the body.

	Defense	Role
_____	2. Nonspecific	a. Destroying harmful pathogens that enter the body
_____	3. Specific	b. Preventing pathogens from entering the body

    4. What is the job of the body's first line of defense? _____

_____

    5. List the four components of the body's first line of defense.

      a. _____   **c.** _____

      b. _____   **d.** _____

    6. Is the following sentence true or false? The body's most important

nonspecific defense is the skin. _____

    7. How does mucus help protect the body from disease? _____

_____

    8. Body secretions contain an enzyme, called _____,
that kills bacteria.

    9. When does the body's second line of defense come into play? _____

_____

    10. Is the following sentence true or false? The inflammatory
response is a nonspecific reaction to tissue damage caused by

injury or infection. _____

Chapter 40, The Immune System and Disease *(continued)*

11. White blood cells called _____ engulf and destroy bacteria.

12. Why does an increase in the number of white blood cells indicate that the body is dealing with a serious infection? _____

_____

_____

13. An elevated body temperature is called a(an) _____.

14. Circle the letter of each sentence that is true about elevated body temperature.

  a. It kills many pathogens.

  b. It speeds up the action of white blood cells.

  c. It decreases heart rate.

  d. It slows down chemical reactions.

15. Is the following sentence true or false? Interferon is a protein that helps fight bacterial infections. _____

Specific Defenses (pages 1036–1039)

16. What is the immune response? _____

_____

17. A substance that triggers the immune response is known as a(an) _____.

18. What are some examples of antigens? _____

_____

_____

19. List the two different immune responses.

  a. _____ **b.** _____

20. Circle the letter of each sentence that is true about humoral immunity.

  a. It is a response to pathogens in body fluids.

  b. It depends on lymphocytes.

  c. It involves antibodies.

  d. It involves plasma cells.

21. A protein that helps destroy pathogens is called a(an) _____.

22. What happens to a clump of viruses and antibodies? _____

_____

23. Is the following sentence true or false? Antibodies can fight viruses but not bacteria. _____

24. Label the antigen-binding sites in the drawing below.

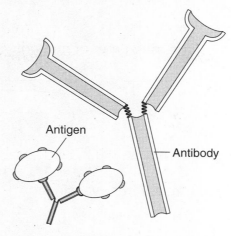

Antigen

Antibody

Match the type of cell with its role in humoral immunity.

Type of Cell	Role
_____ **25.** B cell	**a.** Assisting plasma cells
_____ **26.** T cell	**b.** Producing antibodies

27. Is the following sentence true or false? Plasma cells are specialized B cells. _____

28. How does permanent immunity develop? _____

_____

_____

_____

29. Circle the letter of each sentence that is true about cell-mediated immunity.

    a. It relies on lymphocytes.   **c.** It involves antibodies.

    b. It involves killer T cells.   **d.** It causes pathogen cells to rupture and die.

30. Is the following sentence true or false? Cell-mediated immunity is particularly important for diseases caused by prokaryotic pathogens. _____

Active Immunity (pages 1039–1040)

31. The first smallpox vaccine was produced by _____ _____.

32. What is vaccination? _____

_____

_____

33. How do vaccines work? _____

_____

_____

Chapter 40, The Immune System and Disease *(continued)*

Passive Immunity (page 1040)

34. Complete the Venn diagram comparing types of immunity.

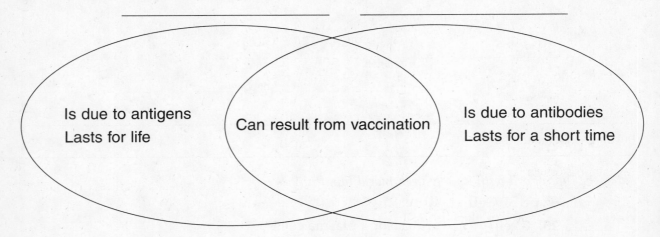

_____   _____

Is due to antigens
Lasts for life

Can result from vaccination

Is due to antibodies
Lasts for a short time

Section 40–3 Immune System Disorders (pages 1041–1044)

This section describes diseases that affect the immune system.

Allergies (pages 1041–1042)

1. An overreaction of the immune system caused by antigens is

   called a(an) _____.

2. Circle the letter of each choice that is a result of allergens binding
   to mast cells.

   a. The mast cells release chemicals known as histamines.

   b. There is increased flow of blood and fluids to the surrounding
   area.

   c. Sneezing, runny eyes, and other symptoms occur.

   d. Antihistamines are released by the mast cells.

3. A condition in which smooth muscle contractions reduce the size
   of air passageways in the lungs and make breathing very difficult

   is called _____.

4. Circle the letter of the choice that is the usual trigger of an asthma
   attack.

   a. A combination of many different antigens

   b. A particular antigen

   c. A drug that is inhaled

   d. Relaxation of the smooth muscles

5. Is the following sentence true or false? The best way to avoid an
   asthma attack is to avoid the antigen that produces the attack.

   _____

Autoimmune Disease (page 1042)

6. What produces an autoimmune disease? _____

_____

_____

7. Complete the compare-and-contrast table.

AUTOIMMUNE DISEASES

Autoimmune Disease	Organ or Tissue That Is Attacked
Rheumatic fever	
Juvenile-onset diabetes	
Myasthenia gravis	
Multiple sclerosis	

AIDS (pages 1042–1044)

8. Is the following sentence true or false? AIDS is a type of disease in which the immune system is weakened by infection.

_____

9. What do the letters *A, I, D,* and *S* stand for? _____

_____

10. List some of the diseases that may be symptoms of AIDS.

a. _____

b. _____

c. _____

11. What made scientists suspect that AIDS was caused by a virus? _____

_____

_____

12. Circle the letter of the choice that refers to the cells that are attacked by HIV.

a. Helper T cells   **c.** Red blood cells

b. Killer T cells   **d.** Helper B cells

13. Is the following sentence true or false? The body does not produce antibodies against HIV. _____

14. Circle the letter of each choice that is true about the spread of HIV.

a. It is usually spread by casual contact.

b. It is spread only by sexual contact.

c. It can be spread by sharing intravenous drug needles.

d. It is spread only by contact with infected blood or other body fluids.

Chapter 40, The Immune System and Disease *(continued)*

15. Is the following sentence true or false? Any sexual contact carries

some risk of contracting HIV. _____

Reading Skill Practice

When you read about new or difficult concepts, making a concept map can help you better understand and remember the ideas. Make a concept map that shows how immune system disorders are classified, based on the material in Section 40–3. For more information about concept maps, see Appendix A of your text. Do your work on a separate sheet of paper.

Section 40–4 Cancer (pages 1046–1048)

This section explains what cancer is, identifies its causes, and describes how it is treated.

Introduction (page 1046)

1. Circle the letter of each sentence that is true about cancer.

   a. It is generally a life-threatening disease.

   b. It is characterized by cells multiplying uncontrollably and destroying healthy tissue.

   c. It is caused by foreign cells invading the body.

   d. Its is easy to treat and to understand.

A Cellular Disease (page 1046)

2. When do cancers begin? _____

   _____

3. A mass of growing tissue is known as a(an) _____.

4. Is the following sentence true or false? All tumors are cancerous.

   _____

Match the type of tumor with its description.

	Tumor Type	Description
_____	**5.** Benign	**a.** Does not spread to surrounding healthy tissue or to other parts of the body
_____	**6.** Malignant	**b.** Can invade and destroy surrounding healthy tissue or spread to other parts of the body

7. The spread of cancerous tumors beyond their original site is

   called _____.

8. List three ways that cancer cells cause illness as they spread.

a. _____

b. _____

c. _____

Causes of Cancer (pages 1046–1047)

9. Complete the concept map.

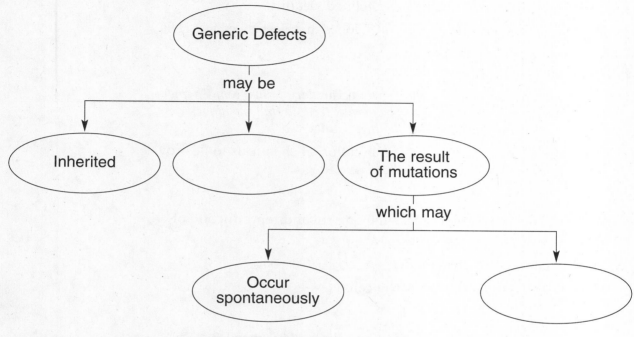

10. What is an example of a virus that causes cancer in humans? _____

_____

11. Chemical compounds that are known to cause cancer are called

_____.

Fighting Cancer (pages 1047–1048)

12. Why is it important to detect cancer early? _____

_____

13. List the three general categories of treatments for cancer.

a. _____ b. _____ c. _____

14. Which types of tumors are often removed by surgery? _____

_____

_____

15. Another name for drug therapy is _____.

16. Is the following sentence true or false? Radiation destroys fast-growing cancer cells more slowly than normal cells.

_____

Chapter 40, The Immune System and Disease *(continued)*

Progress Against Cancer (page 1048)

17. Circle the letter of each sentence that is true about cancer in the United States since 1990.

    a. There has been little progress in fighting cancer.

    b. The incidence of cancer has increased.

    c. The rate of cancer deaths has declined steadily.

    d. Researchers have developed antibiotics that destroy cancer cells.

WordWise

Answer the questions by writing the correct vocabulary terms from Chapter 40 in the blanks. Use the circled letter from each term to find the hidden word. Then, write a definition for the hidden word.

1. What type of treatment uses a combination of chemicals to destroy cancer cells?

   _ _ _ _ _ _ _ _ _ _ Ⓞ _

2. What is a compound that blocks the growth and reproduction of bacteria?

   Ⓞ _ _ _ _ _ _ _ _ _

3. What is a mass of rapidly growing cells?

   Ⓞ _ _ _ _

4. What is a chemical that is released by activated mast cells?

   Ⓞ _ _ _ _ _ _ _ _

5. What is a specialized protein produced by the immune system that helps destroy disease-causing organisms?

   _ _ _ _ _ Ⓞ _ _

6. What is a tumor called if it can invade and destroy surrounding healthy tissue?

   _ _ _ _ Ⓞ _ _ _ _

7. What is the spread of a cancerous tumor beyond its orginal site?

   _ Ⓞ _ _ _ _ _ _ _ _

8. What is a substance that triggers an immune response?

   _ _ _ _ _ Ⓞ

Hidden Word: _____

Definition: _____